The Changing Sister

CONTRIBUTORS

Foreword by George N. Shuster

Sister Marie Augusta Neal, S.N.D.

Sister M. Charles Borromeo Muckenhirn, C.S.C.

Sister M. Elena Malits, C.S.C.

Sister M. Aloysius Schaldenbrand, S.S.J.

Sister Jane Marie Richardson, S.L.

Sister M. Corita Kent, I.H.M.

Sister M. Angelica Seng, O.S.F.

Sister Jane Marie Luecke, O.S.B.

Sister M. Daniel Turner, S.N.D.

The
Changing
Sister

Edited by

Sister M. Charles Borromeo Muckenhirn, C.S.C.

FIDES PUBLISHERS, INC.   •   NOTRE DAME, IND.   •   1965

Library of Congress Catalog Card Number: 65-22150

Manufactured in the United States of America by
North State Press, Inc., Hammond, Indiana

Foreword

The American sister is as traditional as anything in American life. Catholics have long taken her for granted, doubtless too much for granted. And once the weird days of ex-nun fiction had been erased from the Protestant mind, she has earned deep general respect for service and scholarship. On the one hand she was a person through whom many values of European culture came to the United States, and so is closely identified with the period of immigration and all it means for our national history. On the other hand, communities of sisters were formed here, by great women identified with everything that has been "native" in our common life.

But as this book so ably indicates the American sister is acquiring new characteristics. She is partly of today and partly of tomorrow. Though not unmindful of the past — indeed a sufficiently nostalgic tribute is paid to that past — she has her eyes glued to the screen on which the shape of things to come is reflected. Hers will continue to be a monastic formation. Her spirit will derive strength from the scripture and the liturgy. The reality of her virginity will be a guarantee of her integrity, using the word in its highest and best sense.

Nevertheless she will live a wholly different life in a wholly different world. She will be out in the world as an apostle, prepared for the challenges every apostle has to meet. She will understand what urban poverty means, what new contours of the human spirit are fashioned by education, and what the commingling of culture and faith brings with it.

The writers whose essays make up this book have tried hard to assist you and me in seeing what being an American sister is going to mean. It does not require a sympathetic point of view or anything of that sort. It is honest reporting, in some cases equally honest speculation. You will find it interesting and in a very real sense moving.

George N. Shuster

Contents

Introduction

Collegiality or co-responsibility is a key to the vitality of renewal throughout the entire Church. Each member of Christ to the extent that he is converted in his heart to the new attitudes of the Church, begins to work with his fellow men wherever he is. Only such local adaptation through thought and sharing, suffering and joy, can make the marvelous discussions in St. Peter's basilica take on flesh and blood in the human life of suburbs and slums. So far there has been much public discussion about sisters, but very little discussion by sisters. Understandably most of the organizations, conventions and published proceedings on the topic have come from groups of sisters who are in positions of authority. Superiors present an essential point of view regarding sisters. But the same problem often has many facets. The ordinary sister not only sees problems from a different angle than the sister in an official position, but she is often much more in touch with the details of the apostolate as it is lived each day.

The publishers, editor, and contributors hope that *The Changing Sister* will add a new and creative voice to the *aggiornamento* of sisters. Each chapter is solidly based on the personal competence of the sister author. In addition, each author manifests a long personal involvement in seeing the modern sister in the light of some highly disciplined field of training. The basic drive is for insight into truth, not for authoritative directives. Due to the complexity of the questions about sisters' renewal the use of a team of writers seems self-explanatory. The book is by and about the sisters of the United States. There is surely

1

a Catholic consensus about renewal of women religious. However, no realistic discussion, much less effective action, can result from beautifully arranged principles, unless they are pointed toward conditions in a specific culture.

Historical perspective is always necessary for genuine appraisal of any human reality. But in the case of adaptation in the Church, and particularly in women's communities, it has special urgency. Without a sense of history, both religious and their friendly critics can be blaming existing persons, when they should be discovering the historical forces which made the present situation and even formed the persons involved. Communities today are human societies, falling under all the laws of history and sociology, most of all when dealing with group change. Communities are made up of persons of varying ages and backgrounds, who were in the main formed prior to the new attitudes of Vatican II. In its history and structure, the Catholic Church in the United States is almost totally a product of the Council of Trent. And religious women have been one of its most conservative elements. The greatness and weakness of the Church in general and women's communities in particular stem mainly from two historical facts: their basically immigrant origins and their development in isolation from the mainstream of American life.

These truisms were concretized and in some cases canonized in the details of religious life in this country. Sisters stood visibly for the Church; the Church stood for 19th century European Catholicism. Once we grant that the Church has rediscovered itself as the people of God, it becomes obvious that the majority of the American Church have long since adapted to American life and entered the 20th century. The laity, who quantitatively

are the Church, are largely emancipated from the old isolation of Catholic neighborhood and parish life. But since
structures of the old type of Catholicism were more rigid,
more enforceable, more impermeable in religious communities, the adaptation in them is both slower and more
painful.

Two other historical elements must be mentioned, admitting all the while that the whole area of historical
background for sisters' renewal urgently demands professional study. In the early 19th century, women were invisible in socio-political life; their personal existence was
dominated by men. This outmoded style of life has been
preserved until the present *aggiornamento*, in the customs
and mentality of women's communities. The sister's socio-
political irrelevance has been so total that any activity in
this area raises storms of controversy. Many of the problems connected with emotional immaturity, extreme passivity and inability to make decisions comes from masculine dominance, particularly from the clergy. Granting
that all of this is now changing, the fact of its existence to
the present moment is a condition not to be passed over
lightly. Adult relationship with clergy and laity are an
entirely new experience for the average American sister.

More sisters in every community enter, however, as
mature women and receive further adult formation, both
personal and academic. Communities are becoming able
to do their own thinking and governing, in collegial relation to clergy and laity. Certainly, in the future, the religious women of the world will gain some voice in their
own governing through representation of religious women
on the Sacred Congregation of Religious. This book is one
attempt to give sisters a forum for the needed serious
thought about their own deep and effective renewal.

The other historical fact which must be kept in mind is

that American sisters have been more involved in large institutions than their counterparts in other countries. By far the majority of sisters now serving in the American church are in schools and hospitals. This is an understandable fact in the light of the history of immigrant needs. But now the needs of the Church in this country are swiftly changing. The institutions owned by sisters are staffed largely by the laity. Understandably the past devotion of thousands of sisters in these institutions, as well as the immensity of financial involvement make calm discussion of this problem difficult. However, it must be faced and change effected intelligently and for the greatest good of the Church and its people. Otherwise, each institution will change like Topsy in a hit-or-miss way, with sad internal situations evolving and perhaps crucial needs of the Church remaining unanswered.

authorities

Intelligent planning for the adaptation of women's communities will require the pooling of many minds, varied competences, much suffering, great love. But the viewpoint of the psychologist, the theologian, the sociologist exists, not in a vacuum, but in the mind of a specific person. The Holy Spirit is working in persons with no rank in the Church as well as through those in authority. Together, under this impulse the open Church is developing, the Church which makes Christ lovable to men. This book has been produced to offer one of many possible expressions of the Spirit in the religious women of the United States. It is in a sense a concrete example of the charismatic role in the Church as it is now rediscovered in the scriptures and doctrinally reaffirmed by the Council.

In *The Dynamic Element in the Church,* Karl Rahner deals powerfully with this theme. He makes evident the absolute necessity of a return to a balanced practice in the Church regarding true docility to the Spirit of Christ operative in his Whole Body. Respect for the guidance of the Holy Spirit through those in authority and respect for the action of the same Spirit in the vocation and conscience of each Christian are the vital polarity which alone brings about the atmosphere of true freedom of sons in the Kingdom of the Father. The following excerpts are to the point:

"Both [office-holders and their subjects] must realize that in the Church which has this charismatic element, subordinates are quite definitely not simply people who have to carry out orders from above. They have other commands as well to carry out, those of the Lord himself who also guides his Church directly and does not always in the first place convey his commands and promptings to ordinary Christians through the ecclesiastical authorities, but has entirely reserved for himself the right to do this directly in a great variety of ways that have little to do with keeping to the standard procedure and the 'usual channels'. . . . . . " Executive authority in the Church must, therefore, always cultivate the awareness that it is not, and may not be, the self-sufficient planner, as though in a totalitarian system, of all that is done in the Church. It must keep alive the consciousness that it is a duty and not a gracious condescension when it accepts suggestions from below; that "it must not from the start pull all the strings; and that the higher and, in fact, charismatic wisdom can sometimes be with the subordinate, and that the charismatic wisdom of office may consist in not shutting itself off from such higher wisdom." (p. 70-71)

Not only does the Spirit work through all the members of the Church, rather than only through those placed in a position of authority, but to be open to the inspiration of the Spirit, a great respect must be had for the diversity that is present in any community. Father Rahner places

Unity (

great importance on this kind of unifying force that is love. "Ultimately only one thing can give unity in the Church on the human level: the love which allows another to be different, even when it does not understand him. . . . For only then can the Church be one in spite of her dual structure. The principle that charity brings with it implies that each in the Church may follow his spirit as long as it is not established that he is yielding to what is contrary to the Spirit: that therefore, orthodoxy, freedom and goodwill are to be taken for granted and not the opposite." (p. 74) Without claiming charisms, the authors share their insights in the Spirit and his unifying love.

While urging all its members to personal co-responsibility, the Church has also spoken with full authority on the nature of the Church and the various groupings of persons within it. She enters her new era of ever deeper relevance and loving service under the powerful light of the *Constitution on the Church* issued by the Second Vatican Council. In this document the Holy Spirit tells us the special meaning and holiness of religious life.

"The profession of the evangelical counsels, then, appears as a sign which can and ought to attract all the members of the Church to an effective and prompt fulfillment of the duties of their Christian vocation. The people of God have no lasting city here below, but look forward to one that is to come. Since this is so, the religious state, whose purpose is to free its members from earthly cares, more fully manifests to all believers the presence of heavenly goods already possessed here below. Furthermore, it not only witnesses to the fact of a new and eternal life acquired by the redemption of Christ, but it foretells the future resurrection and the glory of the heavenly kingdom. Christ proposed to his disciples this form of life, which He, as the Son of God accepted in entering this world to do the will of the Father. This same state of life is accurately exemplified and perpetually made present in the Church. The religious state clearly manifests that the Kingdom of God and its needs, in a very special way, are raised above all earthly considerations. Finally it clearly shows all men both the unsurpassed breadth of the strength of Christ the King and the infinite power of the Holy Spirit marvellously working in the Church." (para. 44)

With its heavy emphasis on the new concept of the People of God, the Council must find an answer to the question of the place of religious in the modern Church. Against those who would de-emphasize fifteen hundred years of religious dedication, the Council makes it clear that the religious person is very much part of the total picture of the Church's life. "All men should take note that the profession of the evangelical counsels, though entailing the renunciation of certain values which are to be undoubtedly esteemed, does not detract from a genuine development of the human persons, but rather by its very nature is most beneficial to that development. Indeed the counsels, voluntarily undertaken according to each one's personal vocation, contribute a great deal to the purification of heart and spiritual liberty. They continually stir up the fervor of charity. But especially they are able to more fully mold the Christian man to that type of virginal and detached life which Christ the Lord chose for himself and which his mother also embraced. This is clearly proven by the example of so many holy founders. Let no one think that religious have become strangers to their fellowmen or useless citizens of this earthly city by their consecration. For even though, it sometimes happens that religious do not directly mingle with their contemporaries, yet in a more profound sense these same religious are united with them in the heart of Christ and spiritually cooperate with them. In this way the building up of the earthly city may have its foundation in the Lord and may tend toward him, lest perhaps those who build this city shall have labored in vain." (para. 46)

The specialness of religious which the Church so earnestly defends is in no sense a return to the old idea of privileged status or pharasaic "higherness." Rather, in a pilgrim Church, which moves through history in joy and confidence, but as the suffering servant of the Lord, religious will witness more than ever to sacred and not worldly values. The clarification of the role of the Christain in the world means that much of what religious did before may be done by laymen. But the true greatness of religious life stands out more clearly than ever. We offer the chapters of this book as a contribution to the aggiornamento of sisters already begun in the United States. May its contents make a little more realizable the ideal of religious life presented by the Council's *Constitution on the Church*.

1

Sociology
and Community Change

SISTER MARIE AUGUSTA NEAL, S.N.D.

Something has happened to the modern world since World War II, something that had begun to happen long before the war but was, prior to this time, too unconscious to be reflected beyond the art product and philosophical speculation. It is a quest for a new kind of community, a self-conscious community in which an adult can find that kind of psychic support that is necessary to ensure continued motivation to live and which at the same time allows for the spontaneous and creative development of human potential scarcely imagined before general economic and educational upgrading made it possible for us to think more realistically in peer terms rather than in the traditional mass-elite orientation of the older peasant society.

Granted that this search for community is not universal and is often obscured by the problems and concerns about the mass society; still it has been expressed in a sufficient variety of forms to indicate that it is a value sought and that it possesses also a developing shape. Simone Weil struggled to speak of it in *The Need for Roots*.[1] Albert

[1]Simone Weil, *The Need for Roots*, trans. by Arthur Willis (G. P. Putman's Sons, New York, 1952).

9

Camus laid the groundwork for it in brilliant descriptions
of its absence in *The Stranger*, and became its prophet in
The Plague.[2] The social scientist stepped in with Robert
A. Nisbet's *Quest for Community*,[3] while William H.
Whyte expressed his concern in a description of the subur-
banite's attempt to create a community in his bedroom
town, and the company's in the office. The product he
finds inadequate for the man who values his individuality.[4] Schools of business administration have found effective communities within the informal structure of the in-
dustrial plant, communities of a kind with rules often in
conflict with the formal organization rules of the company.[5] A whole applied field of social psychology called
group dynamics had developed rapidly in the 1940's; one
of its aims is to create a sense of community in business
establishments in order to release for work that human
energy that responds to effective attachments rather than
to economic gain. Genuine efforts have been made to
make work such a delightful part of life that it can be
done with joy in contrast to the treadmill-like routines
that have come to characterize production in the assembly
line.[6]

[2]Albert Camus, *The Stranger*, trans. by Stuart Gilbert (A. A. Knopf,
New York, 1946). *The Plague*, trans. by Stuart Gilbert (A. A.
Knopf, 1948).
[3]Robert A. Nisbet, *Community and Power* (Oxford University Press,
New York, 1962). This book was originally published under the
title *Quest for Community*, 1955.
[4]William H. Whyte, *The Organization Man* (Doubleday, New
York, Anchor Book, 1957).
[5]Harvard School of Business Administration sponsored a series of
studies having these findings, under the direction of Elton Mayo
in the 1930's. One example is F. J. Roethlisberger and W. J. Dis-
kon, *Management and the Worker* (Harvard University Press,
Cambridge, 1939).
[6]The National Educational Association and the Center for the
Study of Group Dynamics formerly at Massachusetts Institute of

SOURCES OF TREND TOWARD CONSCIOUS
SEARCH FOR COMMUNITY

1) Industrialism

There are several levels of new concern to create community but one very general one stems from reaction to the overall process of urbanization, industrialization, and bureaucratization that Maurice Stein describes in a book interestingly enough entitled *Eclipse of Community.*[7] The impersonality, anonymity, and monotony of relationships in modern associations structured for efficiency rather than for effectiveness have made an impact on man's psychic structure so that loneliness even in the midst of many is now a common experience. David Riesman captured this experience in *The Lonely Crowd.*[8]

The early 1940's saw within the Church a movement back to the farm to escape this anonymity of the city.[9] This movement sponsored by the Rural Life Conference we now recognize as a temporary effort to escape the realities of our moment in history, but it was significant in that it reflected a Christian condemnation of the highly structured bureaucratic society which, with the help of mass media, has come to characterize not only business, but government, labor, education, social life, and even religion in the large city parish. It revealed the fact that

Technology and now at the University of Michigan, Ann Arbor, established a summer institute for just such training at Bethal, Maine, in 1948. This type training now is being done in about fifty centers throughout the country.

[7]Maurice R. Stein, *Eclipse of Community: An Interpretation of American Studies* (Princeton University Press, Princeton, N. J., 1960). Conrad Arensburg's study of Culture and Community is also relevant (Harcourt, Brace and World, 1965).

[8]David Riesman, Reuel Denney, Nathan Glazer, *The Lonely Crowd* (Yale University Press, New Haven, 1950).

[9]Luigi G. Ligutti and John C. Rawe, S.J., *Rural Roads to Security* (Bruce Publishing Company, Milwaukee, 1940).

there was an awareness among the spiritually oriented that there was something unholy about the modern world. It is interesting that the first reaction to this discovery was to try to escape from the world. Today we are much more willing to accept this highly structured world as our own, and to seek ways of coping with it rather than repudiating it.

This change is to a large measure due to the new attitudes of the Church toward the world. Why this change? For one thing we have begun to discover that the factor that is making the world so complex and highly structured is that it is full of people and that to feed, clothe, educate, employ, establish and order life, and allow for personal development calls for cooperative effort and minute division of labor. This very need for the survival and development of people is the cause of bureaucratization, urbanization, and industrialization. Reluctantly and to some degree nostalgically we are ready to admit that, although the rural society was (at least in retrospect) a delightful society, its natural communities so secure and stable (as they seem to us now) can never be ours again. The modern quest for community must not repudiate large scale organization but make for a richer life within it, for right now it is the only possible structure to serve man's ever increasing numbers and needs.

The modern world is seeking to create communities that are not withdrawn from but are a living part of its complex organizational structure. So far we have not done so well. The Mayo studies are criticized in two directions: (1) They suggest changes that will create a work situation that is so delightful that no one wants to produce. (2) They train human engineers whose task it is to try to manipulate leadership structures to make men feel they are a community in order to induce them to produce or over-produce as loyal members of the firm. It was of this that William H. Whyte was complaining in *The Organization Man*. In *Crestwood Heights*, Seeley, Sim, and Loosley found a residential community over concerned with the emotional stability of their children.[10] Resistance to over-conformity and loss of individuality stem from a genuine fear man has today that he is fast becoming an object rather than a person and that the interpersonal relations in which he participates in his adult encounters are more and more object-like. Some evidence of how far that condition has gone is the response to the reform in the liturgy which is directed to an experience in which we can encounter others as persons rather than respond to them as creatures placed in our way as temptations or obstructions to our personal sanctification. Yet we find many who shy away from liturgical community because it destroys privacy by bringing people into our prayer life and disturbs our communication with God.

2) *Exploitation of Men: Second Factor in the Search for Community*. The division of labor necessitated by production of goods and services for a burgeoning population was not the only source of stimulation for a new search for community in the mid-twentieth century. Another causal factor far more traumatic in its content and more gripping on the consciences of man is the genocide perpetrated in Germany in the 1930's. The concentration camps, prisons, and other locales of human cruelty that have been exposed as products of decision-making in our modern bureaucratic system reveal to us the awful cruelty with which we can treat a human person when, in programing social change, we define him as stranger, deviant, rebel,

[10] J. R. Seeley, R. A. Sim, E. W. Loosley, *Crestwood Heights, a Study of the Culture of Suburban Life* (Wiley and Sons, Inc., New York, 1963).

rival, or burden. This tragic incident is only one of many
perpetrated by totalitarian bureaucratized impersonal
social systems. Looking back over the long tradition of
western culture we rejoice at the fine statements we have
made about the dignity of the human person. We rejoice
in the Greek, Roman, Hebrew and especially Christian
roots to which we can trace its expression. Today, however we have to deal with our own torn consciences when
we dare to contemplate the human cruelties emerging
from the decisions we allowed to be made or the actions
we did not take. This becomes especially acute when we
examine the societies in which these cruelties have occurred. Their heritage is so Christian that we have to admit with Chesterton that Christianity did not fail here, it
simply was not tried. But then we have to ask why, since
we are so tremendously involved in the effort we call
Christian, why we find among us these cruelties to the
Negro minorities in America, the working class in South
America, the native in Africa. Each of these owes his
present status to the decisions Christians made about their
education, training and representation in government. The
treatment of minorities in all the nations of the world is
the case in point, a graphic case to which Pope John
pleaded that we devote serious attention.

Many thoughtful attempts have been made to explain
why, despite our commitments to the dignity of the human person, these things happen. One such explanation
is Martin Buber's *I and Thou*.[11] Here is an effort, obscure
yet clear, to describe how we can encounter the other as
person rather than as object. It sounds strange to say we

[11]Martin Buber, *I and Thou*, trans. by Ronald Smith (Charles
Scribner, New York, 1958). See also Maurice Freedman (Univer-
sity of Chicago Press, Chicago, 1955), (Harper Torchbook, 1960),
Martin Buber: The Life of Dialogue.

must cease to treat others as objects ("Its") and begin
to treat them as persons. We always thought we were
doing this until the genocide demonstrated to us that this
was not so. These were Jews in Germany; but in our cities,
in our towns, in our homes there are others on whom our
hostilities rest in parallel ways. Even as we talk the doctrine of love, we manipulate the system for our own special
interests, or claim it is human nature to think of ourselves
first, or that "you can't beat city hall," or that every man
is out for all he can get and "we've got to be practical."
Even when we do not openly say these things we act as
if we believed them. We cannot really hear the cries of
the Negro, or the Jew, of the working class, or the farmer,
or the peasant, or the student, or the child, or the poor,
or our own neighbor or whoever it is that we have coded
into a category and deprived of the right to be a person
in his encounter with us. The prejudices of the modern
world reveal graphically that our world is full of people
treated as objects who cannot possibly reach the status of
persons with us, because our whole training and life experience has closed our sensitivities to the needs, the
meanings, the aspirations, of many categories of others
who are not meaningful to us because of the way we have
defined the world. And yet the whole message of Christianity asks of us to give that same personal consideration to
the stranger that we give to the dearest self, not as to a
stranger but as to Christ.

This discovery in the world and in the convent of how
very much some people are "Its" to us is gradually revealing to us that our indifference to world peace, disarma-
ment, the economic plight of the underdeveloped nations,
the inner city, the treatment of minorities, those problems
to which Pope John asked that we devote our Christian
efforts, stems from a basic incapacity to feel with the

other, not just the other defined formally by these categories but any other not easily encountered with our present world view. Modern studies in group analysis reveal insensitivity to others, and definitions of the world so narrow that within these it is even possible to convey the existence of problems or needs beyond those to which we traditionally responded.[12]

Each age of man broadens its encounter with the rest of the world. The primitive world defined the little community as the people and all others as nonpeople. Navaho, for example, means "the people." Through the introduction of TV, radio, paperback, newspapers and other media, along with rapid means of transportation the boundary reductions of our encounters with others are limitless. If there is not concommitant development of psychological capacity to be open to many people without experiencing the invasion of our privacy, we will build up psychic walls of exclusiveness to replace the physical ones formerly placed by spatial distance. Christianity does not condone such a stance. In fact the challenge of Christianity is the building of community without walls. This is something different from anything the world has ever experienced before. Folk society, social classes, ethnic groups have always considered themselves legitimate exclusive communities. The effort to develop an openness to the other while at the same time we respect his privacy and never invade his sanctuary is one which we make towards those whose dignity as persons we respect but which we deny to those we treat as objects. This is the main thrust of the Christian message for our times. This is why Pope John XXIII devoted *Pacem in Terris* to concern for separated others

---

[12]Sister Marie Augusta Neal S.N.D., *Values and Interests in Social Change* (Prentice-Hall, Englewood, N.J., 1965). Interest-non-change characteristics.

who are deprived due to our indifference or unawareness.

People vary strikingly in the number of others who are for them persons and the number of others they use as objects. For some, all are persons, for others, all are objects. Most of us fall somewhere between these extremes in our treatment of others. Christ asks of us that we strive to treat all as persons. At this moment in history, as the Church deals with problems of minorities, the under-developed nations, and world peace, these issues come to express the central Christian concern for the other. Their solution rests centrally with the Church's service workers, the religious communities of men and women whose task it is to set the style of living the Christian life. (There are religious who mind being called service workers in the Church, associating this with functionaries and all the impersonality this implies—but the term here is intended to have dignity as when the Pope calls himself "servant of the servant of God." It is also intended to move toward the elimination of the idea of an elite.)

3) *Current Forms Do Not Fit the Need: Third Source of Trend Toward Search for Community.* While the world outside the cloister and convent re-examines the need for community, looks nostalgically back to the folk society or even to the city ghetto when it had become a replica of the old country,[13] and gets ready again to seek ways of creating community, the cloister, the convent, the mona-stery, and the seminary looking back over centuries of "community" living are wondering why there is pressure for them to change today. The reason has to do with the social structure of those communities; the old structure is no longer relevant to new needs. Our religious communi-ties, structured on the family model, have fitted in well in

[13]Oscar Handlin, *The Uprooted* (Little, Brown, and Co., Boston, 1951).

past centuries yet we could not offer them today as models
for the rest of the world to adopt because somehow at
this moment we know they too need remodeling if they
are to meet the needs of this moment of history. We too
have experienced that object-like relationship and something of the impersonality experienced in bureaucratic
structures—but the reasons are different. Our communities today are chafing under their command-obedience
structure and we are trying to figure out why. We know
that obedience is necessary and good. We know that commands must be given; we know that anarchy and excessive
individuality frustrate any common effort. Yet we know
our model is not working. We have heard the accusations
of those hostile to our mode of living that it generates
susceptibility to totalitarianism, that it stresses too much
the dependency of the obedient, that the members are
treated as children and encouraged to obey as the child
obeys his parents.)

Our observations reveal that we have called those in
charge mother or father as the case may be. The younger
members are treated as children; age is highly valued.
Initiative is sometimes discouraged or nipped or resisted
when the initiator is a younger member of the community.
It is true that the vow so beautifully taught and accepted
demands unquestioning acceptance of the will of the
superior, that even the wish of the superior is defined as
the command of Christ. We know that the intent here is
that the superior's command reflect the expectation of
Christ. In practice, however, the superior has been defined
as the head of the local house, the province, the order.
but not the head of the Church. We are beginning to discover that in the course of time this emphasis has resulted
in the deflection of emphasis from the Church as community to the local house as community.) The immediate

needs, the survival interests of the limited group, rather than the preaching of the gospel have in some cases become the focal factor for decisions that determine the direction the apostolate take. We know that such a deflection of dedication from the purposes of the Church has happened many times in history, has happened to many other organizations besides religious orders, and is now happening to us. Hence it needs to be looked at candidly, evaluated in its direction, purpose, intent, and method. There are perhaps no organizations in the world that exhibit as much good will as religious communities. Why then at this moment in history were we caught napping when human needs called out for response? We became religious to bring the compassion of Christ to a needy world. We do respond to the needs we perceive. Why did we miss the social messages of the popes from Leo to John? And why were these messages needed at all if we were on the job?

MINIMAL RESPONSE TO SOCIAL NEEDS

Other-worldly orientation: If you read the rule of religious orders of women founded in the last century and read it rule by rule, chapter by chapter, you will find many reiterations of the need to keep the world out, to withdraw from conversation with seculars, from discussion of the news of the day, from discussing new plans and programs, in general from counseling or initiating any action that deflects from the special end for which the institute was founded, that is, teaching children, medical care, work among the poor, and so forth. Yet if one then examines this special end and the way it is now carried out by the same institute, it will often be found that the pressing problems to which the institute first made its response either no longer exist, or still exist but are not

the focal work of the institute in its present structure.
Where such a condition exists there is need to reexamine
purpose and means for attaining it. Many religious orders
are doing just this at present.

What has happened to make us aware of a need for
change? For one thing professionalization has set in, a
necessary addition to the work in the field of education,
medicine, social welfare, the main works of religious
orders of the past hundred years. Health, education, and
welfare, the latest addition to the nation's programs has
been the work of the sisters. Obviously it has become a
large-scale need if to meet it the whole country is now
organizing, for the poverty program, the medical care for
the aged, the mammoth education bills. Our works have
become the enormous needs of a burgeoning society and
world. When these needs were emerging and no public
facilities served them, then the compassion of the Lord
which the religious order expressed stimulated the fine
works of service that the orders reflected in this past century. It may well be that now is the moment to relinquish
many of these to the laity and to begin other works pressing for response.

Our professionalization follows rather than leads the
laity today. What does this tell us? Somewhere along the
line our focus turned from these works even though we
were doing them. Where was it? It was on the development of our own community life from which we went to
these works as from the in-group to the out-group. These
works became less incorporated into our community life.
Our community life stood apart from our works. How
then is this community life related to the works? Does it
foster the works, prepare us for them, reinforce our enthusiasm and dedication to them or has it become by some
strange turn a source of resistance to them? I think the

latter is the case and now I want to examine how this has come to be, because it certainly did not begin this way.) (These works are people, so the word itself is object-like).

Many of our orders were founded or had redirected their works in the nineteenth century when the general tenor of religious (spiritual writing emphasized an indi-vidualistic and transcendent focus of the road to salva-tion, that is, God and myself.) The world was perceived as dangerous, or delightful but tempting, and deflecting one's attention from the goal which was personal sanctifi-cation. We went to the poor whose neglected condition was the stimulation for our foundations but we brought the poor, the aged, the sick, the little children into our schools, homes, hospitals, and institutions and cared for them with deep compassion, an amazing devotion of time and energy of which the world has little conception. We shared them with our cloistered innocence and they, com-ing from the cruelties of the wrold of whose indifference they were victims, loved this simple concern. We ap-proached the rich to subsidize our work and we loved them for their generous response. We organized guilds, clubs, leagues, to which we invited the rich and the gen-erous middle class to come and pray and relax and give. This they did. We faced two separate worlds. The poor whom we serviced as loving mothers; the rich whom we thanked in many many instances as our betters. We re-lieved pressing problems of the immigrant, and the out-cast. We gave psychic support to the generous donor who was pleased that the good sister appreciated his gift. By this relationship we built up huge establishments that so serviced the pressing needs of the society which created and preserved these poverty patterns that the works, our works, became indispensable to the *status quo* and we were rewarded for increasing and multiplying our institutions, staffing them and servicing them. We did this so intensely we never stopped to ask why these poor were poor, why these needy suffered. (We asked the question but it was rhetorical).

And we did something else also. We developed parallel services for the well-off—schools, hospitals, homes for the retired. And we found when we worked with these more fortunate people that they were good, lovable, and like the poor needed us as much as did the poor. But in time they moved from the central city and they wanted us to come with them to staff their schools, their hospitals, their social centers and we could not say no. We were poor too and had to go where we would be supported. Unwittingly we became their servants and they and we moved from the pressing problems of the poor in the city who could not move out because the rents were too high, the transportation too expensive and the welcome not forthcoming.

Our numbers did not increase in proportion to the needs so in time we had to make decisions as to where we would open new houses. Expediency became the criterion because we had never stopped to assess the structural trends of the society in which we were working. We had neither the time nor the training for this. We answered the calls for help as they came and when two came we answered the one we could afford. Money for both the inner city needs and the poor village needs was not available many times (before the governments became like us conscious that the society of people creates its own poverty pockets and hence must service them). So the poor, not seen, became forgotten to some degree. The people needing help multiplied. The communities of sisters became refuges from the world. Retreat houses, convents, schools, hospitals, became treasured places for those caught up in the anonymity of the bureaucratic society. These people, our alumnae, encouraged our remaining what we were, their refuge from the world.

But then a new voice became articulate, best heard in Pope John, but first heard clearly in Pope Pius XI speaking from the tragedies of the depression of the 1930's and the risings of the totalitarian states. He was saying for the first time (according to a content analysis of our social ethics books) that the evils structured in our modern institutions are our responsibility to change and to bring into conformity with the teaching of Christ, into harmony with the demands of the common good, that is into such forms that those living within society have opportunities for happiness not despite the social structure but because of it.[14] What he was telling us was that our economy had so structured evil that the poor were deprived of an adequate share of the good things they helped produce, and furthermore, that what was produced was not fairly distributed. That this deprivation overflowed into the educational system, and the aspects of the social order, Pope John added later. Karl Marx had said this a century before and blamed it on our two-class system but because he repudiated God and grace and encouraged the revolution to destroy the exploiting class he was not heard. When in time we discovered that despite the error of his therapy he had put his finger on an evil that we could remedy, we heard the voices that encouraged the remedy. Pope Leo and Pope Pius were among the most articulate in *Rerum Novarum* and *Quadragesimo Anno*.[15] The latter,

[14]William Feree S.M., *The Act of Social Justice* (Marianist Publications, Dayton, Ohio, 1951).
[15]Pope Leo XIII, *Rerum Novarum*, first published in 1891 and *Quadragesimo Anno*, first published in 1931. Both can be obtained from the National Catholic Welfare Conference, Washington, D.C.

entitled in English "The Reconstruction of the Social Order," made clear for us for the first time that man must do just this, reconstruct the social order. It will not happen by itself. With the entry of the totalitarian exploiting systems the faith of the Social Darwinists had subsided and we gradually came to realize in the context of our times what freedom really means. We are free to introduce changes and to resist change and neither effort is by its nature good or evil. We are free to succeed and free to fail. It is the content that makes the difference.

RECONSTRUCTION OF THE SOCIAL ORDER

We came with the aid of Pope Pius to realize, at least intellectually, that any reconstruction of the social order would have to be done after consulting with men and women who knew how it was constructed in the first place. Their numbers were woefully few. The field of sociology, stemming as it had from positivist philosophical base outside the Church, left us quite hostile to its findings and quite ignorant of its meanings. In the early 1930's, stimulated by Pope Pius' teachings on Catholic Action, clergy and religious of all types began the development of social action groups. But what could we use as a model for developing leadership when the whole focus of our dedication in our religious orders and seminaries was modeled on a hierarchical structure for our work relations and a family type structure for our away-from-work community life within which the world was seen as evil, dangerous, tempting, and of secondary importance. Secondary to what? To our community life.

We organized Catholic Action groups with a hierarchy of offices, with command coming from the top and obedience expected down the line. We programed a policy, gave it to groups already formed with offices elected and roles assigned before the task was introduced. And what happened? We found ourselves with an overstructured system lacking the dynamism that comes from commitment to a cause which one has personally experienced. Why was this? The studies Kurt Lewin directed in the 1940's suggest the reason. People better carry out a program of action that involves social change when they participate in making the decisions about what is to be changed, anguish over and respond with enthusiasm as the means become visible or possible through shared exploration of need and available means.[16] To initiate change requires a tremendous investment of psychic energy which man does not generate unless motivated by understanding, concern and commitment. These develop only in interaction of peers with peers. These studies came too late to affect the early program. When they were applied in the 1940's this was done in a way in which we made people feel that they were making decisions while we manipulated the lines of command. Again it did not work. Why? We were almost totally unaware of the true psychic structure of man. Machiavelli was more our model than Christ. This picture, of course, is somewhat overdrawn but the point is relevant that the works of lay groups in the Church when working with religious have been a problem because of the role definitions religious have of the laity. The laity are outsiders to our community; they are low status members of the formal hierarchical structure of the Church. We have no experimental model to guide our working together except the family or formal organizational structures and

[16]See Kurt Lewin, "Group Decision and Social Change," in *Readings in Social Psychology*, edited by Guy E. Swanson, Theodore M. Newcomb, and Eugene L. Hartley (Henry Holt, New York, 1952). The article by Lester Coch and John R. French, "Overcoming Resistance to Change," in the same reader is even more relevant. These articles appear also in the recent revisions of the reader.

neither of these generates an equal-status peer group relation needed for exploring problems. A new kind of social
structure is needed for this purpose and it is the thesis
of this paper that religious communities are ideally situated to become this new form.

The 1930's spawned another set of attitudes toward
human problems. Men and women disillusioned by the
destitution of the Jews in Germany and others similarly
disillusioned with their experiences in the Marxist experiment were beginning to reflect on the overstructured efforts toward social change springing up in the West and
wondering why totalitarianism had become so attractive.
Erich Fromm in his provocative study of *Escape from
Freedom* proposed the hypothesis that modern man was
afraid of the new freedom he found when he discovered
that he makes his own institutions and is responsible for
their present conditions.[17] Fromm saw him escaping into
highly stratified organizations which gave him a sense of
security or at least provided him with an excuse for not
taking responsibility and making choices for which he
would be held accountable in the critical and somewhat
hostile environment made so by rapid change. This analysis has stimulated much study and particularly clarifies
some of the unexpressed problems of this man who, in the
face of an evil he perceives to be present in the organizations of which he is a member, can no longer say, "It is not
my responsibility, I am not in charge." In the mass-elite
society of an earlier era, many of the laity lived relatively
free of responsibility. In the convent, religious had done

[17]Erich Fromm, *Escape from Freedom* (Farrar and Rinehart, New
York, 1941). For accounts of the disillusionment with Communism,
etc., see Richard Crossman (ed.), *The God that Failed* (Harper,
New York, 1950); Czeslaw Milosz, *The Captive Mind* (Knopf,
New York); and Arthur Koestler, *Darkness at Noon* (Macmillan,
New York, 1941).

the same. It was quite frightening—all of a sudden to hear from the Church and the world that freedom to do what one wishes includes responsibility for choices made.)It is an awful feeling to lie awake at night and think of all the changes needed in society and to realize that he who knows the need must provide the remedy. Fear of playing this role, thought Fromm, was pervasive when these new insights became part of modern man's knowledge about himself and his world. But why such fear? For one thing the newly-awakened knows how he and his fellow men treated the innovator who upset the even tenor of their ways: the character attack, the withdrawal of psychic support, the economic, political and social sanction— those powerful forms of informal social control he knows would be the lot of him who tried to change things and he was afraid.

But who exerts these sanctions and on whom? We are all familiar with them. Maybe we have not yet seen clearly that these are the mechanisms that preserve a style of life, and which keep man's social institutions in existence. An institution is no more than a set of rules for getting something done. These rules are carried out because members of the group think they ought to be and they punish with scorn, ridicule, or rejection those who deviate from them. Obviously the rules can be changed by reduction of the sanctions, but who are these sanctioners? Those who want the system to remain as it is. Down through the centuries man has preserved an amazing assortment of styles of living through the unquestioning naive assumption that they were natural or controlled by some absolute law. William G. Sumner in his classic study *Folkways* confirmed belief in the unchangeableness of social rules.[18] The Ku Klux Klan's last feeble, grotesque efforts to pre-

[18]William G. Sumner, *Folkways* (Ginn and Co., Boston, 1940).

serve a style of interpersonal behavior based on erroneous
beliefs about differences is also a classic example of the
extremes modern man can reach in his effort to enforce
the institutionalized ways irrespective of their rationality,
justice, or humanity, irrespective of their contradiction of
the belief systems to which the members are committed.

Most men today cannot so easily accept the inevitability
of old cultural forms. They are too conscious of planned
change in Russia, China and elsewhere.

FAMILY NO LONGER ADEQUATE MODEL
FOR RELIGIOUS COMMUNITY

But why have adult groups so feared change and so
ardently persevered in retaining outmoded forms of interaction with others despite the irrationality of some of these
behaviors and their contradiction of shared beliefs? Here
I must propose another hypothesis and explore it. Many
adult groups are consciously or unconsciously modeled on
the family, especially if the group is desirous of creating
community. The family is a community and is also a place
wherein the expression of affection and the freer discharge
of aggression is permitted; it is for the child a refuge from
a strange external world. Its memory for many is an
idealization of a protective environment where he can release his feelings with impunity. But the family is a special
kind of community in which a child learns many things he
does not understand—learns in a complexity of affection-
aggression bonds with his parents who have a unique tie
to him. The things he learns are their ways which he accepts though often he does not understand them. He
learns them in order to be accepted. He dare not change
many of them lest he lose the relationship he has come to
need.

When adult communities operate in the family style, many of the members of the community generate for him the same type of irrational attachments he experiences in his socialization process at home. For old-style adult life this was not too serious a problem but for ours it is. Why is this so? In the primitive and peasant societies of the past the political and economic structures were consciously modeled on the family in a parent-child model relationship. The Church too as made up of God and the family of man took the family ties for its major role players and often thought of itself as a family community. When the roles one played outside the family call for patterns of response dissimilar to those within the family this parallel generates problems in several directions, man comes to confuse God, parents, and other command-givers. The limited authority characteristic of all adult relationships gets confused with absolutes and becomes entwined with problems of faith in complex ways. In modern societies the economy has become independent of the family, the corporation not the family firm has charge of the production and distribution of goods and services. The polity, once a monarchy of tribal father and his children, is now predominantly a representative democracy of peers making decisions for peers wherein status is in terms of special expertise hence not absolute. The educational system is comprised of specialists who are experts in one area and students in another. For roles in these systems the parent roles with their characteristics of pervasive authority have little relevancy. Those trained in the family model are at a disadvantage when they take their limited role set out to a world which requires a more versatile repertoire. Some further explanation of this point is in order at this point, because it is not yet explicit in much of the literature within the Church.

1) *Changing role of the family:* Because of the division of labor in modern society the family has of necessity been forced to specialize in its primary function of (1) care and training of children, and (2) stabilizing adult personalities rather than being an economic productive unit as it was even a hundred years ago. Both of these roles are socio-emotional rather than task-oriented. The family at the same time has become limited to parents and children. This means that most of one's early childhood training is received from two or even one role model who has an unusually deep affection-aggression relationship with the child, being both provider and disciplinarian. The result of this highly specialized function leaves the child, as he emerges into the world of work, and education, with a limited set of value responses to adults: respect, loyalty, love and obedience. Yet the adult world of work requires a resilient give and take, initiative and control, acceptance of discipline and courageous rejection of illegitimate authority, the standing alone on principle, the giving support to an idea man, give and take that the nuclear family does not provide because the family is not a model in its command-obedience and love patterns for the adult community relationship wherein leadership roles are temporary and functionally specific when properly played and held. This new relationship between family and community, family and the world and education, family and peer group requires a discovery of the primary functions of the family, their central purpose and dignity but their new limitations as well. The family today is not the model for role relations in the adult world.

2) *Development of extra-familial roles:* But how does one then develop this enlarged set of role patterns? This is the critical question and what is said in this area has about it the element of the experimental. In the *Moral*

Judgment of the Child Jean Piaget demonstrated why for
two different reasons interactions limited to the family
type are inadequate for the achievement of adult status.[19]
(1) The child is submissive to the word of his parents, believing without question everything he is told. He does
not perceive the element of uncertainty and search in
adult thought. In the same way he believes every thought
that comes into his own head. He does not treat these as
hypotheses that have to be verified. This condition continues until he discusses his ideas with his peers. In this
setting he comes to criticize and be criticized and this
criticism leads to the verification of ideas. But, says Piaget,
discussion, genuine discussion, can only occur among
peers. (If he is right, and much that we have already
said about the parent-child bonds reinforces his point,
discussions that take place in convent settings will be
effective only to the degree that they are based on a peer
interaction.)

These comments thus far refer to the development of
knowledge. The second area to which he refers is the development of moral judgment. Piaget also notes that the
imperatives the child received are for him absolute when
the parents express them. Outward agreement with accepted rules does not constitute morality. There must also
be a recognition of and the appreciation of the value of
the rules that are proposed. Again for a child to develop
this kind of appreciation there must be interaction with
peers. With this type of interaction "unilateral respect
breaks down and the primary personal judgment develops."[20] At the end of his analysis Piaget becomes almost

[19]Jean Piaget, *The Moral Judgment of the Child* (The Free Press,
Glencoe, Illinois, 1951).
[20]*Ibid.*, p. 402.

too eloquent as he predicts the outcome of the peer experience.

> A new morality follows upon pure deity. Heteronomy steps aside to make way for a consciousness of good of which the autonomy results from the acceptance of the norms of *reciprocity*. Obedience withdraws in favor of the idea of justice and of mutual service, now the source of all obligations which till then had been imposed as incomprehensible commands.[21]

Human Relations ✓

In this last statement Piaget strikes the heart of the matter. True human relations are reciprocal. They take into consideration the I and the Thou. Each person comes to know the other as a person. Most of the social structures in which we interact to get things done do not allow the development for such a profound relation. But were there communities in which the development of such an art or skill or whatever it may be were the goal, everything in the gospel suggests that it could become a mode of interpersonal behavior that, mastered by some, could then be shared with others until moving from centers of community into the larger community it could come in time to permeate the whole of society. But this is not all Piaget is saying. He also suggests that the commitment to duty, which we now speak of in terms of obedience to rule or to him who commands, becomes through interaction with peers a commitment to justice and mutual service which is in turn a deeper obedience. It is worth pausing to stop to ponder what the world would be like if the source of obligation were to derive from a deeply internalized sense of obligation to incomprehensible commands. Have we even considered seriously this link of levels of maturity with obedience and justice? This I submit should become the objective of the living together modes of religious communities of men and of women.

[21] *Ibid.*, p. 403.

This extended discussion of Piaget is included here because it seems to express the psychological rationale for a new kind of community experience that is required by the religious women who would respond to the needs of the world in its present encounter with the Church. For centuries the vow of obedience has been stressed in religious orders. The obedience asked, unlike the poverty and chastity, is not a special counsel of perfection, rather it is the same obedience to the word of God that is expected of all Christians, that Christ gave to his Father. No member of a religious order can or should abrogate his responsibility to choose and to respond to an awareness of a need because of his vow.[22] In practice, however, due to the peasant-elite heritage of the Middle Ages a kind of private pervasive omniscience has been assigned to the superior's role along with the expectation that he or she be a loving parent to the community of religious in the old tradition of *noblesse oblige.* In earlier days, too, the leaders were chosen from among members of the upper class of a two class society wherein training in responsibility was given to the nobles and training in loyalty and obedience given to the peasant. Most of today's older religious come from the old peasant stock, however, and the training in the home is to obedience and loyalty as the tradition reinforced, while the training to responsibility has been relatively idiosyncratic and not part of the traditional family training. The result of this historical factor is that the majority of religious come to the convent with deeply internalized trainings in obedience and loyalty (and some with latent hostilities with respect to this training); but a special systematic training to responsibility for making the society in which we live is characteristic of but a few.

[22]See Karl Rahner S.J., "Reflections on Obedience," *Cross Currents*, X, (Fall 1960), pp. 362-374.

This, of course, is just as true of many of the older lay
population served by the religious. Training to reciprocity
and responsibility is not a special style of their cultural
heritage and hence has not been built into the style of
training given in our schools as has obedience and respect
for authority. This does not mean that individual families
did not develop the style but it does mean that those who
move into the authority roles have no traditional community ideal of responsibility worked out and also no
social reinforcement of their own private judgment in this
area. To give this social reinforcement is one of the functions of a cultural heritage. Necessarily then they must
fall back on the family style of command, the only one
they have learned in an experimental way from interaction
with their own parents. Hence their interaction with subjects is attended by all the trauma of their own childhood
and this too they relay to their subjects at the unconscious
level. (Note the mass-elite orientation of the word "subject.")

For some time now we have been aware of the need
for responsibility training but we cannot add a kind of
training just because we discover the need of it. We have
to know how to give it and what it is and this knowing
has to be experienced before it can be shared. The convent offers such a setting.

In summary then it is here suggested that the family is
no longer a model for a religious community mainly because the family has become so highly specialized for the
socialization of children and also because it has become
nuclear, that is, limited to father, mother and children.
The old extended family had many adult role models including grandparents, uncles, aunts and other relatives.
But even further than the model problem, a community of
adults needs experience in peer relations to develop that

critical judgment from which creativity and responsibility develop. The family emphasis in religious communities allows the religious to treat students, patients, clients with an over-protectedness that does not give them full recognition and opportunity to develop their human potential with full realization of their dignity as persons. It also stimulates in many religious an infantilism that leaves them less than spontaneous in their response to the exigencies of this moment in history.

RELIGIOUS AND THE CALL TO COMMUNITY:
1. THE POSSIBILITIES

Changes are coming. There is no doubt that awareness of the inadequacies of dependency training for living in today's world is part of the thinking of current sister educators and that profound changes are in process and under consideration at every level. That is not the issue here. The issue here is that this response to a new need in the world would be better handled if the community life of the sister gave her an experience of the Christian encounter with her peers. Through this encounter she could develop in this process of interaction the fullness of the I-Thou relationship that would not only enable her to live the richness of her own human potential, but also enable her to share the dynamic energy released by this experience with a world seeking now a truly communal encounter with a spontaneity that is the heritage of the people of God. It may very well be that the next era of history will call her to whole areas of new works just as the last era of history called her from the cloister to staff institutions for the poor. (This was the original call even though we have since drifted from it in many circumstances.) Whatever the call to which she responds next,

the kind of person she will be will make the difference in
what she can effect.

Many factors point to the need for and the coming of
this change in sister community relations. Some responses
to the liturgical changes are a case in point. These responses have been in many instances infantile. Some have
tried to make rules out of suggestions, turn directives into
recommendations; some evaded, some denied the new attitude in the Church until its presence was so evident that
non-response appeared ridiculous. In many instances they
were out of harmony with the new *Constitution on the
Liturgy* because in fact they were wishing it away in their
fantasy life. Pressed for the reasons for resistances some
found personal discomfort to be the cause. Commitment to
a ritual, desire for order whether it had meaning or not,
withdrawal from association with people, a reluctance to
respond where they had not initiated, all these were reasons for resistance. Many were abashed to find that their
responses were not in fact unique to them but quite typical of many other religious orders of men and women
with similar old styles of life. Yet the new liturgy has for
its aim the creation of a community of persons facing their
God in deep acceptance of each other as the people of
God.

RELIGIOUS AND THE CALL TO COMMUNITY:
2. THE PROBLEM

Responses to social action programs of the Church
found some of us not only unprepared and unaware but
in many cases actually resistant. Not yet have we become
fully aware of the deep causes of this resistance. Living in
the security of family structured communities just before
and during World War II, some did not experience with
the same trauma as the rest of the world, the gradual

awakening to the fact that the evils they were denouncing
had in fact been caused by them. Some religious did not
learn as well as those not of the convent that we, modern
Christians, and not the devil were responsible for the genocide of the Jews, the exploitation of the Negro, and the
non-education of the really poor in the most forsaken
places—responsible, because our gospel called for more
concern than we gave. Where others developed a new enthusiasm for the Word they could understand, some religious did not develop that passion for the vernacular so
that the Word could be heard. Others learned at that time
that the gospel unpreached must go unpracticed. (And
our social and economic life reveals wonderously the degree of its nonpractice.) Religious when cloistered often
cling, more than the outside world, to the naive belief that
the word spoken is communicated irrespective of whether
the audience understands the language in which it is
heard. Only now as we hear the epistle and gospel each
day do we come to realize with the laity that the gospel is
best heard when we all hear it together. Many in the convent have not yet fully discovered that a whole way of
economic life, of political life, and of social life has developed unbaptized not because we have not been there as
Catholics but because we condoned the structured evil
in its rules totally unconscious that we shared that secular
culture, it values and norms.[23] Religious along with others
sanctioned it by punishing those who deviated from its
secularist content because somehow so many had come to
think of these norms as Christian without examining how
they, by their fruits, revealed that the gospel of Christ was
not in fact practiced. With others many religious experienced no great surge of human compassion (and some real
surge of human resistance) to examine the violation of
[23]On this point see Ferree, pp. 110, 186.

housing codes because in a sense we all owned those houses. The reform of the political order has not become the special concern of religious and some have even rationalized that some of the structured evil must continue for practical reasons. So with the economy. No great zeal is expended on plans for conversion of our economy to peace time uses where we profit by the present mode. Little of our effort is expended on the development of the social sciences because we are only now coming to know that the realm of the interpersonal is the area of man's greatest potential for spiritual growth through the responsible study and use of what can be known by controlled observation and systematic experimentation; that man's spontaneity and creativity are helped by understanding his motivations, his unconscious needs and drives, his secret ambitions, his limited understandings, his deep emotional involvements and inhibitions. Even as we glorified man's free will we became victims of tremendous determinacies because of our fear to know and our reluctance to look. The man we tried to love because God commanded us to love, we could not even come to know because our encounters were so limited to the impersonal and the familial. The in-between encounter of peer with peer in an adult relationship based on respect for the dignity of the person, for his freedom, for his aspirations could become the quest of religious community living. Here each ego learns to set limits on himself to produce that control and responsible action which enables the development of group relations centered on goals through implementation of shared values. The reward received from the other for such treatment will itself elicit the energy from the self to respond with ever more initiative and creativity devoid of exploitation.

What these coments suggest is the need for some serious examination of the structure of religious community life. We cannot adequately educate ourselves behind the walls. We cannot be contemporary Christians fully cloistered. Yet our purpose as religious is to point to another reality beyond the earthly city. We chose our life of freedom in the Lord so we could be free for the world but in time we have allowed the cult of the hearth to absorb our community life. On the other hand we religious need some kind of closed community. We need a home to which we can return to rest awhile where we can pray and talk and love more freely and fully, where we can assess, define and redefine our purpose. The discipline of our lives in freedom is needed in the world; the freedom in discipline at home, where we are wanted, accepted, and repaired after the toil and heat of the day. It is for this that we need a new form of community not peasant but Christian, more mobile yet havens, wherein we become stable persons rather than where we create places of stability. Yet this place of gathering cannot be exclusive on the one hand nor merely a hotel on the other.

RELIGIOUS AND THE CALL TO COMMUNITY:
3. THE CHRISTIAN RESPONSE

The outlook of the Church on the world has radically changed. The transcendent emphasis of the past few centuries has now swung to an immanent emphasis.[24] This is the interest of *aggiornamento*. The historical rationale for this development stems from the fact that the central command of the Christian commitment asks for love of God and love of neighbor. Each moment in history by

[24]Emmanuel Cardinal Suhard, *Growth or Decline? The Church Today* (Fides Publishers, Notre Dame, Indiana, 1948), pp. 54-55.

reason of the decisions made in previous moments emphasizes one of these directions to a more or less greater degree than the other and hence has its own unique style of response. We have come to the end of a long post-Reformation transcendent emphasis and the failures to respond to the pressing problems of the masses in the last century asks a reconsideration of the meaning of the "love thy neighbor" focus which is so explicit in Christ's statement: "A new commandment I give you, that you love one another as I have loved you. By this shall all men know that you are my disciples." This reconsideration needs to be done with a seriousness that will generate compassion for human suffering with the intent of both sharing it now and helping to relieve it. We are just beginning to discover we cannot cure problems we do not experience as problems. This change is without a doubt the work of the Spirit. It took many years to prepare the people of God for this new stage in the life of the Church. Yves Congar has well analyzed this in the *Lay People in the Church*.[25]

This moment asks for massive reorganization of society not only in its distribution of wealth so eloquently described in *Mater et Magistra*[26] but in its attitude toward persons, Buber's concern. The mass-elite orientation with its emphasis on leaders and followers is passé for this moment. Obedience is necessary and loyalty is necessary but neither of these in any static distribution of labor is the essential need of this moment.

Justice, freedom, responsibility, and commitment with focus on reciprocity are the major ideals to be developed

[25]Yves Congar, *Lay People in the Church,* trans. by Donald Attwater (Newman Press, Westminster, Maryland, 1957).
[26]Pope John XXIII, *Mater et Magistra* (America Press, New York, 1961).

in today's community. This does not in any way mitigate the importance of obedience and respect for authority. For the training of children these are as always necessary virtues to develop, but the adult encounter requires that persons move beyond this relationship to its normal adult fruition in reciprocity and justice. The obedience of a religious cannot in any way be equated with the obedience of a child. Commitment generated by the more mature virtues is much deeper, more predictive of order and control, and far more creative, responsible, and encompassing of all concerned. Control will be as great if not greater than what we have but it will be internal not external control. Spontaneity and creativity, warmth and support will be greater. The structure of the modern world with its necessary bureaucratization makes conscious valuing of this cluster of virtues and conscious programing for their development the essential aspects of any community style that is going to be able to meet with the necessary spontaneity the challenges of this moment in history for creating the new people of God. If the creation of a better society is not a need then those values are not essential. But Christianity is a therapy for the social order even as it is man's way to God. And our society in its present form is not the best we could attain, rather it has structured evils we must eliminate.]

THE SISTER'S ROLE IN THE CHANGING WORLD

If these values are necessary for today's Christian response then those working directly with the development of the individual conscience, ought to be most skillful and practiced in the living of them. And religious women are certainly directly involved in the conscience-developing process. This is so true that I would be willing to say that the conscience of the American Catholic population is a reflection of the thinking, believing, and behaving of the American sister. The school and the Sunday school in America have been the extension of the socialization process in the family for the last hundred years. As parents were taught they teach, especially in those sensitive areas of the forming of conscience. There are many American superegos that have not become responsible consciences. If the possession of a responsible conscience is necessary for living in a society of eclectic values then those who work in the area of human development must have built into their own living experience a way of life that stimulates the development of the virtues that grow out of obedience into justice and responsibility. That this requires new role relations in community is evident from what professionalization has done to the convent, that is, it has limited the competence of all to specializations and made the members interdependent.

The experts in the various competencies are no longer limited to the administrators or supervisors in the religious community. In fact they no longer can be because the number of proficiencies necessary to run any kind of organization today far exceeds the possible competencies any one person could master. Of old the superior was expected to be an expert in creating a community atmosphere that idealized rejection of the world. The Church has taken a new look at the world and its goodness and therefore can no longer afford specialization in rejection of it to guide the lives of its service workers. When contemporaries in the physical and social sciences, in the philosophies and arts, and in administration could only be shared with a few, this kind of division of labor and orientation to the world was a necessity. At that time the religious dealt with segments of the Church which did not need these five virtues in any ordered form because even the having of them would have frustrated adjustment to their way of life in a highly structured two class system. Today all the people with whom the religious deals need these virtues and so does she. What better place to experiment with developing them than in the convent? Reciprocity becomes necessary even now when some have tremendous good will and energy to offer, some professional competence, some administrative skill, and all the potential to develop in many directions given the support and encouragement and opportunity that so many new facilities offer.

ANOMIE, APATHY OR RENEWAL

In an age of transition, anomie (loss of commitment to the existing norm) which generates the experience of meaninglessness and anarchy is a great danger. This we can understand once we realize that social structure is commitment to norms, not just the existence of rules. Power and sanction cannot get people to do things a certain way whether it be the training of children, the running of the economy or the worshiping of God, unless the members of the group believe that the method urged is worth doing. It is not by chance that the suicide rate goes up in times of transition. It goes up because some people find life no longer worth living; absenteeism, school dropouts, recidivism, increase in sickness, and mental illness rates, alcoholism, drug addiction, output slowdown, all of these are indicators that man finds his participation unrewarding, meaningless, futile. We call this apathy. Apathy is the major symptom that the system is no longer relevant to the work it claims to do. The world does not condemn an apathetic system. It ignores it. It will die out in time. In the meantime it will attract only those who want to escape the tedium, anxiety, danger of participation in the changes going on in the system. Religious orders at this moment of change in the Church could very well become these anomic systems. The indicators are several and can be used to test the relevancy of current responses to change in the Church. (1) Who enters? (2) Who leaves? (3) Who is satisfied? (4) Who is dissatisfied? (5) What do the satisfied do with the dissatisfied? (6) What do the dissatisfied do about their dissatisfaction? There are adult and childish and adolescent responses to all these questions. Different religious orders will have different responses because religious orders at this moment are strikingly ranged along a continuum of resistance and response to the current needs of the Church.

The demands are somewhat overwhelming but what is called for is a confrontation with the problem and an informed effort to resolve it. The expenditure of effort, the frustrations of failure, the achieving of some insight all done together, using the resources available, will become the bonds that bind the new community. The mutual forgiveness for resistances, inadequate responses, good intentioned failures of the past and of the present will be as much a means of reinforcing the ties as the mutual encouragements. Ultimately this shaping of human efforts, always in some degree inadequate for the new forms, must be created, recreated, modified and revised; will be itself a means of sanctifying the group in its humility and frailty before the Lord. The great work envisioned will ultimately be his saving action and spirit drawing his people in their fully human forms.

2

Apostolic Holiness: The Christian Dynamics

Sister M. Charles Borromeo Muckenhirn, C.S.C.

INTRODUCTION

The Church is already in the midst of the spiritual re-awakening which will transform all her ways of being present to the men and women of the 20th century. Her vision of herself is as the visible extension of Christ, filled with his Spirit and pouring out his life and truth on all men. This is the power that will enable the members of the Church to experiment, to think, to suffer, to communicate, to spend themselves in humble attempts to make Christ known and loved, to serve the human family on its pilgrimage to the Father. But there is something about the renewal so far which reminds one of the apostles on Mount Tabor. The actual work of building the new Church will be unfinished even when Christ returns. Having grasped the new vision, the test of love will be the courage and patience to work for its realization in local realities, to sow without reaping immediately, to suffer in the hope of future, not present, glory.

The first step toward a realistic descent from Tabor seems to be the admission that it is the entire Church as a totality which witnesses to the entirety of Christ's mission. No one person or group or even rank in the Church

45

can show forth simultaneously all the Christian values. The Church is truly the body of Christ. But it is as necessary to stress the great variety of functions, as it is to live in the awareness of the one Christ life in all the members. This chapter will discuss the deepened apostolic meaning and function of sisters of non-cloistered communities in a Church which makes present to men the good news of Jesus as Lord.

On this topic there is already evident a major shift of perspective as sisters think of themselves primarily as Christian persons, not primarily as sisters. Thus the first part of this chapter will present at some length the Church's new apostolic awareness for every Christian life. The sister's special mode of witness cannot be an isolated phenomenon. Rather the religious community is situated at the heart of the Christian community in its very presence to men and their needs. Christians as a corporate body bear corporate witness to a world awaiting Christ's truth and love and life. The variety of forms of such witness can only be understood within the one, complex sign of the Lord which is his Church in history.

The Church has miraculously rediscovered herself as the people of God, the body of Christ animated by his Spirit and bringing human history to its fulfillment and meaning in Christ. This is an insight whose magnitude we do not yet even begin to see. It is the key to everything else that is happening in the Church today. It is the basic reason why we rightly feel that in some sense everything is changing. To live in the Church as the very extension of Christ is to live by his life, and as he lived. We are persons transformed in Christ whose common worship of the Father is liturgy and whose manifestation of Christ to men is the apostolate.

Two thousand years of history have brought the world and the Church in it to a specific point of human and religious development. It is simply unreal to think about any aspect of renewal of the Church in a purely theological way. Much of the present attempt to discuss the apostolic aspect of the Church seems to fall into one of two extreme positions. There is the too common fallacy that identifies Christ's apostolate with certain specific works of external activity like preaching or teaching, running schools or hospitals. This ignores the necessity of an interior life, an insight, and a message which must come through the activities. The other extreme is to substitute beautiful, theological exercises for the hard work of finding out existentially how Christ's message is effectively communicated to contemporary persons, how Christian love expresses itself in the city, the university, the family.

There is a sense in which the spring of each year is truly new. So with the present renewal in the Church. We embrace with joy the aspect that is new, knowing that it is grafted into a living organism which cannot possibly vanish overnight. Also human beings as individuals, and even more as corporate entities, are sufficiently conservative to serve as brake on the demands of action. The Church, while remaining existentially the same human group and the same fundamental structure, is taking a truly new attitude, a new position toward all of reality. It requires only love of truth to see that never since her earliest days has the Church known so profoundly that she is for the world, not against it. She is the "world redeemed." All mankind and the whole drive of human history find their destiny and completion in her because she is Christ.

Thus the apostolate assumes a totally new perspective. The Church is apostolic by her total meaning and life.

Her dynamism is outward, toward God and toward all men in Christ. The Christian dynamic has been diverted, for providential reasons surely, but still diverted, for centuries. How else could we have arrived at a worldwide situation which regards missionary work as a special profession? The average Christian of any state in life had as horizon of reference, until Vatican II, the salvation of his soul, and perhaps the defense and upbuilding of the already existing Church.

To think profoundly about the apostolate means to think in a new perspective about ancient truths. It means to reflect on the sense in which the people of God here and now are the sign lifted up before all the nations to draw all men to personal contact with the living Christ. It means to meditate on the scriptural sources to find out what God means by an apostle, what it means to be sent on God's mission. It surely means to face unflinchingly the revealed notion of love, agape, the apostolic act, which reveals Christ and must inform all deeds done in his name.

The following theological reflections are basic to the new apostolic orientation for sisters in the practical order. Much misunderstanding regarding change in the work done by sisters, has come from a superficial approach to the question. Individual sisters and whole communities are rethinking their apostolic works, not from modern adaptation pressures alone, but even more from the deepest sources of Christian existence. A sister is a specially intense Christian. Her apostolic life should be more constant and more loving perhaps. But it is not essentially different from that of the ordinary Christian. She should be a specially evident radiance and visibility of the invisible life of Christ in his members.

PART I: THEOLOGICAL INSIGHTS

The Church, The People of God, Now

One measure of the miracle of renewal in the Church is that she can rediscover her true nature after enduring a very inadequate self-image for many centuries. No approach to the truth of the Church seems to capture the modern heart as quickly as the image of the people of God on the march to the city of God, the eternal kingdom. The wearying overstress on bureaucratic organization is refreshingly put in its place by the awareness of the Church as people. All the members are grasped as equals, one in Christ, all sons of the Father. Differences of rank, state, and duty remain, but as secondary and of this world. The common life, the common humanity, above all, the common goal become the bonds and needs which all share. Nothing about the Church can upset or shock one who thinks of her as a group of people. Weakness, sins, and failures will flaw all group efforts, just because the group is not a platonic concept, but a gathering of real persons in Christ.

The people of God incarnates on this earth at any moment the full availability of Christ the Savior. His love and life are made present in the same simple human forms which he himself shared during his years on earth. Gestures, words, feelings, human activities of all sorts will be the instruments through which he continues to love and serve men. The whole sacramental system of the Church is seen as heightened language, gesture, and sacred objects. When used in the community according to Christ's commands, these human realities become the means of specially powerful contact with the living Lord now in Glory.

The deepened discovery of the nature of the Church situates her in history, rather than in some nirvana of perfection and repose. It makes the human activity of the Church the very condition of the fulfilling of history. Christ as individual man, glorified now, achieves his work of personal salvation in each man through the human gestures and words of his bodily extension on earth, his members. Christ did not redeem us spiritually, and he does not sanctify us spiritually. The whole plan of salvation from Abraham to the parousia is the unfolding of God's merciful, compassionate, and utterly understanding love. This love comes to men to fulfill and transform them. And men are simply not spirits.

It is becoming evident that it would take centuries of deformation to have arrived at many attitudes of the pre-Vatican II Church. Christ's Church withdrawn and hurling anathemas, though historically explainable, is theologically monstrous. Perhaps this is why historical understanding is so essential for those who do see the new insights in the Church. Without this historical perspective in one's own awareness, there is a temptation to view clingers to the old ways as intentionally obstructing change and movement. Actually they are the result of a long and sincere tradition.

What light does the concept of the Church as people of God throw on the understanding of her apostolate? It seems that this notion of the Church immerses her members in the reality of the present, makes them the leaven of each moment of time. Christ acts now in history through each and all of his people. They are now what Christ is and wants to be for men. In other words, the Church sees herself as intrinsically the living instrument of a mission. She is a corporate body with a message to proclaim, a light to shine in the darkness, a heart to love and serve all human needs. She is apostolic; that is, here and now she is the reality that Christ entrusted to the apostles and first Christians.

"The people of God on the march" signifies movement, sharing, fellowship with all who want to journey together. This image cancels completely the notion of the Church as a fortress, a ghetto, a haven from life. It seems accurate to say that between Christ's ascension and his return, the very meaning of the Church is her apostolate. Men hear the message. They respond in faith or make their refusal. Those who believe pass on the message and the life it brings, for living faith is universal and dynamic. A static universe, a rigidly established Church and salvation, as being in the state of grace, somehow all went together. Now, in an evolving universe, the Holy Spirit recalls to us the growing, life-giving Church for men who are not in a state, but rather on the way to a destiny.

The people of God are such because they are sons in the Son, Jesus Christ. Thus their earthly pilgrimage, their journey to eternal happiness, must resemble the earthly life of Christ himself. Here are restored in all their power and depth the themes of the suffering servant of Yahweh, the anawim of post-exilic Judaism, the accent of the beatitudes. One travels light for a difficult journey. One dwells in simple places. Freedom to speak, to act, to be, can be smothered more quickly by affluence and vested interest than by opposition and rejection. The apostolate of Christ's Church will become actual and effective, a leaven in society only in proportion as the Church sees herself as witness to another city. She cannot preach poverty to the rich if she depends excessively on their support. She cannot teach humility to the highly cultured if she values worldly learning more than faith. The people of God, no matter how numerous, must be a shock, a scandal, for they are on their way to another world. Paradoxically, it is the apostolate by which they arrive at their goal, the same apostolate which makes them love and serve the simple daily needs of this earth.

To view the Church, as the *Constitution on the Church* does so beautifully, as the people of God is to view it both vertically and horizontally at once. There is the horizontal movement, detached yet committed to advancing man's forward movement. There is at every instant the vertical relation to the glorious Christ, living in the heart of each believer and guiding his whole people in the tasks and decisions of the moment. What Christ was on earth, the Church is now and until he returns. He achieves his mission not in his one humanity only, but in that of every person who gives himself to the kingdom, to the people of God, and to mankind's common destiny.

Biblical Notion of Prophet-Apostle

A different approach to a revealed notion of the apostolate is offered by meditation on the scriptural data. From the beginning to the end, the bible recounts movement, dialogue, vital exchange between the living God and living man. The great men of the Old Testament wrestle with their calling, their mission, their apostolate. God sends his messengers to elicit the free response of men. This is the steady beat underlying all of salvation history. It is not so much the nature of the sending on a mission which differentiates the old and new testaments. Rather, they are in contrast as to the universality and depth of the message, proclaimed in earlier times by mere men and finally by the Incarnate Word.

Prophetic or apostolic activity in scripture flourishes only in the atmosphere of personalism and freedom. The total initiative belongs to God, but the cooperative response must be completely free on man's part. Nothing could be further from conclusions arrived at by human reasoning than the shattering and uprooting message of the Holy One of Israel. The events of sacred history vibrate with feelings, reactions, conflicts, the whole rich array of actual human existence. The living God erupts into human history, breaking its seemingly determined flow. The words given demand not mere assent, but the gift of the entire being of the hearer.

It would seem helpful to note some of the elements common to the prophetic role throughout the bible. Then it is possible to come to grips with the question of the relevance of this scriptural data for deepening the present day discussion of the apostolate.

1) The terms "prophet," "apostle," "witness" are all essentially relational terms. That is, they necessarily imply that one person has been sent by another. There is dependence, submission, self-surrender implicit in the very words. Etymologically the terms are constructed from words meaning to speak for another, or to be sent by another on a mission. The person who prophesies or witnesses is precisely aware of having been acted on by another, of being intermediary between one person and another. In fact there are really three persons involved; the sender, the one sent, and the one to whom the messenger comes. In each person, interior free activity is demanded, adding qualities of complexity and unpredictableness to an already highly involved human situation.

2) The second element in the scriptural notion of prophet-apostle is the message to be communicated. It is evident that persons sent by God are not sent for merely mundane activity, to get certain jobs done. Rather, they are sent precisely to deliver a message. Their mission or task is clear, inexorable. They may refuse to do it. But if it

is done freely, the task itself is defined not by the messenger, but by the sender. Here enters the bearer and doer
theme. The message must be heard, though not necessarily understood fully. It must be accepted with the
heart as well as the mind. The message and not the messenger becomes the focus of the mission, the object of
belief or rejection. The dynamism of prophetism and apostolate becomes a question of communication, of presentation so effective that the hearer must respond one way
or the other.

3) The mode in which the prophet-apostle carries out
his mission is interestingly different from any merely academic approach to the truth. The prophet, having heard
and accepted the message, lives it and proclaims it simultaneously by example and action, united with meaningful
utterance. While being at an opposite pole from purely
intellectual communication, the prophetic sharing uses
words and language with the power not only of God's
truth, but of human commitment. His actions call attention to the message, often demostrate its demands and
blessings. But the actions are vitally united with speech,
with humanly graspable meanings. The whole man, the
embodied spirit, the total person of the prophet communicates the message to other total persons. The response
must not be merely intellectual, though profoundly involved with intelligence. The message given, since it concerns always some vital relationship of man with God,
must be heard and responded to by establishing or refusing a new personal relation to the divine sender.

4) A crucial and intrinsic element in the apostolic complex is the experience of suffering. The entire bible cries
out to us that God is infinitely different from man; his
ways are not our ways. When his Word comes existentially
to a man or a people, there as an agony of personal

readjustment of values. The prophet first of all suffers intensely in order to be open enough to hear the Word. Then he suffers for all those to whom he is sent and who refuse the message, a message he now knows experientially as a message of mercy, love and transformation. Usually the messenger suffers at the hands of those to whom he is sent. He becomes the sign of contradiction for each person who hears and sees him. If his relation to God, expressed by obedient love, submission, and unselfish service, is the true one, then he becomes a finger of guilt for all who refuse his way. The prophet-apostle in the entire Judeo-Christian tradition is the man sent by God, transformed by God. He witnesses to the necessity and availability of such transformation for every man, through his personal living of the message of the living God.

All of this is a rather generalized commentary on the notion of witness and apostolate in scripture. Actually the notion seems to be concretized in three related but analogical notes. The Old Testament prophets blazed the trail of divine communication with men. They used human speech and human actions to convey to their fellow men what God had mysteriously made known in the depths of their minds and hearts. With the incarnation of the Word of God, the messenger and the message became existentially one. Human speech and actions are used by Christ to fulfill his prophetic role. But they are words and deeds of the God-man; theandric realities which heal forever the split between man and his heavenly Father. The men sent by Christ, one with him in the mystery of his Mystical Body, are yet individually only men. They recapitulate in a higher way the prophets of Israel as they take a universal message to the entire people of God.

For the uses of this chapter it seems important to spell out somewhat the mode in which the apostles of Christ

exemplify the general revealed notion of the prophet-apos-
tle-witness. Unlike Jesus, their Master, they must receive
the message they are to share. Unlike the Old Testament
prophets, the message they receive is somehow God himself as communicated in Christ. They proclaim Christ, not
merely a message of Christ. They do not teach primarily
a doctrine, but a person. However, the extent of their
ability to share the Christ-Truth will be correlated with
their personal, total hearing of Christ the Word.

The bonds of oneness with Christ make the apostles profoundly conscious that they are sent on a mission, that
they have been given a task which is the very task of the
Savior himself. Thus the early apostolic consciousness is
dialectically suspended between Christ sending them out,
and a world desperately needing their proclamation. It
would be inconceivable to them to hear Christ for oneself
alone. A message is given in order to be passed on.

The apostles differ from Christ in that they and their
message are not identical, in the sense that Christ is God
revealed to men by his very existence. However, their
method of presenting the message must be like Christ's.
In this aspect, there is in some sense a fusion of the prophetic person and the truth he is trying to convey. Christ
points this out in all his remarks which touch on the necessity of doing and teaching. He demands a profound integrity between principles and action, between mind and
heart. In fact, Israel's notion of the heart is simply a symbol for the unified interiority of the human person, out of
which come the words and deeds which alone are of the
person in a genuine sense.

There is a deep reason for the oneness of message and
messenger in the various senses in which it is essential to
Christian witness. The burning center of the fullness of
divine revelation is that God is Agape, the love that pours

out being and goodness, even unto incarnation and redemptive death. So a truth can only be proclaimed by being lived. Christ loves to the limit, and thus reveals God's
inner reality. The disciple who hears of and surrender to
this love, lives by it and becomes its very proclamation before men. Sometimes the apostle-prophet misunderstands
the message and turns it into a religious philosophy, a set
of abstract truths. Then, he not only loses the message,
but fails to communicate even the doctrine he does see.
For God did not reveal truths. He revealed himself. Only
by personal involvement in faith and love can a man hear
Christ and be his living messenger.

There is an unfathomable mystery involved in the
apostolate of Christ as shared with the persons who are
his Church, his Body in time and space till he returns. It
is the mystery of the inevitability of suffering. Christ was
the project, the apostle, the witness. His message was love
and the cross was the sign of the extent and nature of that
love. Those with whom Christ shares his mission and
message will always find it painful to be misunderstood,
rejected, afflicted with the sense of failure and inadequacy. The subtle desire to link up human acceptability
with the successful proclaiming of the gospel is a perpetual temptation. Excellence in witness brings suffering
and death, not acclaim and prestige. The very content of
Christ's message implies suffering. A sinful human race
finds pain in the slow growth in holiness even where
Christ is earnestly sought. Completely unselfish love is as
stupid from a worldly point of view now as it was in
Christ's time. It is not the service it demands which is
foolishness to the world. What is ultimately unacceptable
is the very notion that such love is possible, much less that
it is the very nature of the living God.

We who are the Church of mid-twentieth century must
start our plumbing of what it means to be sharers in
Christ's apostolate now by meditating on what Christ was
as apostle, what he meant his apostles to be. Such reflection will bring a more balanced attitude toward receptivity
of the Word of God, of the need for silence, prayer and
discipleship as always underlying the outward sharing of
what resounds in our hearts. We must be receiving, sur-
rendering to a person who is God's message to men, before
we can be the voice and gesture through which he continues to speak to men. The inseparability of doing and
teaching, of living and saying the message at the same
time will undercut the false dichotomies of interior/ex-
terior life; prayer/action; contemplative/apostolic. These
are existentially rhythmic like the inward and outward
motion of breathing. There is a real priority for the creature in receiving what God gives. Yet if what is given is a
message of life, it must be shared in order to be sure one
has heard it right.

Agape, the Apostolic Act

Reflection on the Church as the people of God yields an
awareness of the Christian life as intrinsically apostolic.
God in Christ has manifested the notion of an apostle as
a man sent on God's mission, with a message to be lived
and taught by divine power. A third theological perspective on the nature of the Christian apostolate can be
gained by insight into divinely revealed *agape*. This is the
love that comes from on high to reveal the very being of
God and to make man divinely holy.

Christians have always known that the infallible sign
of divine life in men is consistent love of God and neighbor. But the precise meaning of this love and the ways in
which it has been expressed would involve an elaborate

historical study. Today, due mainly to the scriptural renewal, we can understand better than ever that love in the Christian context is a unique and necessarily revealed type of love. It is a love which is of God, comes from him, and returns to him. The monumental three-volume study of Ceslaus Spicq, O.P., *Agape dans le Noveau Testament*, now in the process of translation, makes available the wealth of biblical sources for a solidly based theology of divinely revealed love, *agape*. In these few pages we hope only to indicate that the existential solution to the question of the apostolate when it is actually taking place will be found in an understanding of *agape*.

The English word "love" is frayed from overuse and from variety of meaning. It seems almost necessary to use the word *agape* for revealed love, and then take the time and care necessary to distinguish it from every other kind of love which can enter into human life and experience. The Greek word *agape*, used by the scripture writers in the New Testament, was intentionally chosen to move away from the more common word *eros*. The culmination of the new testament revelation is found in the simple statement, "God is love"; God is *agape*. This completes the old covenant and opens out into the infinite reality of God's inner life. Obviously, everything hinges on understanding and communicating what this love is like. The God of revelation is the God who pours out being and life to all creatures; who is merciful and forgiving forever. He is source, generous and outgoing. He demands man's love, but only so that man may share in God's own life and happiness. The love revealed as the very being of God is utterly selfless, communicated eternally between the three persons who are the divine community, the one living God. In other words, love, *agape*, as the revealed reality of God is something man can never know from merely human experience.

God, the Father
becomes tangible
to us through
Christ.
//

The whole of salvation history unfolds not only the mystery of God as love, but also the mystery of his desire to share this love and life with all men. In Christ the love of God assumes tangible form. It is revealed to the utmost in the humble obedience and saving passion of Jesus, the perfect Son and servant of Yahweh. The sign that a man is in Jesus, that he is a son of the Father, will be that he lives, like Jesus, a life of loving service and adoring obedience. Divine life is unselfish love. Divine life in a man will be expressed in unselfish love of others. It becomes immediately obvious why Christ made the practical love of neighbor the standard of final entrance into the kingdom forever. It is the only certain sign that a man has God's life in him and can live with God forever. The new law is truly new. It is a new heart, a new interiority, transforming all actions and relationships from within.

Agape, in God and in the man who has received it from God in Christ, will be focused on the good of the one loved. It is never self-seeking, but rather strives to find ways of doing good to others. It is disinterested, reaching out, sharing without any reflective turning back on self. It neither seeks nor expects human thanks. Finally, *agape* does something. It effectively serves, heals and enriches. The last thing to be confused with true *agape* is the merely good intention, the avoidance of "uncharitableness." The complacency of this latter notion has done great damage to the dynamism of Christian love by stifling any serious personal involvement in the sufferings and needs of real living persons. There are fourteen traditional works of mercy; only one of which is prayer. Holiness, *agape,* and gritty reality are one thing in this world until Christ returns.

The deeper understanding of *agape* is already leading to greater awareness of the presence and activity of the

Holy Spirit in the man who has divine life. Somehow he
plays a special role in pouring forth in our hearts the very
love power of the Triune God, for the Spirit is the very
love which unites and proceeds from Father and Son. The
sign of divine life, of the Spirit of God in a man and in
the Christian community, will be the visible presence of
the works of *agape*. The Christian community as the
visible extension of Christ is also the visible localization of
his Spirit of love. The bond of the members is their mutual
fraternal love. When lived authentically, it truly makes the
Christian community "the sign raised up among the nations."

Even such a brief recalling of the revealed nature of
Christian love, *agape*, enables us to deepen and make
more existential the contemporary awareness of the Christian apostolate. Three perspectives suggest themselves:
agape as the message to be given; *agape* as the revelatory
sign; the psychological structure of an act of *agape* as the
divine reality permeating and giving value to all apostolic
"works."

1) *Agape* as message: To many Catholics, until the
present renewal in the Church, the first task of the Christian was to accept with docility a series of truths divinely
guaranteed by the Church established by Christ. These
truths were only too often accepted as a sort of pledge of
membership in the group. One was not supposed to think
about them much, or try to see how they related to each
other. Even worse, the collection of truths proposed often
ranged on an equal scale, fundamental doctrines and matters of secondary importance. The presence of Christ in
the Eucharist and the appearance of Mary at Fatima
could seem to receive equal assent. The notion of message
to be communicated was lost in the notion of infallibile
doctrines to be held.

Actually, God revealed not truths, but himself and his love and his power. The whole series of great events in Israel and in Christ were revelatory, visible signs communicated divine reality to living witnesses. God and man were historically involved in dialogue, communication, call and response or non-response. The religion of the living God from Abraham to the present instant is a moment by moment interweaving of God's loving initiative and each man's free decision. The message throughout revelation is the good news that God loves man and wants to save him. But this message must be heard and accepted and lived with all one's heart, all one's life. In Christ the good news achieves a form of gift and call beyond which even God cannot go. A man is free to reject the message of the *agape* of God in the dying Christ. But he is not free to call it just a doctrine to be held.

As we discussed above, the apostle is a man with a message. The message he must pass on in word and deed is the tremendous news that God is infinite love and saving mercy for every man who turns to him in Christ. The whole history of doctrinal and theological formulations is the necessary privilege and task of the human mind which, having accepted the message, thinks about it, penetrates it and teaches it in human language. But it has been a near disaster for the Catholic Church that the formulations have too long been substituted for the living message which demands one's life, not just one's assent. In any discussion of the apostolate today, one must start with the message given by Christ, the message of saving love which, when properly proclaimed, is a sword and a scandal.

2) *Agape* as sign: Limited experience of life makes it evident that even good persons usually act with some degree of self interest. Human beings are creatures, limited

and needy. It is normal and perfectly understandable that we act to fulfill ourselves, to develop our powers to become educated, cultured, useful persons and members of society. The very joy of human love is somehow deeply rooted in its mysterious mutuality, in the sense of mutual recognition of the other. Even the most generous human love knows that generosity itself is the quickest way to balanced and happy human living. Our experience of life and love at their noblest hinges on the relation in each person between need of others and gift of self. The whole drive of the human person is toward love and ultimately toward unselfish love. But this love seeks another human being who will return and complete the love.

The troubling mystery of man is that he tends to think that he is made for human love alone. But only divine love can totally transform him. God has offered himself, his life and his love to men. He has in fact made the free acceptance of this gift the everlasting happiness and sole destiny of man. But God's love is pure gift, pure gratuity. It does not depend on man's efforts. Rather it comes to man and lifts up his entire being. Man's free role is humble openness, receptivity, the single role of the creature before the generosity of the creator. One of the deepest mysteries about sin is that it is a refusal to be enriched, a refusal to admit dependence and insufficiency. God wants only to give a share in his life forever. But the condition is that it be wanted. The message of *agape* must therefore be offered in such a form that it leaves the one who hears it free to accept or refuse. Christ was the messenger of *agape* in the most perfect way, offering his life and his love without protection or defense. His hearers could follow him or kill him.

The apostle then is a man who personally has accepted the message of divine love for himself. But the message is for all. So he will in some way spend his life in sharing the message. The message is not an abstract doctrine, but a mode of being, a love relationship between God and man. Therefore, only acts of personal love can be the means of showing, of teaching the message. Precisely here is the point of insertion for the entire new testament focus on fraternal charity as the sign of the presence of grace in the believer. God's very life is unselfish sharing. Grace will make a man like God as he appeared in Christ. It will turn him toward constant love and concern for each person he contacts. The message is love; acts of love are its proclamation.

This theme "love of neighbor" as the new commandment and the whole of the law is a source of endless personal meditation and insight. No other means are available for understanding this theme. It cannot be forced or proven or imposed from the outside. It is no use telling others to love their neighbor until the message of divine love has been communicated in word, and most of all, in example. Once a believer grasps personally that he does not have any certitude that he has divine life unless he is actually serving others, he may begin to look for the needs and sufferings of others. As long as he thinks that keeping certain laws is a sign of divine life, he will become the Pharisee type enmeshed in what Christ proclaimed to be the most terrible sin of all. Thus actual service of neighbor is a source of peace and joy to the one who practices it in simplicity and genuine concern. The suffering entailed in realistic service overflows with humble awareness that one is truly trying to be open to divine life and power.

On the other hand, to those who witness consistent and sincere service of others, a universal and realistic love, the actions become signs of the presence of some new element in the door. Divine life, even if not so named, is being proclaimed. Human beings unredeemed do not burn out their lives immersed in the joys and sorrows of all who come into their sphere of activity. This is probably what Pope John meant when he called the Christian the eighth sacrament and the only one that an unbeliever will receive. Unselfish love makes visible in the world a new set of realities. It tells those who witness it that man can be more than human; that there are sources of power and kindness that come not from the man, but are gifts to him from some other source. The one who loves may never know his impact, for this is not what he notices or seeks. But the viewer may be changed forever by being faced with a mysterious and new element in human life. God's grace in each man's heart normally is effective only when coupled with visible signs. These signs are the effects of grace in the lives of those already living under its light and strength.

3) *Agape* as message and *agape* as sign are insights confirmed by experience, but also clearly taught by Christ. We may lack personally convincing examples of the effectiveness of divine love in our own effort to share, but the very words of Christ oblige us to live in service and compassion, in effective love of our brothers. The last perspective on *agape* is from a different point of view. It is an attempt to approach more closely the psychological realization of how a person operates from the inside when actually trying to be apostolic. What does a person do in his heart when trying to witness consciously to the good news of love, by loving as Christ did?

Perhaps it is good to note that the ultimate and constant object of the *agape* in a human heart is the living Triune God. The response of the divinized man is one of adoration, gratitude, obedient and loving surrender to the God who is his beginning and his end. However, in this chapter we are focusing on the love of *agape* when its immediate object is a fellow man to be loved and served for God as Christ has shown us. The word "apostolate" for too long has tended to be used exclusively as a type of activity, necessarily religious in content, usually organized and too often aggressive in tone. Our thesis here is that only concrete acts of *agape,* directed to specific persons can literally be called apostolic, that is, acts of living witness to the message of Christ, shown existentially in the very being of the messenger. Only in these cases is the good news communicated in the vital and potentially transforming sense in which Christ meant it.

Ideally, what should go on in an interpersonal encounter so that there is some sort of apostolic influence possible? The most basic attitude, it seems, on the part of the one who is trying to love and serve another, is a direct and sincere awareness of the other person. The whole richness of modern psychology and counseling is invaluable for the apostolate and is presupposed here. The gospels radiate the uniqueness of each human person. Their need, not Christ's greatness, dominates every event. This awareness of the other person in a Christian way requires some consciousness of the other as a member of Christ, as a son of God, or some other reference placing the relationship into not only a natural, but a supernatural perspective. *Agape* for this person would mean loving him just as he is, as a unique reflection of God, a fellow traveler to eternal joy. It would mean being concerned to find out his need *as he sees it,* to seek with compassion and empathy to enter into his problem or situation. Then together the two persons can try to find a solution, or at least an alleviation. *Agape* would mean unself-consciousness in the apostle, gentleness, genuine concern. There would be no temptations to impatience, pressure or prefabricated solutions. In other words, the first conscious requisite for the apostolic act, *agape,* is awareness that one is Christ, is acting for Christ, and is serving Christ. Not that such inwardness radiates irresistibly. But unless it is there, genuine apostolic effectiveness seems impossible. How can a message, not even intended or adverted to, come through?

In discussing the apostolate in the broadest sense, its implications are true for every mode of Christian existence. Whenever a Christian is trying to bring Christ and his love and message to others, this witness must be an overflow of his own commitment and intensity. There is increasing sensitivity to the extreme institutionalizing of the apostolate in recent centuries. Perhaps there is a connection between this problem and the overstress, since Trent, on the objective validity of the sacraments. Surely a priest, no matter what his personal holiness or lack of it, can administer valid sacraments. But does he really have a deepening effect on the holiness of his people, if his ministry and his personal life are not of a piece? The liturgical renewal has changed the sacramental stress to inner dispositions by which the living Christ and his grace can transform the Christian. The same problem is obvious in treating the mere teaching of doctrinal formulas as if it were an apostolic function. The good news of salvation has been missed completely in many well organized catechism sessions.

If actual *agape* is the essential reality of an apostolic act, then the interior life in a person becomes the constant and simultaneous source of his activity for his fellow man. Growth in personal contemplative prayer should increase personal consciousness of the presence of Christ, of the Holy Spirit in one's self and others, of the impulse of grace and the providential directives of God. These are the very interiority of the mature Christian person, making him increasingly sensitive to the needs of others. Openness to the Spirit means the Spirit in all his manifestations. Openness to others means increasing ability to sense the unexpressed suffering or confusion of another. Service and all its external manifestations become genuine signs of love and care to the person for whom they are done. They are matched to unique human needs and not imposed out of some disguised need to feel zealous and active. Christian service is gentle and joyous. It produces peace and serenity, the real healing of real wounds.

There is a tremendous unifying effect in the personality when one sees that actual *agape*, not its external acts, is the core of Christian love. All types of activities can be freely used to serve genuine charity. The rigidity of forcing persons into "apostolic activities" vanishes. All attitudes, all virtues, all contacts, become mediations of love. Love directs and forms and orders one's whole life from within. This is precisely the liberty of the children of God. It is also the bond of perfection and the single law. Joy increases with opportunities of service. One never feels unjustly burdened or put upon. The peace of the Spirit accompanies the tranquil awareness that, even if imperfectly, one is moving toward Christ by trying unselfishly and realistically to serve him in his members. Perhaps safest of all, the facts of daily encounters keep one from pride and any premature sense of success. *Agape* leads to interpersonal involvement and suffering. Its power and its purification are simultaneous.

A few practical remarks remain on the psychological aspects of *agape*, viewed as the apostolic act in the deepest sense. It seems to involve an increasingly heightened sense of presence in the believer, a sense of the personal reality of Christ, his life and his love. It is this mysterious plus value that comes through the human activity through which *agape* is mediated to another person in the form of loving service. The holiness of the witness, the presence of the message of Christ, the power of divine love and its apostolic externalization, all seem to co-exist and increase in direct ratio to each other. Here we are at the heart of the false, superficial dichotomy between "the interior life" and the "apostolate." Only an extremely conceptualized and non-existential approach to the question could come up with such a division. Genuine apostolate is the outward manifestation of one's inner life and relation to Christ. We might simplify discussion along this line by speaking of the apostle and the apostolic life, rather than the abstraction "the apostolate." Persons who think they have been assigned to a previously organized external project called the apostolate usually do it by withdrawing their real selves. Then they tend to think of their interior life as taking place during formal acts of religious and prayer.

It is obvious that the Christian apostolic endeavor simply must be person to person, in some sense. This does not mean necessarily one to one, for genuine group action can be intensely personal. But there must be genuine openness and sharing of one's own self, not a mask of formulae or actions which separate and confuse. Also, due to the ambiguity of human external activities, it usually seems necessary for apostolic effectiveness to have some rather extended time span. For example, a teacher makes his final impression as to attitudes and spirit, not just the first day, but at the end of a semester. His virtues and vices will have had ample room for display and a deeply-rooted *agape* will or will not have been manifested.

Rarely is the revelation of what is deepest in a person a one-act situation. But those who live together in whatever type of human group have ineradicable effects on each other, for better or worse.

The attempt to view the actual conscious practice of *agape* as the apostolic act would seem to be a powerful help toward dynamic devotion to the Holy Spirit. This would be true at any rate, because he is love and because he is the special source of our personal holiness. But, in addition, the attempt to love and serve others in the concrete needs of every day means acquiring the fortitude to drop formulas and preconceived solutions. It means depending on grace and faith, inspiration and the use of one's own common sense and intuition to make decisions moment by moment suited to the unique instant and the unique person. This is one of the attitudes, crucial to the whole of the Christian interior life, that a truly apostolic life should develop. Holiness always means an increasing dependence on the Holy Spirit at each moment. Ironically, it is the defenders of the superficial, dualistic notion of the interior life, who fear freedom and existential dependence on God in the apostolate. They advise caution, hesitancy, and rigid categories of safe activities; But the human person grows all in piece. His deepest commitment to Christ is expressed in service of him in his neighbor. Then the whole person is bound ever closer in the Spirit to the whole Christ, the whole family of God on the way together to their common Father. "If we love one another, God dwells in us, and his love has reached its fullness in us." (1 John 4:11-12)

Some Contemporary Philosophical Principles

The understanding of the Christian life as dynamic, of holiness as apostolic has been enriched by natural insights as well as by the theological truths already discussed. The following remarks merely indicate contributory ideas and insights, without any attempt to discuss or validate them.

The restressing of the body-soul unity of man underlies

most other points of seeming newness. If man is a bodied spirit, then to be involved in either aspect is to be involved as a total person. Belief and commitment cannot be fully human and remain merely intellectual. States of soul and attitudes of the heart will mold the body and its modes of expression. The whole man becomes a visible sign of his inner stance in regard to God, the world and other men. It is whole persons who are Christians. If their acceptance of Christ and his message exerts no visible evidence of outward-going love and service, then either the message is inadequately grasped, or the commitment is facile and ungenuine.

The personalist renewal, general now in all the philosophical and humanistic disciplines, sees as self-evident that the very meaning of person is a being in vital relation to another person. The structure of consciousness is a vital unity of subject-object. The "problem" of subject-object dichotomy vanishes before the experiential awareness of coexistence in consciousness of the other, and of the self as aware of the other. This is surely the death blow to many varieties of false "interiority," withdrawal spirituality, and canonizing of muteness and unconcern as signs of spiritual depth and recollection. Awareness in unself-conscious love of the other is simultaneously and obliquely the most penetrating and serene awareness of one's self.

Perhaps the tendency to separate in reality what the mind must distinguish in thought is a consistent reminder of the weakness of the human mind. At any rate, the either/or mentality is a snare for all of us. It can be particularly insidious in Christian thought which is necessarily complex, but often demands in reality that two things be united which are separable in thought; for example, love of God and neighbor. For this constant problem of the "both/and" instead of the "either/or," much in modern thought is helpful as an antidote. Reality is seen as historically conditioned, existential. It demands a moving point of view, which must keep many things together instead of sacrificing one concept to another. If love is the heart and center of Christian existence, then it is always and at once love of God and of all men in one's very being in Christ with others. The liturgy and the apostolate are two different modes in which Christian life and love overflow from the Christian community, one reaching upward to God; the other reaching out to human need, to heal it in Christ's love.

Form and function are two facets of any living thing. It is usually through the second that we come to understand the first. The activities of a being give a clue to its inner nature. One does not choose to know form and ignore function or vice versa. To know Christ fully, for example, is to know that he is the God-Man who came to save and sanctify. His Church is surely his mysterious divine-human extension. But it is this precisely to carry out his saving functions. The renewed insight into the Church approaches her existentially in terms of what she must be doing, how she must be functioning among men. The older stress was on the truth of her divine establishment, her structures, and rights. The current form-function oneness brings both stresses into focus. Because the Church is Christ, she is everywhere and always apostolic. Much of the too timorous approach to the apostolic life could be helped by meditation on the unity of function and form in Christian life.

Of great importance for realistic understanding of the apostolate is the revival of the scholastic reminder about everything being received according to the mode of the receiver. Here at the root is the deepest reason for adaptation. A message, a life to be conveyed by free communication and free acceptance, simply cannot be meaningful only to the messenger. What else is modern catechetics all about except a profound attempt to face this fact. The understanding of the message, the understanding through love of the one to whom one is sent, and the creative uniting of these two awarenesses is essential to any effective apostolate at any time in history.

The unique writings and vision of Father Teilhard de Chardin have had an impact on every field of human thought; an impact which is constantly gathering strength. He is surely the Christian thinker who most aptly speaks to the modern mind with its scientific, evolutionary bent, and its man-centered view of the universe. For those who respond to Teilhard's vision, all that is valid in the modern attitude finds its fullest meaning in the acceptance of the Christ who is the Lord of the Universe, a personal center drawing all men into a final destiny of unity in love.

Teilhard's thought opens up the possibility of a new perspective for a Christian synthesis, different from, though not in conflict with, the medieval synthesis. Rather his vision offers to the Church a modern frame of thought in which the Church can present herself as she really appears in revelation. The developmental themes like the people of God, the leaven, the growing vine are easily grasped in evolutionary terms. The scriptural themes about the return of Christ, the whole of eschatology, become in Teilhard's view, dynamic, central, magnetizing all of history as it is actually lived, in incompleteness and yearning.

In terms of the apostolate, Teilhard's vision offers hope and courage, challenge to build God's world in and with and for him. It gives meaning to the apostolate not only in the sense of supernatural value, but also the genuine values brought into being by loving service of the multiple needs of human society.

PART II: SPECIFIC RELEVANCE FOR SISTERS

There is much joy at the breaking down of artificial barriers in the Church. This can lead to a tendency to blur some important distinctions. To be in Christ or not is the only eternal and radical cleavage. Modes of Christian existence should surely be seen as modes, that and no more. However, in the unique personal destiny of each member of Christ, the differences in modes make great differences in day to day reality. To be married is a different way of being a Christian than to be a religious.

Our immediate task here is to try to delimit as different within the oneness of Christian existence the apostolic witness of the sister today. The old cliches about higher and better states seems particularly useless. Whatever truth such phrases used to convey, they do so no longer. Rather, they cause resentment on the part of other Christians and can present a subtle temptation to pharisaism on the part of religious. We prefer to look upon the Christian community, priests, sisters, and all the other faithful gathered around the Eucharistic table. Made one body and one people, each member carries his witness into his world. How in our times, in our country, are sisters going to do this with increasing effectiveness?

The first sign of newness is the very discussion of the question, a discussion which seems to be entering a new phase. The opening up of problems, the challenging of superficial rigidities and the emotional reactions pro and con are mercifully on the decline. Since the admission that women are persons in the Church, it is becoming obvious that sisters too should be treated as persons. Thought and shared discussion are taking the place of defensiveness. It is becoming clearer that there are profound theological principles, scriptural data even, at the heart and center of the meaning and role of sisters. No individual sister, housewife, or even parish priest can just decide what sisters are and what they should or should not do. Sisters are consecrated to God. They are sacred persons in some special way in the Christian community. If the whole Church is renewing and refocusing herself, it is no surprise that sisters personally and corporately must be concerned in the same way. The Holy Spirit and the magisterium of the Church are clearly on the side of renewal, reform, adaptation. Any group of Christians not deeply involved in renewal manifested by serious discussion and courageous experimentation is somehow out of touch with the present day currents of life in Christ's Mystical Body.

The Christian life is a life of corporate worship, personal prayer, apostolic service. These great human realities must be found in any and every life which can be called even minimally Christian. The question for sisters, as they join the human race and the renewing Church is not, "Shall we do these things?" Rather, they are asking, "How shall we do them as specially consecrated members of Christ?" Too many communities unintentionally had substituted the community for the Church, the superiors for the hierarchy, private prayers for liturgical life and the survival of community projects for apostolic service. It is with the latter area that we are concerned. What type of apostolic spirituality must be developed in religious so that they share in the contemporary mission of the Church.

Two basic insights must be kept in view throughout this discussion.

1) The very nature of the Church, divine-human, eternal-temporal, other worldly in this world, demands some radical polarity in her public witness. The Church as a whole must simultaneously and in balance witness to the goodness of God's world and to its radical incompleteness.

Men must hear that the world has been redeemed in Christ. It can and must be used properly and transformed in Christ as preparation for the new heavens and the new earth. The incarnational aspect of the Church is absolutely fundamental. She can never appear mainly as withdrawn, aloof, negative. Christ entered into all that is human so as to elevate and sanctify it through the cooperation of free persons. This transforming role of the Church is her basic mission to and in the world of man and matter. The fact that for centuries this has been somewhat obscured is a historical problem due to a tremendous complexity of causes.

The more we stress the need for Christians to be leaven, to enter into reality to raise it up in Christ, the more we sense the need for an opposite witness within the one Christian sign. Some persons must make visible and shocking the fact that this world as we know it, is not ultimate. Men must be constantly reminded that we have here no lasting city, that the world of supernatural reality, the Triune God, eternally glorious life with him are not available in this world even if through it and its struggles. This has been the traditional understanding of virginity and poverty when embraced freely and lived publicly in the Church. Numerically those totally consecrated to God and the world to come, will always be very small compared to the total human group whose vocation is sanctity through and in this world properly used. But the smallness of the number does not affect the essentialness of this special witness. In other words, only the married couple and the consecrated virgin together really constitute one adequate sign of the total mesage of Christ. The former proclaims the holiness of this world when lived in as a Christian; the latter is a visible reminder of the transcendent common human destiny and the relativity of everything in this world. Everything of the earth can be sanctifying means to the world that is to come.

2) There is another insight which underlies a new apostolic spirituality for sisters. It is that human renewal of any kind and most of all religious and spiritual renewal comes from an interior principle. As the inner change takes place it expresses itself necessarily in the whole psychosomatic reality of the human person as an embodied spirit. From the changed individual and even simultaneously, the relationships, cultural patterns and institutional arrangements will gradually change. The Catholic Church has tended to be externalized, rigid and intellectually uncreative for many reasons since the reformation. The new sap of freedom, interior life in the Spirit and openness of communication seem almost subversive to some in the Church. But calm observation makes evident that all living growth is from an internal life principle. One simply does not change living things from the outside. Least of all can free spirits, human persons be pressured and forced into genuine development. This is why the most crucial need at the moment in Church is the mutual creating of a new spirituality, a new heart, a new interiority. This will transform in love and joy from within, the patterns of life and custom left from a period which understandably lived by a different spirituality. Without this understanding there is no danger of a type of person appearing in the Church who would force on others the "new attitudes" with as much lack of respect for the person as that which corroded the old conformist pattern.

If these two insights are accepted some interesting conclusions are evident. Within the one Christian liturgical-apostolic spirituality of the new Church, there needs to be an opposition by way of stress in modes of living. Laymen should incarnate the Christian life in a different style than

that manifested by consecrated virgins. Their differences
will enhance the Church, enable them to collaborate
honestly by doing related but different function har-
moniously. Surely this is more edifying than mere dis-
placement of one group by the other in terms of lack of
sisters and growth of population. There are many changes
that have already occurred but without thought, order or
theological meaning. Surely this sort of adaptation does
not even touch the question of the Church as corporate
witness to anything. It is the witness of the whole Church
that is necessary. This means in the concrete the whole
local Church in a specific time and place. For example,
the apostolic witness of a Christian community like a
parish, will be clarified for our times by priests, sisters and
laymen meeting, sharing and discussing in order to find
complementary roles so as to be a corporate and attractive
sign to those not yet in Christ. Think of a parish in which
the priests are visible concretizations of the power of the
living Word of God in scripture and sacrament, prophets
of God's crucifying and transforming truth; a parish in
which sisters are convincing and joyful reminders that material things, family life and personal independence,
though good, are not man's destiny, but the means to its
achievement through loving service; a parish in which the
whole Christian community somehow lived in this world
with a meaningful message, one with all men on their
pilgrimage through death to life. Sisters, I fear, are on a
dead end road, if they want to decide their meaning and
witness only in terms of their personal religious life in
their community. Sisters are ecclesiastical persons, belonging to Christ and therefore to his Church. To witness,
they must not only mean something, but manifest it to
others.

Before trying to indicate some of the main traits of the new apostolic spirituality as it may develop precisely for sisters, it seems important to admit that sisters have a special problem in regard to such apostolic renewal. It is a problem not shared in exactly the same way by either priests or laity. Sisters are women and therefore also members of the laity. On both counts they have been "subjects," treated as minors, mainly by the Church officially, but also to some extent within the communities themselves. Religious women, isolated in convent patterns, have with few exceptions lived outside the stream of the emergence of women into civic life all over the world. This means that sisters in this day are women in not quite the same sense, culturally, as their secular sisters. Much of the superficial business of adaptation for sisters is simply admitting that the Victorian era made sense only in its historical setting. The canon law mentality has had such strong effects in every area of Catholic life. It was particularly effective in the day to day life style of sisters. Until recently sisters were not educated, were governed passively, and were formed to think that every slightest rule and regulation was a major part of Christian holiness. This means that the actual present situation in religious communities is an unusual combination of unrelated elements. There are the artificially preserved and extremely rigid cultural forms, of the 19th century, which are religiously sanctioned. Somehow these are to be assimilated by normal American women trying to love and serve Christ in the here and now. This agony of conflicting forms and spiritualities is possible only due to the historical fact of communities existing as rigid and dead forms of a culture bypassed decades ago in the ordinary world. It must be admitted humbly in the light of the

Spirit, that communities have for many years been de-
forming young persons when they sincerely thought they
were forming them.

The strange attitudes which puzzle ordinary persons
come from this artificial formation. We have all been
sometime or other stopped short by the extremely self-
effacing manner, the blandness of personality, the naivete
about obvious things, a sort of bloodless living, extreme
deference to authority, and panic in the face of honesty
and criticism. These are simply not qualities of the normal
20th century American young woman. Is it any wonder
that there is a vocation crisis? Should there not be, until a
new and truly Christian spirituality is clarified and held
up as the ideal? One quite consistent stress in the thinking
of many middle aged and older religious is that they are
preserving the works of their founder. Even limited reflection indicates that founders were vitally related to their
times, in fact saw far ahead of them. They founded precisely because none of the existing institutes seemed to
be adequate. Founders, if anyone, would be in full throes
of experimentation both out of obedience to the Church
and out of love for the needs of real living persons.

Renewal of individuals and of groups is never easy. One
of the special obstacles is vested interest. The more a person or group is involved financially and materially, the
greater the tendency to bless the status quo, to work on
merely material problems, to view with alarm all creative
thought and discussion of change. This must be admitted
to be a very special problem in the renewal of the
American sisters communities. If renewal is essentially a
question of a new heart, a new spirituality, then time and
personnel must be given to intangibles like thought, planning, study of psychology, sociology, theology. Money
must be expended on things like travel, released staff,

lecturers. The allotment of time is an almost infallible indication of values, perhaps even more so than allotment of money. Much of the time of those who should be the spiritual leaders of the religious women of the country necessarily goes into the managing of large institutions. This is an understandable drain on creative thought and genuine dialogue. Even more subtly, a spiritual renewal will surely revive gospel values. Those on whom we are often overly dependent due to our vested interests might not like sisters as well, if sisters began to be apostles of poverty, detachment and social justice.

These things must be said if we are to come to grips realistically with the qualities of a new apostolic spiritual-ity for American sisters. Truth is the heart of Christian witness. To face the present with respect for the historical past is absolutely necessary. To see why patterns which worked before are outmoded now, is not to blame, but to attempt to heal. The urgent crisis of the American sis-ters lies in the fact that their greatest need, a deeply apos-tolic holiness, is a most difficult achievement. Both as Americans and as Catholics we tend to be externalized, superficial and far too trustful of the goods of this world as the means of Christian renewal. However, there are hopeful harbingers of thought and discussion among American sisters. Which way do the signs point in terms of a new spirituality, an apostolic notion of holiness for sisters? Here we will indicate trends in four areas which are surely essential to traditional religious life no matter when or how it is lived.

1) Love and not fear will be the dominant force, mo-tive, goal and atmosphere of the life of a sister. Love of Christ brings her to the community at all. If she is in a non-cloistered community, some type of actual loving service of human beings was probably involved in her re-

sponse to Christ's grace. Love will be the purpose of the rules and constitutions which govern the living together of many sisters, all of whom are focused on actual love of the whole Christ. Love, *agape*, the very divine life grows in her daily. It must express itself in genuine Christian love and fellowship with all the sisters and with all those who are contacted in any way. The variety of human relationships will be learned and lived as in any normal Christian life. Divine charity will reach out to all, while sanctifying those gifts of human love and friendship which God may provide.

Sisters will be aware of being a vital part of the people of God, of being prophets, apostles by sacramental command, even before making vows. They will enter into and live religious life as a constant and privileged group witness to the reality of love, of *agape*, of unselfishness and joy through service. In all these attitudes, sisters are merely manifesting more ecclesially the great Christian attitudes common to all believers. They will no longer consider themselves a breed apart, living a completely different life. Rather each sister will be the candle lighted and on the candlestick, each convent will be the city on a mountain, open and welcoming to all.

2) The specialness of the sister and her meaning in the Church will lie not in the fact that she loves Christ and her fellowmen, but rather it will be found in the fact that she has been given the grace to seek Christ and his love in a specially total and public way. She has been called to a personal intimacy with Christ which paradoxically is lived in public view of the Church. She proclaims by her giving of the only life she will ever live that Christ exists, that he is the divine fullness of all that human realities only faintly reflect. The vow of virginity will be the existential center of the new spirituality of the sister in the

Church. For the renewal is primarily personal, not organizational. But the human person is fulfilled through love. The miracle of consecrated holiness, when it is achieved, is that the love of Christ, which is every man's destiny and glory, becomes the sole concern and satisfying reality of these human persons. Christ is all that any man needs. But this truth is, to say the least, easily obscured. Consecrated virgins should be powerful witnesses to the presence and lovableness of the Lord. Their foregoing of marriage now is in expectation of the perfect union of Christ and the human person in eternity. The image of the religious as vital and consecrated spouse of Christ needs to be made meaningful again. Surely no culture needed more desperately a proper valuing of sex and human love.

The vow of poverty needs a whole new orientation in religious life. The religious should stand before the world as proclamation of spiritual riches, attained through detachment, generosity and liberation from material necessities. To see the sister as witnessing to evangelical poverty, is to see her again within the context of the Christian community. Obviously, she must have minimal necessities. The reason for this minimal material existence must be obvious in terms of greater freedom to proclaim Christ's truth through loving service, to remind all that the real treasures are not on earth. But this witness to material minimalness can never be an indirect criticism of the great majority of the human race who must be very concerned about material goods. In other words, the witness of vowed poverty must have a powerful and clear message about it beyond the mere fact of being poor. For one of the great works of the freely poor is to alleviate the lot of those who are deprived of this world's goods. Another work is to be a goad, a sting and a scandal to the rich of this world, who try to be both Christian and wealthy in spirit. Certainly, the sister in the Church will practice a more and more meaningful and literally true poverty. It will cry out God's power and providence, as well as developing an interior spirit of trust and humility that may produce again the anawim of Israel. Surely, here the providential meaning of St. Therese of Lisieux is a largely unexplored field for active religious. The question of apostolic poverty will force honest examination of large and tremendously expensive institutions owned by religious communities. Only the sisters who are personally and corporately poor dare play a role as prophetic conscience in American society.

3) The vow of obedience has had a quite different proportionate stress than it will have in the new apostolic spirituality. Surely it will always be important, a powerful sign of mature freedom and serious commitment. But it is the vow of the group, the vow necessitated by community living. In the centuries in which the Church herself overstressed her organizational and authority aspects, this showed up also in religious life. But obedience will take its right place in ordering the living and activity of a group of Christians who have vowed themselves to the evangelical life, the apostolic life of virginity and poverty. This stress will give back to obedience its personal and consecratory character, so long overshadowed by infantile submissiveness and confusion between human and divine authority. The obedient sister will be totally given, totally open to the Lord Jesus and his Spirit. She will welcome the direction of the Church and her community. But this direction must itself be of the Lord and ordered to furthering his mission on earth. As some thinkers have pointed out, the present crisis in obedience in religious communities is really a crisis in the proper understanding and constructive use of authority.

Since obedience is a social virtue, it presupposes a society, a living community. In a religious community which is truly bound together in genuine *agape* between the members, all of whom are consecrated to the Lord, the task of those who must exercise authority and direction is made not only easier, but more meaningful. Authority again becomes, as in the gospels, a ministry of service of the brethren, of service to the Church's mission as existential witness to all men. That this witness be harmonious and well planned, authority is obviously necessary. It would seem that the limited idea of obedience and authority in the old spirituality is actually one of the biggest obstacles to the quicker development of the new spirit. Some in authority at present conceive obedience as purely ascetic, even if the commands are minute or meaningless. They seem genuinely unable to comprehend that sisters took the vow of obedience precisely to be directed corporately in a community task of witness and apostolate. They wonder at restlessness in the ranks. But the Church in her highest authorities is calling communities to renew. Sisters are sometimes paced very slowly by those who should be leading a renewal already overdue.

4) The new spirituality will find ways of achieving a much deeper contemplative life of personal prayer which will be carried out into the daily tasks of the sister. The old notion of a schizoid alternation between prayers and activities, work and retreats, God and human beings simply has to go. The theological basis for its demise is precisely the doctrine of *agape*, God loved and served in Christ present in every man. The existential cause of personal growth in a unified interior life will be each sister's involvement into contemplative prayer, liturgical worship and meditative reading of scripture. As faith is increasingly experienced as transfused with hope and love, as a per-

sonal encounter with Christ, the living Lord. His presence
carries over more and more into daily activities and contacts. The apostolic work is carried out in conscious love of
Christ in the one served. Contemplative prayer which increases love of Christ impels the sister to actual service of
Christ in the real needs of his members here and now.
Thus the sister will become the living mystery to men of
an interior presence, of a religious life which is constant
and consistent. It is true that sisters have had a tremendous effect on the American Catholic notion of the Church
and Catholic life. Then we must humbly admit that love
of prayer and the interior life, to which we are supposedly
dedicated, has not been one of the main things we have
transmitted. In fact, in the era of government support of
what used to be works of mercy, the sister may find that a
living witness to the depth and joy of the interior life of
personal love of Christ will be not only her holiness, but
even her apostolate. Who will teach the lay Christian how
to pray and serve if not those who are dedicated full time
to both?

The world is changing, the Church is changing, sisters
are beginning to change. They move out from a period
which was very different from the present. It was a period
of history which enfolded great women, great holiness and
great dedication to the works which the Church needed in
past decades. Today the most important directive for
change for sisters is that they change profoundly and
genuinely. This means that as persons, as women, as Christians, as consecrated virgins sisters must change their interior attitudes, must plunge more deeply into the spiritual
realities which are the innermost being of Christ's Church.
As sisters personalize their own inner awareness, the experiments and discussions in their communities will gain

in depth and relevance. It is not going to be easy to adapt the works and institutions and customs which have served well in past generations. It is not going to be easy to become perhaps less acceptable, by middle class standards even in some cases rejected for our message. It is difficult to form flexible and consistently adaptable, yet stable personalities. However, these are the tasks Christ and the Spirit ask of sisters now. Never before has the world needed more the balanced and total apostolic witness of the people of God. The privilege of the religious sister is to play her role in the Christian people as a consecrated reminder that we are all on the way together to another world yet to come. It is a world whose light is the Lamb and whose only law is love.

3

The Meaning of Virginity in Religious Life

Sister M. Elena Malits, C.S.C.

"Are sisters married to God or do they just work for him?" a high school freshman recently asked the panelists at a religious vocation program. With the disarming directness of youth, she posed the question raised by modern women who think seriously about or try to live the religious life. The girl was really asking if consecrated virginity offers a person the unique development and fulfillment that comes through a mature love commitment, for which marriage is the usual model. Her naive formulation may be amusing, but it captures a rather typical feminine attitude: there is a pejorative stress on "*just work* for him." School girls, along with their mothers or the sisters who teach them, like to think of relationships in interpersonal rather than functional terms. Few women prefer the prospect of "having a job" to "sharing a life," whether in the natural order or analogously applied to the supernatural.

Recently a wave of valid criticism has been directed against the "feminine mystique" (that too-facile view of women as females instead of persons).[1] An uncritical acceptance of certain personality traits or social roles as

[1] Betty Friedan, *The Feminine Mystique* (W.W. Norton & Co., Inc., New York, 1963).

distinctively feminine would risk limiting the specifically
human potential of women. Nonetheless, some broad tendencies seem to characterize women's approach to reality,
whether attributable to the biological-psychological differences of "nature" or to the sociological factors of cultural conditioning. Most women are person-centered
rather than role-oriented. Even when completely dedicated to a professional field or enjoying the satisfaction
which comes from any task well done, women are inclined
to regard their work as an expression of love for persons
more than as an accomplishment of objective value. They
seem to evaluate activity more in terms of its self-actualizing effects than in its social productivity. Normally,
women assume those functions which best symbolize their
love relationships and serve the mutual development of
themselves and others. To be realistic, therefore, any discussion of women's roles and activities must take into account the way the feminine mind relates these to the inner
demands of love and personal fulfillment.

For this reason, the current movement of renewal for
sisters must deeply explore the significance of consecrated
virginity. The welcome debates about the concrete forms
that apostolic work of religious women should assume will
miss the mark unless they proceed from a profound understanding of what virginity means in the life of a person and
in the Church as a whole.

To a woman, her virginity appears as the most significant facet of her religious vocation. Obedience may be
logically prior, but in the sister's inner awareness of herself, her relationship with God, and her responsibilities
toward others, the vow of chastity carries more psychological weight. From a negative point of view, she perceives her human situation as that of a woman without a
husband and children more immediately than she thinks

of herself as someone with limited independence or lacking possessions. And while the pain of religious obedience cuts deeply and sharply, it is felt more intermittently and less diffusely than the pervasive sense of loss and unfulfillment which is the price of virginity. In its positive aspects, the sister sees her virginal consecration as the very basis for her particular relationship with Christ and her meaning in the Church. Obedience and poverty appear as concrete expressions of fidelity to a supernatural marriage.

Although the concept of religious life as a sponsal relationship with Christ can degenerate into cheap sentimentality, it is rooted in the authentic tradition of the Church. Baptism has always been understood as an espousal to the Lord; and each baptized person, man or woman, physically virginal or having sexual experience, can be said to be wedded to him. The Eucharist, moreover, is celebrated as the marriage banquet of Christ and his Church; and every Christian who shares in the feast enjoys a nuptial association. Nonetheless, the Church speaks of the consecrated virgin as married to Christ in a special way. While masculine celibacy constitutes a relationship with Jesus as exclusive and intimate as that of women vowed to virginity, the sponsal imagery is appropriately feminine.

Canon law seems to devote more attention to obedience and poverty in the religious state, but the liturgy focuses on virginal chastity. Profession rites for men stress friendship with Christ, while those for women usually take the form of betrothal ceremonies. It is precisely virginity, not poverty or obedience, which places the woman in that condition the liturgy calls "bride of Christ." The liturgical texts seem to consider poverty and obedience only in reference to the virginal consecration which creates the marriage bond. Poverty appears as sharing the life situation of a spouse who is poor, and obedience as total responsiveness to him. The Roman preface for the consecration of Virgins emphasizes this:

> In You may she possess everything that she wishes to love, and to love You above all. Through You may she keep that which she has promised. Made pleasing not through the body but through the soul to him who looks within the heart, may she be numbered among the wise virgins and await the heavenly Bridegroom.

The liturgy is well attuned to the psychic perspective of the woman religious in stressing the central role that virginity plays in her life.

Virginity is, moreover, the aspect of the religious which seems apparent to everyone. Far more easily than obedience, or even evangelical poverty, it is recognized as a distinguishing feature. Those who know little else about the Church in general or religious in particular will be sure to know that nuns do not marry. Children are conscious of it: "How come you don't have any kids of your own?" is a familiar question to the sister in school. These are the most obvious circumstances about a religious, especially a woman.

Although the fact of consecrated virginity may be evident, it is not self-explanatory. Unless it is to be identified simply as spinsterhood, virginity is a sign which needs to be interpreted. But this interpretation must be in the light of the whole Christian mystery and not merely a reasoned justification.

The Rational Defense of Virginity

Of course the reasonableness of virginity can be defended. It is possible to make a case (and a good one, if rightly stated) for the usefulness of virginity in encouraging single-minded pursuits and its social utility in releasing from family obligations for the sake of a wider service.

Christian virginity can and has been explained in these terms—*ad nauseum*. Moralistic arguments tinged with some form of Manicheanism or blatantly egocentric are all too familiar. So, too, is the rhetoric of those who extol virginity merely on the plane of its benefits to education, hospital service, and the care of parish rectories!

But these "arguments from reason" do not answer the frank objections of people today who question the value of virginity; neither do such arguments satisfy those who sincerely seek to know its true significance. Nor does this approach help those women, increasingly educated in contemporary attitudes, who consider or have already embraced consecrated virginity as their vocation in life.

College students, for example, are unimpressed (to say the least!) by a demonstration of the effectiveness of virginity for securing an "undivided" mind and heart. They are apt to reply by quoting statistics on the incidence of personality disturbances among celibates. Any interpretation of virginity as "freeing from the responsibilities of marriage" is intolerable to the New Breed's philosophy of fierce personalism and commitment. Today's sophisticated students will reject such views of virginity as self-centered and anti-social. They will prefer the Peace Corps to religious life. And they will be more right than rebellious in refusing to equate whole-hearted dedication or humanitarian effectiveness with consecrated virginity. A pragmatic presentation of consecrated virginity remains at best insufficient and at worst misleading. For contemporary young people, however, it is always unconvincing. If done in their idiom and with consummate skill, a few psychological and sociological merits of virginity may be acceptable to them. Such a handling of the matter, unfortunately, never answers their real, though perhaps unexpressed question: what does virginity mean?

But it is not just a hard-to-satisfy college crowd which insists on knowing the inner significance of virginity if it is to be accepted as meaningful in human experience. Today, people in general are irked, if not appalled, by an apologetic approach. They are impatient with arguments for either the ethical superiority or operational efficiency of celibacy.

Contemporary-minded Catholics in particular will endure no pious moralizing about the merits of the "angelic condition." They belong to an age which is discovering the positive values of human sexuality from a psychological and even a theological point of view. While deeply concerned about the sexual dimension of love, they are nonetheless eager to appreciate all valid forms of human love, whether in its natural or supernatural expressions. Christian couples are interested in learning what consecrated virginity tells them about Christ, the Church, and their own married vocation. And they have a right to an answer which is more than a puritan polemic.

Thinking American Catholics, moreover, are unimpressed with a defense of virginity based on its assets to the Church's institutional life. Sensitive to the deficiencies of parochial education, to take but one example, they are not inclined to judge contributed service necessarily as an asset. The vocation to consecrated virginity will never justify itself to twentieth-century people on the grounds of organizational profits. Too often the operations of religious communities in our highly skilled, professionally-managed society appear pathetically ineffectual and incapable of competing with institutions powered by means other than "dedication." Even when successful, the race to keep up with secular institutions exacts a price so high that the effort risks destroying the objectives. Involved in a type of administrative work which appears only remotely apos-

tolic to them, religious women could turn into cold functionaries instead of witnesses to Christ. Pressured by impersonal circumstances, their very sense of living a consecrated vocation could be endangered. The effects of such
a situation are tragically experienced by too many sisters
and easily observable to other people. No, the explanation
of virginity on the level of ecclesiastical expediency will
not serve.

How then is consecrated virginity to be explained in
today's world? Obviously it must be communicated in the
language of contemporary people. And the presentation
should be set against the backdrop of their present interests and concerns. To be convincing, a consideration of
virginity would utilize the penetrating insights of existential philosophy into the nature of a man as an embodied
being in the world who develops in a network of inter-subjective relations. Furthermore, an effective treatment of
virginity would recognize the contribution of depth psychology in establishing the normal relationship between
personal maturity and sexual love. A thoroughly contemporary view of virginity would face squarely the real difficulty: virginity is more than a problem of "avoiding temptations"; it involves the question of human growth—a
moral issue in the widest sense of that term. How does a
person who freely relinquishes the ordinary means of self-
completion and self-giving through marriage and family
life insure an authentic human development? The question
is crucially important if one takes seriously the principle
so often glibly quoted: grace builds on nature.

A presentation of virginity suited to today's needs must
then be fully cognizant of the role of sexuality in human
existence. There can be nothing naive about it. An adequate treatment of voluntary virginity would honestly admit that it could be potentially dangerous to emotional

health. Perpetual continence could be a threat to mature personality expansion. Yet a competent presentation would be able to show that psychic stultification is merely a possibility, not an inevitable consequence of the virginal condition.

The sexual elements of any human being's experience must be synthesized by his rational powers at the specifically human level. A person can be prevented from achieving this synthesis by sinful appetites, emotional disorders, or even plain childishness. But morally culpable or not, the fact remains that such a person's sexuality fails to achieve its properly human orientation.

In married love, although sex is something more than physiological or even emotional appetite, it is but one important aspect of a multifaceted relationship. Sexual expression, therefore, has to be harmonized into the whole pattern of a love which is proper to persons, that is, one which is ordered by the spiritual powers of intelligence and will—a love which serves the good of the other instead of self-gratification.

An analogous process should be at work in the case of virginity. The sexual aspects of life have to be integrated into a mode of existence which, in this instance, is ordered by a reasonable decision to remain perpetually continent.

If the behavior of a celibate is neurotic or simply juvenile, this deviation is not caused by the lack of sexual activity as such. It is in some sense attributable to the person's warped perception of reality and mixed motivation (this may be not a moral failure, but a matter of unconscious predisposition). Nonetheless, such a person reveals an inability to deal with himself and to relate to others in a manner which properly integrates sexual aspects into the total scheme of human life.

To achieve such integration, however, the sexual aspects must be recognized, accepted, and properly related to all other aspects of life. In freely foregoing the legitimate use of sexual powers, the celibate cannot obliterate his sexuality. Whoever attempts to ignore it does not escape the human condition; instead he will be victimized by the very sexuality he flees. A person who irrationally fears sex does not live (as he may mistakenly imagine) at a superhuman level. Such paralyzing fear hinders him from dealing with his own sexuality in a truly human way. In order to sublimate sexual inclinations they must be first acknowledged and appreciated as healthy and good in themselves.

Neurotic concern about sex and a virginal chastity have nothing in comon. The mere abstention from sexual experience is neither the *cause* of the emotional abberation nor of the positive virtue. The neurotic concern results from an uncontrollable emotion about sex; and the virtue from a free rational decision in regard to its use. To the degree that the celibate fails to integrate his sexuality realistically and peacefully in accord with the purpose of his life, to that degree will his experience be dehumanized. Just as sexual relations fall below the human level unless synthesized by mature and generous love in marriage, so the abstention from them in the state of virginity can be something less than human if it is not fitted into the finality of another order of love.

These are but a few ideas which a contemporary treatment of virginity would need to explore and expand. However, while full attention must be given to these facets of the problem, that is not enough. Merely explaining psychological processes, even when it is a question of sublimating sexual inclinations for the sake of a greater love, still fails to probe the mystery of Christian virginity. Although a psychological explanation of virginity may help to explain why some persons remain unmarried in order to dedicate themselves to their work, it does not shed light on that state consecrated by vow and publicly professed in the Church. Such an approach is simply a subtler and more sophisticated version of what was previously termed inadequate and misleading.

What is necessary today is a theological interpretation of virginity which utilizes contemporary thought yet is genuinely traditional—not in the short-sighted range of post-reformation theology—but according to the full biblical, patristic, and liturgical tradition. As existential as the bible, as concrete as the liturgy, it would be as historically relevant to our times as the Fathers' thinking was for theirs. Such a theology of consecrated virginity would recognize the meaning of sexuality in human life and would show how sexuality is incorporated into God's revealed plan. Consecrated virginity would be approached as a Christian mystery and a sacramental sign. Set in the whole context of salvation history, it would be treated as a mystery revealing Christ in his death and resurrection and manifesting the presence of his Spirit in the Church. Understood within the whole complex of the Church's life, Christian virginity would be considered a sign in relation to the other sacred signs which constitute the sacramental nature of the Church.

Of course, more than a verbal explanation of consecrated virginity is needed. It must be lived in such a way that the significance of virginity as a vocation within the Church is evident. The concrete living of consecrated celibacy will, however, be conditioned by people's conception of it. If the constitutions of religious communities, their houses of formation, retreat conferences and spiritual reading books reflect a predominantly moralistic and egocentric view of virginity, it will produce some tight-lipped sisters afraid of being women, not knowing how to be fully adult, and incapable of making their full contribution to modern society. On the other hand, if religious are given an orientation to virginity which is scriptural and sacramental, and at the same time psychologically sound and related to the development of women in our times, there will be a new flowering in our religious communities. In fact, a burgeoning has already begun because such a theology of virginity, at least in its broad outlines, is now available.

The rest of this chapter will be devoted to the development of a few theological ideas about consecrated virginity and will suggest some ways of practically implementing them.

VIRGINITY IN THE BIBLICAL TRADITION

The Old Testament presents the story of God's salvific plan unfolding in the realities of human experience such as conjugal love, begetting children, family life, belonging to a people. The bible opens with an account of God making "man" as the pair, man/woman, not an undifferentiated or isolated individual: "Male and female he created them" (Gen 1:27). Human sexuality is adversely affected by sin (Gen 3:16), yet the victory over sin is bound up with the process of generation (Gen 3:15). Upon it, the promises made to Abraham (Gen 15) and David (2 Sam 7) depend. In the New Testament those promises are accomplished through the birth in the flesh of the Son of God (Luke 1-2).

Repeatedly in salvation history the divine power and mercy are revealed in removing the reproach of sterility. God takes away the barrenness of Sara, Rebecca, Rachel,

Anna, and Elizabeth, blessing their marriage. He fructifies
the womb of Mary by the overshadowing of the Spirit and
gives the world a Savior through her virginity. God's redemptive plan works itself out through the realities of
marriage and virginity. They are constitutive elements in
the story of salvation.

The bible is filled, moreover, with themes metaphorically dealing with marriage and virginity. The prophets present Yahweh as the faithful spouse and Israel as his adul-
terous wife (Osee 2; Joel 1; Isa 54; Jer 3; Ezech 16). St.
Paul speaks of Christ as the sacrificing husband who delivers himself up out of love for his bride, the Church
(Eph 5).

"Virgin Israel" is a term used by the prophets to emphasize the misery of God's sinful people (Amos 5; Lam 1-2;
Joel 1). According to the Semitic mentality, to die a virgin
is to die unproductive and deprived of the purpose of a
woman's life (Jgs 1:37-40). In calling Israel a virgin, the
prophets are far from complimenting her on her purity;
they are reproaching Israel for being unfruitful and threat-
ening that the divine punishment will make her perish
like a woman who leaves no descendants.

The virgins of the Apocalypse who "follow the Lamb
wherever he goes" (Apoc 14), are a symbol with a very
different meaning. Here virginity is used as an image of
fidelity and single-hearted devotion to God. Even in this
text, however, virginity does not represent sexual innocence as such, but is a metaphor describing the condition
of those who have remained faithful to the Covenant and
are unsullied by any form of idolatry. The virgins are
God's people who are "pure of heart" (Matt 5:8; Ps 24:4),
in the biblical sense of being sincere and constant toward
the Lord.

The messianic wedding feast pictured in the last book of the bible (Apoc 19:7-9), symbolizes the estblishment of the heavenly kingdom in the final age. This scriptural image brings together the theme of marriage and that of virginity: those whose fidelity to God has been kept pure can be espoused to the Lamb.

In his parables Jesus speaks figuratively about a wedding banquet (Matt 22:1-14), the bridegroom (Matt 9: 15), and virgins (Matt 25:1-13). But he also teaches about marriage and virginity in themselves. The Creator of male and female is the author of the institution which unites them as two in one flesh with an indissoluble bond (Matt 19:1-9). Yet there are persons who do not enter into the union of marriage which has been established by God as the ordinary way of life for men and women. Some are incapable of it because of birth or circumstances. Others deliberately forego it, choosing to be "eunuchs" for the sake of the kingdom of God (Matt 19:12).

St. Paul develops the implications of the Lord's teaching. He too refers to marriage and virginity metaphorically: addressing the Corinthians he says, "I betrothed you to one spouse, that I might present you a chaste virgin to Christ" (2 Cor 11:2). His primary concern, however, is the reality of Christian marriage and virginity.

Paul characterizes the love that should exist between husbands and wives (Eph 5:21-33) and specifies their marital duties toward each other (1 Cor 7:1-11). While he appears to stress the moral value of marriage from the negative point of view as a safeguard for the weak against fornication (1 Cor 7:2, 9), and would prefer virginity as the norm rather than an exception (1 Cor 7:6-7, 36-40), Paul clearly commends marriage as good and a worthy vocation in the Lord (1 Cor 7:28, 39). It is more than that;

like virginity, marriage too is a divine favor: "For I would that you all were as I am myself; but each one has his own gift from God, one in this way, and another in that" (1 Cor 7:7). The benefits of virginity stem from the fact that "the time is short" (1 Cor 7:29). The virgin enjoys a certain liberty of action and prayer. But virginity is something more than a condition favorable to the spiritual development of the person or the apostolic life of the Church. According to St. Paul it anticipates the coming of the kingdom and is a concrete witness that "this world as we see it is passing away" (1 Cor 7:31).

Christian marriage is called by Paul "a great mystery" (Eph 5:32). In the typically Pauline sense a "mystery" is a sign which reveals God's plan of salvation in Christ. The loving, permanent bond between Christian spouses and the fruitfulness of their union is a human image of the relationship between Christ and the Church. It points to and discloses in a veiled way certain aspects of the total mystery of our redemption through Christ's Passover which establishes the New Covenant.

The whole context of Paul's teaching indicates that he considers virginity also a sign revealing God's salvific plan. It proclaims the death and resurrection of the Lord and testifies to man' share in the paschal mystery now and in the life to come. Marriage, to be sure, is a sign of the love between Christ and the Church. Virginity, however, is a sign that this love belongs to the life of the Spirit who transforms men through the sacraments and ultimately in the resurrection.

Throughout the history of salvation, God reveals himself and his relationship with man through various *signs*. The created universe is a visible manifestation of the Creator's invisible attributes (Rom 1:20). The events of the Exodus are the revelation of Yahweh's saving activity in behalf of

Israel; they constitute the great "signs and wonders" of the Old Testament (Ps 105). Men, too, act as signs of Yahweh's presence in the midst of his people. Moses and David were living disclosures of the Lord's mercy and fidelity. The prophets in particular were flesh and blood signs: by what they were, as well as what they said and did, the prophets revealed to Israel the meaning of the present and at the same time pointed toward the future fulfillment of God's promises.

Jesus Christ, the incarnate Word, is himself the pre-eminent Sign. For St. John, he is the revelation in the flesh of the Father's glory (John 1:10-18) and the divine love (1 John 4:9-10). St. Paul calls him "the image of the invisible God" (Col 1:15). St. Augustine admirably sums up the biblical viewpoint: "There is no other sacrament (i.e., 'sign') of God except Christ" (Ep 187:34).

In the New Testament the deeds of Christ are described as signs which unveil his true identity and elicit faith (John 5:31-47, 30). The victory of Jesus over the demons and his miracles, for instance, are signs that in him the kingdom of God is already present, though not consummated until the end of time (Matt 12:22-28; 24:23-31). Similarly, the announcement of the gospel and the missionary preaching are signs that the kingdom is at hand (Matt 10:1-8) and the final age imminent (Matt 24:14). The powers of the apostles to cast out devils and to cure are also presented as signs that the messianic times have begun with Jesus and his work (Luke 9:1-6). Replying to the question of when the kingdom is coming, Jesus says: "The kingdom of God is among you" (Luke 17:20-21). The future fulfillment of God's salvific plan is already breaking into the present. In the coming of Christ and his establishment of the Church as the earthly phase of the kingdom, the past promises of salvation are being accomplished and their eschatological realization is now actively unfolding like a seed. This is the meaning of the "parables of the kingdom" (Matt 13; Mark 4).

The Church with its apostolic and liturgical functions is itself a collective sign. The community of the faithful is the visible witness of God's desire to gather all men into ultimate union with himself (1 Cor 15:28) and with each other through his risen Son in the New Jerusalem (Apoc 21). In response to the proclamation of the good news, both Jews and Gentiles become heirs of the divine promise (Acts 2:37-41; Eph 2:11-22) and are justified by faith in the resurrected Lord (Rom 4:23-25). Through baptism, Christians share in Christ's Passover from death to life (Rom 6:1-11) and are incorporated into his body which is the Church (1 Cor 13:13-31; Eph 3:13-22). The old divisions are obliterated and there is neither "circumcised and uncircumcised" (Col 3:11), but only one New Man (Eph 3:15), the prototype of recreated humanity (2 Cor 5: 16-19). Through the eucharistic celebration, Christians already anticipate the eschatological banquet (1 Cor 11; 26), the "marriage supper of the Lamb" (Apoc 19:9). All separations are dissolved in the perfect *agape* and men enjoy eternal life in their risen bodies (1 Cor 15:35-37) in the society of the elect. The Church is the sign lifted up among the nations, inviting men to unity (Isa 11:12) and pledging the destruction of death (1 Cor 15:22-28; Apoc 21).

But the Church can be the sign of man's redemption only because it is the earthly body of the glorified Christ. "He is the head of his body, the Church; he, who is the beginning, the firstborn from the dead . . ." (Col 1:18-20). By his resurrection and ascension the man Jesus has been "exalted by the right hand of God" (Acts 2:33), who has made him "both Lord and Christ" (Acts 36).

The resurrection of Jesus is the sign of signs; it is the ultimate revelation of God's salvific intent to regenerate mankind. The resurrection is the decisive event of all history, the greatest of God's redemptive actions which are signs of his saving will. The raising of Jesus from the dead testifies to man's reconciliation with God (Rom 4:24). It is an eternally enduring act, the unique event (Heb 10:10) which establishes Jesus as immortal in his humanity (Rom 8:35; Heb 9:23-28). "I am the First and the Last, and he who lives; I was dead, and behold, I am living forevermore" (Apoc 1:18). The glorified *Kyrios* is the divine witness that the Spirit of love has been poured forth upon all flesh (Joel 3:1-5; Acts 2:16-21; Rom 5:1-11), calling men into the community of the redeemed (Eph 1:3-14), regenerating them as sons of the Father (Rom 8:14-17), and transforming them in the likeness of Christ's risen life.

The resurrection is, therefore, the sign *par excellence* of God's work of salvation among men. In announcing this good news, Peter proclaims that the risen, exalted Lord is the living evidence that the Old Testament promises have been fulfilled and that the "last days" have arrived (Acts 2:14-36). Through the Spirit of the risen Christ, everything in the past history of salvation is accomplished and in the future is already achieved by anticipation.

Various biblical signs have been mentioned: the universe, Old Testament events and persons, the incarnate Word and his actions, the powers of the apostles, the whole Church itself, the resurrection of Jesus Christ. There is a common denominator among them. In biblical thought, a sign is something visible which contains within itself and manifests an invisible, supernatural reality. But more than that, a sign is a pledge in the present of a future fulfillment. A sign is not simply a symbol or image of a distant reality, but it *is* that reality in its initial expression. The future is already contained, although still hidden. A sign is a promise, yet more than a promise; it is an earnest, a first installment, an embryo which possesses the essentials of a reality not yet fully developed.

Thus in the biblical narrative not only does creation reflect the goodness and beauty of the Creator; but the first day of creation, marked by the stirring of God's breath, presages the last day of transformation of the universe by the Spirit of Christ. Thus the Exodus, as a journey from slavery to freedom, is for Israel an experience of redemption which anticipates Christ's journey from death to life. Moses, David, the prophets not only foreshadow the work of Jesus; they really embody it in a nascent form at the Old Testament stage of development. The incarnation is already the seed of the resurrection. The resurrection of Christ and the whole life of the Church is an anticipation of the *parousia* and the society of the Heavenly Jerusalem.

THE SIGNIFYING CHARACTER OF
MARRIAGE AND VIRGINITY

Set within this pattern of salvation history, the meaning of Christian marriage and virginity as *signs* begins to emerge. A recent study of the biblical concept of marriage by Pierre Grelot[2] and one by Lucien Legrand on virginity,[3] provide an excellent treatment of the signifying character of these states from an exegetical point of view. Karl Rahner has developed a formal theology of the married and religious vocations based on their nature as signs expressing two aspects of life in the Church which is sacra-

[2]Pierre Grelot, *Man and Wife in Scripture* (Herder and Herder, New York, 1964).
[3]Lucien Legrand M.E.P., *The Biblical Doctrine of Virginity* (Sheed and Ward, New York, 1963).

mental through and through.[4] A few of the insights of these men will be presented here because they prove helpful in achieving a deeper understanding of the role of virginity. Since virginity and marriage are complementary signs, however, both must be considered together if either one is to be well understood.

Since the Church itself is a visible sign manifesting a supernatural reality, says Rahner, its qualities as a sign must be evident in all aspects of the Church's life. He distinguishes what is called its "sacramental functions" (in the strict sense of liturgical activities) and the "daily life" of the members of the Church. In the sign of baptism, for example, the Church confesses its belief that its life comes from God and is not of the natural order. In baptism the Church professes hope in the salvation that is to come in its fullness at Christ's return—the total salvation of which baptism is the pledge. However, Rahner continues, the daily life of the members of the Church must also be permeated with awareness of the supernatural and and expectancy of the definitive salvation which is to come with the return of Christ and the resurrection from the dead.

Because the Church is a society made up of men, visible creatures, the total supernatural life of the Church must be manifested in a tangible way. There are two essential characteristics in the Church, Rahner asserts, and each must find expression in the daily life of the Church's members as well as in the moments of sacramental encounter.

The first characteristic is what Rahner calls the "cosmic" aspect of the Church. The Church does not destroy nature. Since the Church communicates God's life, it necessarily loves what God has made. The Church reveres the whole

[4]Karl Rahner's thought on this subject is available in English in summary form in John D. Gerken's *Toward a Theology of the Layman* (Herder and Herder, New York, 1963), pp. 54-81.

order of creation. Rahner says that this cosmic characteristic of the Church is manifested primarily in the life of
the layman and, it might be added, specifically in Christian marriage.

The layman's vocation in Christ is realized in the world
through normal human activities. The lay state in the
Church is a witness to the goodness of the natural order
and is a sign of the intrinsic worth of human values. Ideally, the layman's use of the goods of the earth, his exercise
of personal freedom, and his love for his family testifies
to the truth that the world and man's basic human drives
are from God. The state of the layman indicates that the
Church exists in the created universe and that it is into
this natural order that God infuses his own supernatural
life. The vocation of the Christian layman gives new meaning to material things, self-determination, and especially
human love. Rahner's view of the theological significance
of lay life (in which marriage is the normal condition)
has the advantage of showing that the layman can truly
love God by means of these terrestrial values which are
highest in the natural scheme of things.

Nonetheless, the Church's daily life must also show that
these supreme human values are not absolutely the highest
goods of man as redeemed by Christ. And so in accordance
with its sign-nature, the Church must make this truth evident in the lives of certain members. In order that the
Church give a true impression of itself, the Spirit calls
some Christians to relinquish the preeminent goods of
human nature. The person's response to this call is a sign
to all men of the reality of the supernatural order. It is a
living testimony that the Church, while in the world to
sanctify it and lead it to God, is not *of* the world. The person who willingly surrenders the greatest human joys, in
answer to the divine summons, witnesses to the Church's

belief that man's ultimate happiness lies beyond the merely human. As Rahner views it, the religious vocation is a sign that the Church is waiting for the fulfillment of God's redemptive plan at the end of time in the Heavenly City. The religious vocation complements that of the layman since it expresses what Rahner terms the "transcendental" or "eschatological" characteristic of the Church. In other words, the religious life concretely embodies the goal toward which the Church is moving—the coming of Christ in glory, the bodily resurrection of men, and the final accomplishment of the divine plan in the New Jerusalem. The religious vocation shows that the center of human existence lies not in itself, but in the risen Lord and the life he communicates to his body.

Each of the evangelical vows expresses something of the prophetic aspect of the religious vocation, but it seems most clearly evidenced in consecrated virginity.

Virginity, along with the apostolic and sacramental functions of the Church which the New Testament presents as signs of the kingdom, is an anticipated realization of the ultimate transfiguration to come. The glory of a world recreated in the Spirit and fashioned in the likeness of the risen Christ is already present in the baptized soul. The seed of immortality already germinates in the bodies of men nourished by the Eucharist. All the sacraments are signs of the eschatological life, and every Christian who participates in them becomes a witness to man's future destiny. But consecrated virginity, as a state of life, testifies that the resurrection already stirs in the Christian and the community which is the Church. Man's final destiny does not make him asexual by turning him into a pure spirit; but in his risen body he transcends the exigencies of sexual activity. As Legrand explains:

The life of resurrection is no more a life "in the flesh," a life doomed to death. It is a life in God, a life of the sons of God, life "in the Spirit," in a body transformed by the divine glory. Hence the functions of the flesh become useless; procreation loses its meaning, which was to make up for the ravages of death.[5]

The risen life of heaven is, moreover, a life of perfected love between Christ and the Church and among all persons united in him. It is a communion in the Spirit, and even conjugal love will be transformed into the *agape* of which virginity in this life is a prophetic sign.

Grelot develops the thought that virginity embodies the eschatological wedding between Christ and the Church which marriage prefigures. The nuptial mystery of Christ and the Church is incarnated, in the case of consecrated virginity, in an institution which exemplifies that this union is one of charity:

> Total abstention from the use of sexuality not out of contempt, or impotence, or fear, but through self-mastery and renunciation, has as its most profound purpose, that of being an eschatological witness. It affirms the actual presence of the mystery (the messianic marriage of Christ and the Church) in time. It translates the situation, which is that of every Christian, of the "bride without spot" betrothed to Christ (2 Cor 11:2), into terms of the flesh. It is in a special sense a participation in the condition of the Church herself, spouse and virgin. In this case it is no longer the rightly ordered sexuality of man and wife which represents the mystery of Christ. It is the consecration of sexuality by a human person who thus integrates his whole life with that of Christ, the bridegroom.[6]

Virginity is, then, a sign of the future. As an embodied promise of the hope that is to come, it has a social sig-

[5]Legrand, p. 46.
[6]Grelot, p. 116.

nificance in the Church. It points to man's eternal destiny and is a living reminder to all, not just the consecrated virgin herself, that the Christian life is even now a recreation in the Spirit and a communion of love in him.

Yet like all sacramental signs, virginity is not only a pledge of future glory. It is also a commemoration of the past history of salvation. Virginity is a memorial of the entire paschal mystery of Christ—his death as well as his resurrection—since that death is the condition of the resurrection.

Virginity is a sign that exists in the real order of man's sin and its consequences, as the redemption itself is worked out within that order. Because of sin there is death, and the whole history of God's dealings with man reveals that he brings about a new creation only when the old one which has been perverted by sin is destroyed. In the narrative of Genesis the waters of the flood must wipe out a sinful humanity before God begins again with a regenerated race (Gen 6-9). Thus the Day of the Lord must fall upon unrepentant Israel in the crushing doom of the Evile (Jer 4:15) before he can revivify her with his spirit and clothe the dry bones with living flesh (Ezech 37). And thus the old world under the reign of sin and death must be annihilated in the sinless flesh of Jesus on the cross before the universe of man and nature can be reconstituted in the likeness of his risen body.

According to the divine dispensation, the redemption is worked out through the incarnate Son's free acceptance of suffering and death. He bears the full weight of alienation from God which is the existential situation of a sinful race (Phil 2:5-11; Heb 4:14-15; 5:7-10; Rom 5-6). There is no resurrection without the crucifixion, and Christian life essentially involves sharing in Christ's passion and death (Gal 2:19; 5:24) in order to share his glory (Rom 6:5-1).

Virginity is a kind of death, in that it takes away the possibility of generating new life and seeing one's own life continued in one's offspring. Virginity entails pain of unsatisfied desire, the suffering of human loneliness, the extinction of potential fruitfulness. In this perspective, virginity is sheer negation and the denial of value; it appears as self-destruction and a distortion of nature. Sought for its own sake and nothing more, even on the level of natural motivation, virginity seems masochistic. But such is not the meaning of Christian virginity.

Voluntary virginity has always been regarded in the Church as a martyrdom. It is a sharing in Christ's sacrificial death, a dying with him for the sake of rising with him. While that "dying" does indicate a moral effort of asceticism aimed at bringing unruly passions under the control of reason, it involves much more. To die with Christ through virginity is to be associated with the priestly offering of Jesus on the cross. And that priestly offering must be understood according to the biblical notion of cultic sacrifice wherein the victim is consecrated. Legrand explains:

> To understand this sacrificial consecration of virginity, it must be remembered that, in the biblical sacrifices and especially in the holocaust, the victim was destroyed, but the destruction was not an end in itself. It was a way to place the offering in God by transferring it into the field of the invisible. As appears from the Hebrew name of the holocaust (*'olah*: elevation), the disappearance of the victim was only the reverse side of its exaltation. . . . Thus does virginity 'sanctify.' The privation it entails is not the sign of a destruction but of an ascension. Like the holocaust, it is an "elevation." Through the holocaust of virginity, man's life is sanctified and divinized. Imbued with the radiance of the divine presence, burnt by the fire of divine charity, man sees his deepest urge and power turn into an act of

love for God, as the victim was turned into smoke "to
ascend" into the divine glory. Man's vital energy is sacri-
ficed, that is, not cut off but consecrated and transfigured.
In terms of modern psychology, it is sublimated. But whereas psychology, when speaking of sublimation, refers to an
effort of self-purification, the sublimation of Christian celibacy is of a theological order: it means assumption; it de-
notes primarily the action of God accepting man's offering
and lifting it up to himself. This sublimation is the work of
the livine love, consuming body and soul, apparently destroying but really assuming and transmitting their longings.
This transforming holocaust is nothing else that the individual application of the sacrificial exaltation of Christ.[7]

Consecrated virginity is an immolation, then, but one
which signifies a transference from the sphere of the profane to that of the sacred, just as this is the meaning of
Christ's sacrificial act (Heb 9:7-12; 10-12).

Like Christ's death on the cross, virginity represents a
dispossession of self into the Father's hands (Luke 23:46).
Again like the death of Jesus, virginity is meant to testify
to the utter poverty of the "flesh" apart from the Spirit. In
the biblical idiom the "flesh" is not identified with man's
body or bodily functions. Rather the term expresses the
condition of sinful man apart from God. To belong to the
flesh is to belong to the world where death reigns. To be
in the Spirit is to be renewed in one's whole being by the
presence and power of God (Rom 8; Gal 5:16-23).
Through his death and resurrection, Jesus passed from the
condition of the "flesh" which he had freely embraced to
a glorified humanity permeated fully with the life of the
Spirit (1 Cor 15:45). Thus the destruction in the sacrifice
of Calvary is not the destruction of the human nature of
Jesus, but precisely the destruction of man's sinful condi-

[7]Legrand, pp. 82-83.

tion. It is a redemption from the world ruled by death and
an ascension into the life of God where humanity is transformed and glorified by the Spirit. And thus the destruction signified by Christian virginity is not an annihilation
of man's bodily life, but an attitude which relies on the
strength of self rather than on God. Virginity is a crucifying denial that there is any enduring life outside of God.
Virginity is an affirmation in faith that God will make
good our losses in the natural order and will transform the
ravages of sin left in us. As a sign of the paschal mystery
of Jesus, virginity proclaims an end and a beginning, a
destruction and a creation, a death and a life. The prophetic character of virginity as manifesting the entire
economy of redemption is summed up well by Legrand:

> The last days are not only days of doom: they are also
> days of resurrection. Jeremia was not only the prophet of the
> fall of Jerusalem: he was also the prophet for the New
> Covenant (Jer 31:31-35). Similarly for St. Paul the last days
> are only secondarily days of woe: primarily, they are the
> days of the parousia when Christ will come and hand over
> to the Father the world revivified by the Spirit (1 Cor 15).
> The Apocalypse ends its enumeration of the eschatological
> calamities by the resplendent description of the heavenly
> Jerusalem where everything is made new (Apoc 21).
> Christ's death on Calvary was only the beginning of his
> Exaltation (John 3:14f; 12:32f). The full prophetical mean-
> ing of virginity is to be understood in reference to the whole
> mystery of death and life contained in Christ. Celibacy is not
> only an enacted prophecy of imminent doom; it announces
> and also anticipates the life to come, the life of the new
> world in the Spirit.[8]

According to Rahner's distinction, the layman's life
epitomized in marriage is a sign of the goodness of the
natural order of creation, while the life of the religious

[8]Legrand, p. 37.

is a witness to the supernatural order and the eschatological goal of the Church. But, of course, Christian marriage also signifies the paschal mystery of Christ as does
virginity, although in a different manner. Marriage too is
a sign of the total redemptive activity of God begun with
creation and completed at the parousia. As the "great
mystery" (Eph 5:32), marriage for Christians is the sign
of the new and everlasting Covenant (Jer 31:31-34) between God and man sealed in the blood of Christ (Heb
9:15-28), experienced in the Church (Eph 1:22-23), and
fully realized in the eternal dwelling (Apoc 21:1-4). Marriage is a sign which points to the consummation of the
relationship between Christ and the Church as the wedding feast of the Lamb. And since he is a Lamb who was
slain (Apoc 5:6), marriage inevitably involves suffering.
As a sacrament, Christian marriage is a sign of death and
resurrection in Christ and that community of life which
expresses not *eros*, but *agape*. As Grelot says:

> As far as the Christian morality of marriage is concerned,
> the relation between the sacramental institution and the
> nuptial mystery which is its archetype explains the rule of
> perfection which is henceforward binding on the couple.
> The respective attitudes of Christ and the Church deter-
> mine those of the husband and wife (Eph 5:21-32), since
> the conjugal union represents and signifies the whole mys-
> tery, introducing a sacral value even into its physical con-
> summation. Created in a certain order which was destroyed
> by sin, this union is recreated in Christ at a level of perfec-
> tion which it could only attain with the help of redemptive
> grace. The marriage partners still have to bear with the
> profound defects left in sexuality by sin. They will learn to
> know their moral weaknesses. They will know too the bit-
> terness of both willing lapses and almost involuntary falls
> from grace in the face of apparently insoluble problems . . .
> In spite of these drawbacks of a rebellious nature, their
> sexuality, taken up into a supernatural order which relates

it to the mystery of Christ and the Church, will, nonethe-less, be saved from the wretchedness which it may still feel, but which is overcome by the medium of grace. In this way a communion of love will be realized between the husband and wife which will restore for them the lost human unity, not in a perfect sense, since there will still be lapses, but, nonetheless, in a real sense, because they have together been joined to God: even physical love will be encompassed by charity.[9]

Both marriage and virginity, then, are signs which ex-press various aspects of the total life of the Church. They are signs which are fully intelligible only in relation to each other.

Marriage proclaims that Christian life must be fully human—but in order that it be authentically human, life must be supernaturalized. Given the incarnation, there is nothing genuinely human without Christ. An attempt to live on the merely human level ends in falling below it.

The dangers in marriage and virginity are different. As Rahner shows, the layman loves God in and through the human goals he pursues. The risk is that he might rest content in a purely natural love, thereby ultimately per-verting it. The married person must guard against natural-ism, which actually destroys the goodness of truly human values by deflecting them toward sin.

On the other hand, the consecrated virgin loves God through a renunciation of conjugal love. A scathing re-mark of Rousseau, hateful as it is, puts the finger on the danger that the religious faces: "The love of God serves them as an excuse to love no one; they do not even love one another. Has anyone ever observed real friendship among the devout? But the more they detach themselves from men, the more they demand of men; and one could

[9]Grelot, pp. 113-114.

say that they do not raise themselves to God except to exercise his authority on the earth."[10]

The consecrated virgin is helped to escape such pharaisaical religiosity by seeing the earnestness of the layman's family love, his conjugal tenderness, the generosity of father and motherhood. The great pitfall for the virgin is thinking that sacrifice consists in giving up, rather than in giving. The testimony of married Christians aids her in avoiding such ascetical sterility.

Christian marriage will demonstrate that love is only truly human when it issues in the fruitful communication of life. Christian virginity quietly announces that giving life in the fullest sense depends not on the flesh, but on the Spirit.

The complementary character of marriage and virginity is summed up by Grelot:

> Virginity and celibacy on the one hand and Christian marriage on the other react upon one another and influence each other. Both belong to the same order of truths: that of the kingdom of God, of redeemed creation, which has a vision of its eschatological fulfillment but has not yet finally reached it, a vision of its absolute liberty which it does not yet fully possess. Both have their source in the same life in the Spirit, both to a different degree and in different ways. Seen from outside it might appear that one fulfills human nature, while the other sacrifices it. In fact, marriage corrects nature by introducing it into the new world of grace, while celibacy introduces nature into that world in order to consecrate it completely to it. If these two aspects of the question are not fully appreciated, there is a great risk either that marriage will be despised in the name of an inhuman and illusory purity or that celibacy and virginity will be rejected in the name of marriage which is extolled to the

[10]Jean-Jacques Rousseau, *Nouvelle Heloise*, 6th Part, Letter 8, quoted by Y. Congar in "The Theology of Religious Woman," *Review for Religious* (January, 1960), p. 26.

point of abuse; as if, on the one hand, marriage was something evil or now completely transcended, or as if, on the
other hand, virginity was useless in a world restored to the
perfection of the original Eden. The Christian conception
of sexuality exorcises both these errors, since it is aware
both of the reality of life in the Holy Spirit and the real
wretchedness of the human situation, in which this life must
be lived.[11]

Christian marriage and Christian virginity mutually illumine one another in signifying that duality in unity which
is the heart of the mystery of the Church—the human-di-
vine, natural-supernatural, historical-eternal community of
many persons united in one Lord.

THE SOCIAL ASPECT OF VIRGINITY

Now if the Church is of her essence a *community* of *men*
in Christ, its social nature must be made visible. It will be
reflected, although imperfectly, in the family where unity
in diversity is achieved through human love. It is meant
to be most properly signified in the religious community,
where oneness in variety can be accomplished only
through fraternal charity—love based on a supernatural
relationship in Christ rather than on natural bonds alone.

The human civic group—that society of many persons
and families called the "city"—is a symbol of ordered multiplicity and differentiated unity. There are natural ties
which bind the members together. But over and above
ethnic and cultural similarities, the complex relationships
which make the city must be entered into freely. Dialogue
is its very life blood; the city is sustained by communication—the exchange of words and goods.

It is surely no accident that the final stage of God's
salvific plan is pictured in the Apocalypse under the figure

[11]Grelot, pp. 99-100.

of the *city*. "And I saw the holy city, New Jerusalem, coming down out of heaven from God, made ready as a bride
adorned for her husband" (Apoc 21:2). The heavenly
consummation of the divine plan is a *society* or persons
united to God and to each other in the risen Christ whose
glorious life they share even in their bodies. It is a family
of one Father, a communication in the incarnate Word,
and a gathering of free persons in the Spirit. The eschatological Church is described as a bride, that is, a virgin-
spouse. The men and women who will compose this community will be those who anticipated the life of charity in
Christ in their earthly associations as married partners or
consecrated virgins.

Marriage is necessarily a community of two. But the
husband and wife must reach out beyond themselves if
their love is to be perfected. Married love will be fulfilled
in generating new life and nurturing it. In married love
the family, not the couple, is the unit; it must not, however, be a closed unit. Love, although most intense within
the family, should radiate beyond its own circle. If married love is genuinely Christian, it will seek to create relationships similar to family bonds in the neighborhood, the
nation, the world. Christian family love should open out
in a universal charity; it will exclude no one.

Similarly, consecrated virginity is normally lived in a
community. The virgin belongs to a society of virgins
bound together by the evangelical vows. This is her family
in Christ. With her virginal love she must serve the other
members, support them in their needs, help them grow to
spiritual maturity. But she must join with them in going
beyond their own interests and those of the religious
group. As a community of consecrated virgins, all should
be commonly "concerned about the things of the Lord"
(1 Cor 7:32). That does not mean withdrawal from or indifference to human affairs:

"The things of the Lord" which should be the virgin's only concern are not the suprasensible ideas attained by contemplation. The "Lord" in St. Paul is the risen Christ, endowed with power and glory after his resurrection. "The things of the Lord" are therefore the whole order which has the risen Christ as its center, the New Creation, the kingdom and, here on earth, the Church.[12]

Together in a shared endeavor which, like their virginity itself, is "for the sake of the kingdom" (Matt 19:12), Christian virgins will be apostolically fruitful. Not only the individual person, but the community of virgins united in spiritual marriage with Christ becomes the sign of the heavenly kingdom. Aloysius Mehr has pinpointed this truth:

. . . the religious community exists at the point of encounter between two great lines of force and destiny which are the Church and the world. Its being calls out to the total human community from which it arises and in whose service it acts; and its being is a response, deep and creative, to the call of the Word of God. The religious community sums up, symbolizes, and is an eikon of the human community and of the Church.[13]

PRACTICAL IMPLICATIONS

A number of practical conclusions follow from the theological view of virginity which has been sketched. Here it is possible only to indicate areas where the ideas could affect religious life. Some specific ways of implementing these ideas are dealt with in other chapters of this book; the rest must be worked out through the thinking and discussion of sisters everywhere.

First, to live the vocation of virginity most fully and to make known its richest meaning to others, religious need an ever-developing biblical and liturgical spirituality.

[12]Legrand, p. 99.
[13]Aloysius Mehr, "Community Exercises in the Religious Life," *Review for Religious* (July, 1962), p. 301.

God's life-giving Word and transforming Spirit are encountered in prayerful reflection on scripture and in liturgical workshop. It is primarily through experiential contact with Christ in the bible and the liturgy that the consecrated virgin will grow in understanding how God reveals
his plan of salvation through signs. Concurrently, the
awareness of her own virginity as one of those signs will be
deepened.

Sisters who appreciate the biblical attitude toward virginity will be little inclined to exalt, for its own sake,
physical virginity. In the bible that counts for nothing.
The Old Testament does not attribute any religious value
to virginity; rather, like the married women who is barren,
the virgin's status is that of weakness, poverty, humilia-
tion (1 Sam 1:1-10). Mary's prayer magnifying the Lord
(Luke 1:46-55) echoes this attitude; she regards her virginal condition as "lowliness" (Luke 1:48).

But Mary's virginity assumes a religious significance: it
becomes an expression of utter dependence on God, the
characteristic attitude of the poor people of Yahweh, those
whom the Old Testament calls the "anawim." An acknowl-
edgement of human impotence apart from God, Mary's
virginity manifests a disposition which is the very opposite
of a longing for ethical perfection through self-mastery.
Her virginity is "for the sake of the kingdom"; it is a sign
of the power of the Spirit to give life and transform man's
wretchedness, a sign that God chooses the foolish and
weak and base things of this world (1 Cor 1:27).

Such an appreciation of virginity by sisters will en-
gender a spirit of prayerful humility and will counteract
possible temptations to presume a moral superiority. While
this attitude usually presents more of a danger for male
celibates, religious women are not immunie. In men such
an attitude appears as self-reliant pride; in women, a form
of petty snobbery.

But there is another danger probably more common among sisters. It is the problem of feeling the sacrifice of virginity so acutely that the person yields to a pervading sense of unfulfillment. Life becomes marked by a lack of vitality, hope, and gladness.

Of course, because of her virginity, any sensitive woman experiences a natural sense of loss that no spiritual motivation or religious orientation can remove. In the Christian dispensation, the grain of wheat has to die in order to yield fruit (John 12:24); and the fact that it will yield fruit does not remove the painful character of dying. The Christian virgin remains a woman unfulfilled as a wife and mother, and nothing in the order of nature can change that. It is quite possible for the woman religious to feel so overwhelmed by emptiness, that like Jephte's daughter, she withdraws "to bewail her virginity" (Jgs 11:37). Such a person has not gone beyond the Old Testament.

In the New Testament, virginity appears as something optimistic and joyous. Like Mary, the Christian virgin trusts the Lord in his mercy to regard her lowly condition and to transform her barrenness by his mysterious power (Luke 1:46-47). Such an attitude springs from the vision of faith which affirms that "nothing shall be impossible with God" (Luke 1:37); such an attitude expresses total confidence that "God is able out of these stones to raise up children to Abraham" (Luke 3:8).

The sister whose attitude has been molded by the bible will not minimize the deprivation virginity entails. On the other hand, she will recognize this as a condition for the fructifying action of the Spirit, and thus be able to accept the deprivation with peace and supernatural joy. The biblically wise virgin looks forward to the fulfillment of her womanhood in the resurrection and believes that through the Spirit she is already participating in it. Be-

cause faith gives her the assurance that this absolute fulfillment does not depend on sexual love or physical
motherhood, she will not make the mistake of the Sad-
ducees. Christ had to correct their view which he termed
unbiblical: "You err because you know neither the scriptures nor the power of God. For at the resurrection they
will neither marry nor be given in mariage . . . Have you
not read what was spoken to you by God, saying, 'I am
the God of Abraham, and the God of Isaac, and the God
of Jacob'? He is not the God of the dead, but of the living" (Matt 23:30-33).

Because God is the God of the living, the virginal consecration of the sister will be a vital, dynamic principle of
action. Her consecration means that she is "set apart" for
the worship of God, and her life bears a special relation to
the divine cult. Through her active participation in the
liturgy, the sister will be doing now what she will be
doing for all eternity: praising the Lord in body and soul.
But her special vocation to worship God is not something
she accomplishes in a private little world apart from the
whole Church. Rather, the sister's virginal consecration
implies that she is to help God's people everywhere discover the common Christian vocation to worship and that
she join with them in doing it. In order to be totally free
for God's service, the virgin renounces marriage (1 Cor
7:23-36). Her very consent to this particular vocation in a
certain sense sets her apart. According to God's designs,
the sister is singled out and placed in special circumstances. But, as in the biblical notion of "separation from
the profane," the "setting apart" which religious life entails is not meant to be a physical isolation from people
nor a withdrawal from their affairs. Rather this separation
is a *consecration* to the Lord which is intended to enrich
the totality of his people. Although the virgin is set apart

by God, she is to have the interests of the Church at heart. Her very dedication to God should make her vitally concerned about the individual and collective needs of his people. If the virgin, at the call of the Lord who has chosen her, has to leave the "ways" of the people, it is precisely in order that she might communicate to them what she herself receives.

The virgin, through her consecration, can help the members of Christ's mystical body better understand the vocation which is common to all persons in the Church. The virgin's specific religious consecration through public vows can enhance all Christians' sense of the sacred. Her particular "setting apart" should remind Christians in all walks of life of the baptismal consecration which set them apart from the profane world and made them members of the "laos"—the Holy People of God.

Consecrated virginity, then, has a profound social function in the Church. The religious vocation stands as a reminder to all Christians of the liturgical and apostolic powers with which their baptism endowed them—powers which must be operative in each specific mode of life in the Church. The sister, therefore, has a special responsibility to lead people to a deep sacramental life and an active participation in the apostolate. In some cases, this will be accomplished through teaching; in others, by working with lay people in social action groups. The sister who understands the apostolic possibilities of consecrated virginity will discover many ways to encourage liturgical participation and to foster ecumenical understanding, social justice, and missionary witness.

Finally, consecrated virgins need to deepen their understanding of Christian marriage if they are to grasp the full dimensions of their own vocation. Reading some of the many excellent books on marriage now available will help to achieve this, but it is primarily through sustained contact and discussion with Christian families that insights will develop.

A truth which has emerged from the contemporary ecumenical dialogue may, perhaps, be helpful here. Those engaged in this process affirm that when a fundamental commitment to one's convictions can be presumed, dialogue strengthens rather than weakens those convictions. Exposure to another point of view or another way of doing things stimulates a re-examination of one's own tradition and encourages an evaluation of one's fidelity to it.

Could not open discussion between sisters and married couples offer similar benefits? Innumerable issues are of common concern to all Christians. There are, moreover, problems specific to married or religious life which can be illumined by the insights of persons in the other state.

The consecrated virgin has something to teach married people—and she has much to learn from them. Human love remains the analogy for divine love, and the sister can grow in understanding charity through a close observation of conjugal life. Such contact will help the consecrated virgin interpret her own family and community experiences in the light of God's love for her. And if she learns this well, the sister will be able to lead others, especially young girls, to view their own friendships and romances in a similar way. To the degree that the consecrated virgin can show that she understands a woman's longing for completion as wife and mother, she can convince people (through the sign of her life, not just her words) that the sister is the spouse of Christ and mother of his life in men.

Virginity and marriage are complementary vocations within the Church. If today's consecrated virgins compare their role with that of married women's, however, it must not be in terms of some vague, unhistorical ideal. The

comparison ought to be between the sister and the contemporary wife and mother. There was a time when
women were content in a submissive role within marriage and would not think of venturing beyond occupations of the home. But that is not the reality in present-
day America. As Ignace Lepp says in *The Psychology of
Loving:*

> Not so long ago women were very proud of their mission
> to be the servants of the species. Today they are conscious
> of themselves as persons, and desire for themselves all that
> goes along with being a person, namely, independence,
> freedom, the right to happiness and the right to individual
> development. Men have been animated for a long time by
> the same desires, but from now on they will not be able to
> satisfy these desires except in relation to those of their
> feminine companions.[14]

Contemporary wives relate to their husbands as equal
partners, assuming a full share of adult responsibility in
marriage. Moreover, they somehow manage to raise their
families and still take an active role in the community—
and their families can be all the richer for it.

Contemporary sisters are urged to be thoroughly modern women and plunge into the full, rushing stream of the
Church's present life. Consecrated virgins have always
been witness to the mystery of Christ in his Church. Today's sisters are not being asked to discard that role; they
are being invited to enlarge it. The Church in this era is
begging her consecrated virgins to realize their full power
as signs of redemption in the twentieth century. Sisters are
being moved by the power of Christ working through his
intermediaries in the Church. "And the Spirit and the
bride say 'Come'!" (Apoc 22:17).

[14]Ignace Lepp, *The Psychology of Loving* (Helicon, Baltimore,
1963), p. 183.

4

Personal Fulfillment and Apostolic Effectiveness

SISTER M. ALOYSIUS SCHALDENBRAND, S.S.J.

The American sister today can hardly evade the questions so pervasive, so prominent in our time: how become myself? how fulfill myself? These are not academic questions, and the honest questioner refuses to consider the easy expedient of the textbook answer. For these are existential questions, and the only answers that will do are existential answers.

Yet is it right to raise them? Should those whose lives are dedicated to God be concerned about themselves at all? Is it not precisely by being unconcerned about themselves, by losing their lives, that dedicated religious are to find their lives? Preoccupation with the self is surely the greatest enemy of true self-fulfillment.

There seems no denying the evangelical truth that one's life is found in the losing of it. But to ask whether it is right to raise an existential question is to miss the whole point. An existential question is raised despite us. Or, better, we *are* that question and cannot help raising it once we have reached a certain degree of self-awareness. And that seems to be what is happening in our time. Aware of ourselves in a new way, we find the questions of self-becoming and self-fulfillment inseparable from ourselves.

Not, of course, that everyone raises these questions in so many words. Relatively few people do that—psychologists, perhaps, and philosophers. However, everyone who is "of the times" is at least silently "worked by" these questions.

Indications of this existential concern are, I believe, not lacking in the renewal movement among American sisters today. For the renewal movement is more than a reasoned decision to confront the apostolic needs of a new world; it is that, of course. But it is also a mighty wave of restlessness. The book of Cardinal Suenens did not create its audience; it found it. It did not initiate impatient stirrings; it simply gave them shape. To be more precise: the questions raised by the renewal movement have meanings in addition to their obvious meanings. Asking the question: What is the apostolic value of teaching mathematics all day? means also: How can teaching mathematics all day fulfill my desire to be all that I can be and do all that I can do? Asking the question: Are not sisters being "wasted" in administrative and clerical tasks? means as well: Can such impersonal, functionalized tasks fulfill my longing to be fully a person and not just a job?[1] The point of these remarks is simply this: an existential self-concern energizes also, although perhaps secretly, the renewal thrust and explains the impression that there is "more here than meets the eye."

Forthrightly facing existential self-concern, its questions of self-becoming and self-fulfillment, is urgently the task of American sisters today. How an apostolic religious stands with respect to these irrepressible questions of our time is a vital issue, not only for ourselves but for our

[1]Insistence on the primacy of the interpersonal throughout this chapter is not meant to indicate any reserves toward administrative-type apostolic works. Rather, the high degree of social organization makes it desirable that sisters serve in these offices, for their sphere of influence is thereby greatly extended.

contemporaries. What dissuades so many of them from accepting the Christian message is perhaps not so much the failure of our arguments as the failure of our lives to persuade them that the Good News means having life— rich, full, truly adult human life—and having it more abundantly.

In any case, this chapter proposes to raise the questions of self-becoming and self-fulfillment, first in themselves and then in their relation to an apostolic religious life. I hope to show that what is at stake here is more than a better understanding of ourselves, although such understanding is certainly a gain. What is at stake seems to me nothing less than a new, deeply transformative vision of an apostolic religious life.

But it may be asked: is it not ambitious, even dangerous, to speak of transforming our vision of religious life? Has not the essence of religious life been defined and codified, and have not religious been explicitly warned that, despite and throughout any updating process, the essence of religious life is to be preserved intact?[2]

Obviously, everything depends upon the meaning of the word "essence." An eminent *peritus* of Vatican II, in reporting the first session, traced the conflicting views expressed there to basically conflicting attitudes toward essences. Those bishops, a minority, who took an "essentialist" attitude held to the view that the realities of our faith and life are abstract essences to be formulated exactly in an unchanging language because they are unchanging truths. On the other hand, the majority of the bishops took an "existentialist" attitude toward the realities of human life and faith. That is, they were persuaded that truth is no abstract, changeless essence which has nothing to do

[2]Address of Pope Paul VI to the General Chapters of religious orders and congregations: May 23, 1964.

with time and place. Positively, they were persuaded that every vision of the truth emerges in a concrete, historical situation. Thus, they held that the truths of human life and faith are continually unfolding in terms of new historical experiences and that, therefore, no particular age is a norm for all further insight into truth. Implied in this view is the further arduous conclusion: "Expressing the truth is a never-ending task which has to be begun anew all the time."[3]

In general, then, the case for speaking of a new, deeply transformative vision of religious life seems very supportable. Whether my claim is justified in fact depends, of course, upon the strength of the argument which follows. In brief, this argument consists of three parts: A first part will draw upon contemporary thought and experience in order to show that personal fulfillment occurs only in and through genuine intersubjectivity, that is, the co-presence of subjects in a "we." In a second part, I will try to show that the apostolate and religious life are revealed in a new, essentially transformative light when they are seen from the contemporary viewpoint of intersubjectivity. From these parts, which can be compared loosely to major and minor premises, the conclusion follows that—if taken intersubjectively—an apostolic religious life is preeminently self-realizing. But I do not wish to minimize the difficulty of the condition stated in the phrase "if taken intersubjectively." The third part will therefore draw out the implications of this decisively important condition.

PART I: SELF-FULFILLMENT AND INTERSUBJECTIVITY

If ours is a time distinguished by an existential concern for the self, its becoming and fulfillment, ours is likewise

[3]Edward Schillebeeckx O.P., *The Layman in the Church and Other Essays*, trans. Colman O'Neill O.P. (Alba House, New York, 1963), pp. 69-73, 82-6.

a time distinguished by an explicit and increasing awareness that self-becoming and self-fulfillment are possible only in and through the "being together" of persons in a "we." It seems to me that recent developments in psychology and philosophy, as well as certain intimations of contemporary theological thought, affirm persuasively the fact of this awareness and, I would add, its truth. Accordingly, I offer here some indications of these developments.

More dramatically than other areas of psychological inquiry, psychotherapy asserts the decisive importance of intersubjectivity. For it seems plain that a growing number of therapists regard the patient-doctor relation itself as the principal therapeutic agent. What restores the patient to himself, these therapists are saying, is the communication between doctor and patient. Neither the patient alone nor the therapist alone suffices for a cure; cure appears to depend upon the quality of what occurs between them, that is, upon the quality of the patient-doctor dialogue. And this clearly means that restoring the patient to himself is a matter of restoring him to some form of mutual presence or, equivalently, to some form of intersubjectivity.

Why is this so? Dr. Hesnard, perhaps the best known of French analysts, suggests the reason. Commenting wryly on the efforts of a philosopher to demonstrate the existence of other persons, he observes:

> It would have been enough to question a psychiatrist and to have learned from him that every morbid alteration of the mind (that is, of consciousness or behavior) consists in a *lived solipsism* called Psychosis, which isolates the subject in a fictional intersubjectivity, one fashioned out of the débris of his ruined intersubjectivity.[4]

From this side of the Atlantic, another world-famous

[4] A. Hesnard, *psychanalyse du lien interhumain* (Presses Universitaires de France, Paris, 1957), p. 6 note 1.

theorist and therapist confirms Hesnard's diagnosis: "The failure of basic trust and mutuality has been recognized in psychiatry as the most far-reaching failure undercutting all development."[5] To multiply like observations on the part of practicing psychotherapists would not be difficult. Agreement is steadily growing: In its fundamental sense, psychic disturbance means a breakdown of co-presence or mutuality. There is, then, nothing illogical about present emphasis upon the therapeutic relation as being, insofar as it is promotive of co-presence, the curative factor *par excellence*.

In a 1963 publication, *The Presence of the Psychoanalyst*, Nacht argues that unconscious fear plays the preponderant role in all forms of psychopathology. At the same time, however, he insists on coupling the pathogenic factor of fear with the curative factor of "presence": "The appeasement of fear or its eventual elimination is principally a function of the profound unconscious attitude of the analyst in the analytic situation." And he further asserts: "No technical strategy can lead the treatment to a satisfying conclusion if the reality of the doctor, his 'presence,' is not there to protect the subject against his unconscious fears and progressively to deliver him from them."[6] In the end, it appears, Nacht does not differ from Hesnard and Erikson in his conclusion: What is finally curative is the deliverance from unconscious fears, but this deliverance is achieved only in and through an intersubjective experience.

In her recent work, *The Psychoanalytic Dialogue*, Dr. Levy-Valensi interprets therapy entirely in terms of an intersubjective drama. At the beginning of treatment, the

[5]E. Erikson, *Insight and Responsibility* (W.W. Norton & Company, New York, 1964), p. 231.
[6]S. Nacht, *La présence du psychanalyste* (Presses Universitaires de France, Paris), pp. 1-2, 19.

patient is "walled in," unable to communicate, a subject incapable of presence. When treatment is successful, its end finds the patient liberated from his prison. How is liberation achieved? The dialectic of "transfer" and "counter-transfer," a highly subtle interplay, is complex indeed, but this much is to our point: The patient is liberated in the act of discovering the doctor as a "presence," a subject. From being "other," other even to the point of blurring into utter unrecognizability, the doctor has become present as a neighbor. Thereby the patient is delivered from his self-fascination, his "game of mirrors," and the path to participation in a world of presences is opened to him.[7]

Psychotherapists, by underlining the ruinous consequences of its failure, record the fact that intersubjectivity is crucially important for psychic balance. Contemporary philosophers, as we would perhaps expect, lead us to the reason of the fact. Nor is it surprising that this reason lies in the deep places of human being.

A first point is a striking coincidence: both Gabriel Marcel and Martin Buber, each independently of the other, affirm the correlation which psychotherapists find between self-alienation and an absence of co-presence. According to Buber, the self must assert itself either in relation to a thing, an "it," or in relation to another person, a "you." Related to an "it"—whether the "it" be a thing or a person treated as a thing—the self experiences itself as an "it," which means that the self is not a presence for itself. Reversely, when related to a "you," the self experiences itself in "you" fashion, which means that it is for itself an immediate, intimate presence.[8] Marcel speaks in a manner remarkably similar: if the other is a "third party" for me,

[7]E. Levy-Valensi, *Le dialogue psychanalytique* (Presses Universitaires, Paris, 1962), pp. 145, 192-4.
[8]*I and Thou*, trans. Ronald Gregor Smith (Charles Scribner's Sons, New York, second edition, 1958), pp. 4-16.

I am a "third party" for myself; if the other is intimately with me, I am intimately with myself.[9] Self-presence, for Buber and Marcel, appears as rigorously correlative with presence to others.

Yet Marcel, unlike Buber, hesitates to speak of inter-subjectivity in the language of "relation." To relate things, Marcel points out, is always to distinguish or unite them, and this means that they ought to be somehow "outside" one another and "before" the one who relates them. That is, terms of a relation are really terms only when they are given as "objects." Now, things given as "objects" are, as the etymology of the word suggests, thrust out before the mind like boulders on a path. But subjects, precisely as subjects, simply cannot be given to one another in the manner of boulders. A subject cannot be reduced to what is observable, to what is "out there" before others, to the sum of items that fill the questionnaire. Or, in Marcel's preferred language, a subject is not a problem to be solved but a mystery to be encountered.[10]

It is important to see that Marcel is not merely quibbling over fine points of terminology. When he insists that the subject is not a problem but a mystery; when he maintains that subjects are never opposite one another as things that can be observed, defined, manipulated; when he warns that making a problem of the subject is not only a possibility, but an ever-present and never fully vanquished temptation, he is defending the very heart of intersubjectivity. For, to treat the subject as an "it," to submit him to calculations and techniques, to exclude him from the hu-

[9]*Creative Fidelity*, trans. Robert Rosthal (The Noonday Press, New York, 1964), pp. 33-4.
[10]*Ibid.*, pp. 19-20; 182-3. I have developed these ideas more fully in an essay "Gabriel Marcel: Philosopher of Intersubjectivity" which is in press for 1965: *Thinkers and Makers: Studies in the Work of Sixteen Twentieth-Century Philosophers* (Alba House, New York).

man community, this is the beginning of a host of aliena-
tions and the end of intersubjectivity.

In more positive terms, what Marcel wants to say is:
subjects, since they are on the side of mystery, are really
given to one another only in the supra-relational unity
which we call "presence." That is, they are given to one
another really only when they are "with" one another.
It can be said, I think, that Marcel's entire philosophic
effort is a searching inquiry into the meaning of this
"with."

Even if it were possible, there would be something in-
congruous about attempting to summarize the "results"
of Marcel's brilliant but sinuous reflection. What I propose is more modest: four perspectives on the "with"
which seem to illumine it at successively deepening levels.

1) Every subject is worked by an "exigence of the
   with." An exigence is more than a psychological
   need, more than a simple aspiration. So urgent is this
   pressing toward the "with," so imperious this requirement of "presence" that, if it is consistently
   thwarted, the subject "goes to pieces" or becomes
   a statue-like caricature of human being. Indeed, as
   psychotherapists underline so heavily, the subject
   who is really and constantly not "with" others is not
   only not "with" himself but is "sick" over it.

2) No exigence is more fundamental than the exigence
   of the "with." In the end, this exigence is equivalent
   to the desire to be. For the human subject, the desire
   to be and the desire to be "with" are the same because the human *esse* is *co-esse:* to-be-human is to-
   be-with.

3) Inasmuch as being-human and being-with are equivalent, the fulfillment of a human being cannot be

other than an intersubjective fulfillment. Of course, this fulfillment is always provisional and partial for *homo viator*, but this much seems incontestable: to the extent that subject-being is fulfilled, its fulfillment occurs in the being-with of intersubjectivity.

4) But this intersubjective fulfillment occurs only in a mutual gift of presence. No subject can force another to be "with" him in the significant intersubjective sense of that word. Self-fulfillment is therefore always achieved "thanks to" others; herein lies the profound reason for the correlation between self-presence and presence to others: self-presence or self-intimacy is a gift from the other whose freely given presence or intimacy is its essential condition. To paraphrase Marcel: from the hands of a beloved "you," I receive my being.

But if my "self" is received as a gift from "you," how does such giving take place? What happens in the "I—you" communication that is creative of a "self"? Why can I not be "myself" without "you"? These difficult questions are taken up, implicitly at least, by the distinguished French philosopher of a later generation: Paul Ricoeur. I will complete this sketch of a philosophy of intersubjectivity by referring briefly to his thought which, it seems to me, throws new light on the intersubjective coming-to-be of the self.

According to Ricoeur, the self comes to be in the event of mutual recognition. Precisely, the *act* of recognizing affirmatively is the self-creative, the self-giving act. To recognize another affirmatively is to approve of him, to declare him worthy of esteem, to appreciate him as a "self." Under the warm sun of the valuing regard, impersonal consciousness becomes self-consciousness. For the valuing regard is both *affective* and *affecting*. It does not coldly calculate the worth of the other; it *feels* it. And that is why the subject whose worth is appreciatively felt is himself *affected*. Thanks to this being-affected, he feels toward himself as the other feels toward him: which is to say, he appreciates his existence-value or, what comes to the same thing, he esteems himself as a "self."[11]

It may come as a surprise that the experience introductive of the self is an affective experience. Affectivity, there seems no denying it, has had a bad press: Religious persons tend to distrust it; are not sentimentality and the passions to be feared? Scientific minds usually write off as "subjective" whatever is non-measurable about it. Philosophers of a rationalist persuasion archly dismiss it as belonging to the under side of human existence, namely, "animal nature." Fortunately, however, not all philosophers are of this persuasion. One of the most solid achievements of contemporary European philosophers is precisely their reappraisal of affective life.

For we should make no mistake about it: A just appreciation of affectivity is of prime importance to the fundamental task facing every human being, a task which religious dedication makes more rather than less imperative, namely, the task of becoming human. If religion is to lead us to the "more than human," it cannot do so by way of the "less than human."

To this critically important right appreciation of affectivity, Paul Ricoeur contributes impressively. His searching analyses dissolve two ancient and venerable prejudices: the notion that feeling is "merely subjective" and, worse still, that it belongs to the "animal" part of us.

[11]*Finitude et culpabilité: L'homme fallible* (Aubier, Paris, 1960), pp. 136-40.

1) First of all, feeling is not subjective. Like knowledge and no less than it, feeling is initially turned toward the world; affective qualities are read *on* things, *on* persons. What is distinctive about feeling is that it refers back again to the subject and delivers to him the existential meaning of objective reality. Thereby feeling "personalizes" or "interiorizes" the reality which, in abstract knowledge, perforce remains impersonal and exterior. Through feeling, things or persons put at a distance for knowing's sake return to touch the subject, reveal to him their meaning for him, instruct him experientially on how he "stands" in reality. Indeed, far from being the enemy of knowing, feeling is its achievement.

2) Similarly, far from being an appendange of "animal nature," affectivity is the apex of the specifically human. Why feeling has been mistakenly relegated to "animal nature" is especially significant: Ancient treatises on the passions missed the *intersubjective* character of human feeling; their concupiscible and irascible cycles fully and unequivocally apply only to the digestible good. What brings to light the properly human quality of our feeling is precisely the immeasurable distance between affective responses to persons. Understood humanly, which means intersubjectively, feeling opens to us the fundamental meaning of being a "self."

Close description of affective response to persons reveals the self as fundamentally a request of recognition. More than anything else, it appears, the self wants to be esteemed, approved, recognized. "It is remarkable," Ricouer writes, "that the self is never assured . . . when will I ever be appreciated enough, recognized enough?"[12]

[12]*Ibid.*, p. 142. For Ricoeur's analysis of affectivity, see: *Ibid.*, pp. 99-148.

The esteem which the self tirelessly and rightly seeks for itself should be carefully distinguished from egotistical and pathological forms. Here, too, it is intersubjectivity which permits the distinction. For egotistic self-esteem is by no means intersubjective: it is a direct attachment of the self to itself; it does not pass by another person. Authentic self-esteem, on the contrary, is mediated by another person; indeed, the esteem which the self rightly seeks for itself is not different in quality from the esteem which it feels for other persons. The words of Ricoeur here strikingly recall those of Marcel: "If it is 'being-human' that I esteem in the other and myself, I esteem myself as a 'you' for the other; I esteem myself in the second person."[13]

To seek and give esteem on the genuinely intersubjective grounds of "being-human" is immensely difficult. Not only do we begin our life-journey as thoroughgoing egoists, but we begin as quite uninformed about the meaning of being-human. Thus Ricoeur observes that, if the recognition of the self is to have "density" or "concreteness," it requires the mediation of those countless cultural works which attest, in their several ways, the meaning of being-human. VanGogh's "Chair," Beethoven's "Fifth," indeed, all the monuments of law and literature, of science and technique, must give to self-esteem its existential richness, its form and substance.

Whoever consents to the "long detour" of cultural works will, in the patient deciphering of their messages, come to see something of what being a self means. No one, of course, ever sees *all* that being a self means. For, to recall Marcel, the self is never something "given" as objects are given. The self is rather an "intention," a "project." Or, more simply, the self is not a fact but a task, not "a being" but a "to be."

[13]*Ibid*., p. 140.

If it is asked: of *what* is the self a project? the answer is bound to be incomplete. Not even the long detour of all the signs of being-human can "say" the totality, the infinity, to which the self aspires. Yet this much is certain: The totality must be intersubjective which fulfills, not the particular projects which the self *has*, but the existential project which the self *is*. How fulfill in any lesser way a self whose affective experience already reveals it to be an insatiable request of recognition?[14]

For the Christian, it seems likely, there is nothing new in the notion that self-fulfillment should be infinite and intersubjective.[15] What the philosopher sees but darkly and only after sustaining the rigors of an exacting reflection on the signs of being-human, the believer has "at hand" in the revealed truth. To a superficial mind it may even appear that here again faith demonstrates its utility by sparing the believer so much "waste motion."

Of course, things are far from being so simple. There is first of all the obvious mutuality whereby, on the one hand, prolonged reflection on the human "with" hollows out and immeasurably deepens our understanding of revealed truth which otherwise might remain largely verbal and, on the other hand, the revealed truth gives positive significance to our incurable inquietude which otherwise might prove unendurable. These reciprocal benefits are clearly not slight. But there is, further, a less obvious and more specific mutuality whereby, on the one hand, the contemporary viewpoint of "being with" opens up new possibilities for our understanding of the essentially intersubjective revealed truth and, on the other, the revealed truth opens up new possibilities for our understanding of an infinite and intersubjective self-fulfillment.

[14]*Ibid.*, pp. 86-9.
[15]I use the term "infinite" in the broad sense of "inexhaustible" or "having no assignable limits."

Already in fact there are signs of this mutual clarification:

1) Theologians are finding in the intersubjective viewpoint of "encounter" a key to the full and rich reality of sacraments. Viewed in the light of "encounter," sacraments appear as incarnate meanings designed to effect a "coming together." Moreover, this light dispels at least two confusions: the "magical" confusion which makes the sacrament into something dangerously like a "charm," and the "physicalist" confusion which puts all the reality of the sacrament into a thing-like, literally conceived "substance." For the believer, an intersubjective understanding of sacraments means not only a right appreciation of certain sacred signs in relation to a "with," but also and thereby an appreciation of the relation to sacred reality which every significant symbol comports. In this way it becomes possible for the believer to live in a world where his essential relatedness to the sacred is ever before his eyes.[16]

2) Similarly, the viewpoint of "encounter" saves the scriptures from being reduced to the role of mere "container" or "framework" for a series of impersonal truths. In more positive terms, "encounter" enables theologians to draw out the thoroughly intersubjective meaning of the scriptures as the revelation which God makes of himself to his people. For the believer, in turn, understanding the scriptures as "revealing encounter" means a beginning of the "being with" that ultimately fulfills the self, for every revealing encounter supposes some measure of co-presence.

[16]P. Ricoeur, *Finitude et culpabilité: La symbolique du mal* (Aubier, Paris, 1960), pp. 324-32.

3) The intersubjective viewpoint, by sharply focusing on the revealing encounter, brings out in sharp relief what is truly its fundamental import: namely, its being a revelation of, and a call to share in, the divine intersubjectivity. To indicate this meaning it is helpful to contrast two formulas for the mystery of the incarnation, the first: "God became man," and the second: "The Son of God became man."[17] The first formula leaves unremarked the divine intersubjectivity, whereas the second unequivocally affirms it. "Son" includes "relation to the Father." Thereby the heart of the revelation comes into view: The Son is "with" the Father in the unity of the Spirit, and we, through him, are also "with" the Father in the unity of the Spirit. When the believer begins to glimpse something of this ineffable "with," he no longer talks about self-fulfillment but loses himself in marveling.

The climb to these heights has been rather strenuous. Yet I believe that each step of the way is well-founded. If psychotherapists record disastrous effects for the self when co-presence significantly fails and curative effects when it succeeds, if philosophers base the correlation between self-becoming and co-presence upon the essentially intersubjective structure of self-being, if the scriptures reveal the divine intersubjectivity as origin and ultimate fulfillment of the self, it seems justifiable to assert: The existential concern over self-becoming and self-fulfillment is equivalent to a concern over "being with," for it is only in and through "being with" that the self becomes and is fulfilled.

[17] I am indebted to John M. Verkuylen O.S.C., professor of theology at Nazareth College, for this incisive contrast.

PART II: INTERSUBJECTIVITY AND
APOSTOLIC RELIGIOUS LIFE

For two reasons especially, the apostolate invites an intersubjective interpretation. First of all, as bringing to others a "saving truth," it is accomplished only in and through co-presence. The "with," in other words, is a necessary condition of apostolic effectiveness. Secondly, inasmuch as the saving truth is intersubjective in meaning, the "with" is the very substance of the apostolic message. Not only, then, is intersubjectivity an essential condition of apostolic activity; it is its inmost sense.

But is there anything really new here? Have we not always known that "interpersonal relations" are very important in apostolic action? And have we not always said that apostolic action ought to manifest the Triune God? In all this talk of "being with" and "intersubjectivity," it seems that what we have are simply new words, not new realities.

To this objection it could be said that new words may signify new understandings and thus, in a certain way, "new realities." In any case, there is a great difference between a vague or simple awareness that the interpersonal is important to apostolic action and an intersubjective interpretation of apostolic action that draws on precise meanings and discovers significant implications. What follows will, I hope, suggest something of this difference.

The meaning of the "with" as necessary condition of apostolicity, together with its important implications, can be approached step-wise:

1) The bearer and the hearer of the apostolic message must be together as *subjects*. For, as a "saving truth," the apostolic message is nothing like mere "information." Information requires only a segmental or pe-

ripheral awareness. On the contrary, a saving truth addresses the subject in his intimate being, as an immediate self-presence. Now, as I have tried to show in Part I, the person can be present to himself in an immediate and intimate way only when another is with him as a "you."

2) The "I—you" mode of presence which apostolic action supposes is, moreover, neither automatic nor easy. Nothing is less a matter of course than the triumph over our inveterate narcissism which genuine "being with" demands. Counterfeit forms of copresence are, in fact, all too common, and these are hardly ever recognized by the naive or egotistical "apostle" who readily mistakes possessive entanglements, dependency relationships, or romantic infatuations for the "with" of intersubjectivity.

3) The "I—you" mode of presence, seen from its positive side, supposes a liberation from self-fascination and a corresponding "openness" to the revealing Christ and human persons. Thus, when the essential condition of the "with" is fulfilled, it is always thanks to a two-fold receptivity: first, receptivity to the saving truth which, for bearer and hearer alike, is always received as "gift," never held as "possession"; secondly, receptivity to the truth of being-human which, in bearer and hearer alike, is not destroyed but achieved by its destination to divine intersubjectivity.

Here again, however, objections are foreseeable. Does not the foregoing analysis insist too much on the human conditions of apostolic action? After all, apostolic efficaciousness is finally from God; it is he who gives the increase, and his grace is not bound. Besides, if the intersubjective "with" is so dificult to achieve, must we not conclude that fruitful apostolic action is rare?

I am not at all inclined to take these objections lightly. Certainly it is true, and happily so, that the grace of God is not bound. Nor would it be wise to interpret the preceding analysis as "proof" that God's salvific purpose is ever being thwarted by a failure of the "with." An analysis like the foregoing, always oversimple, must speak in terms of idealized absolutes: of the "with" as a condition fulfilled or not fulfilled. Concretely, of course, the "with" is a condition more or less fulfilled.

But when all this is said, it remains true that the "with" *is* a necessary condition of intersubjective dialogue. Insofar as apostolic activity is a form of intersubjective dialogue, the "with" is its essential condition also. Thereby, without doubt, its dificulty and mystery must appear enormously increased. To illustrate: it was simpler and more comfortable to count children in schools, patients in hospitals, dependent children in homes, and to account all this "apostolic work"; it is less simple and less comforting to inquire about the quality of the "with" in all these situations. The price of increased understanding is perhaps just this loss of comfortable simplicity.

When the "with" is taken, not simply as the condition of any subjectively significant communication, but as the inmost sense of apostolic action, the mystery and difficulty deepen immeasurably. It seems possible to distinguish in this "with" a two-fold reference: (1) the reference to the union of Christ with the Father in the Spirit, and (2) the reference to the human vocation of sharing in the divine intersubjectivity through Christ. Only a few major implications of this dual reference are touched on here:

1) If the apostolic message is to be what it ought, it should reflect as faithfully as possible the divine

community as Christ reveals it. Nor is fidelity here simply a matter of exact formulas. For the awesome thing is that, in communicating subjectively significant truth, we communicate less in terms of our essentialist formulas than in terms of our existential attitudes. That being so, an "apostle" who existentially understands the Sonship of Christ as a relation of fear and whose religion accordingly tends to morbidity and compulsivity is, apostolically speaking, dangerous.

2) Manifesting the human vocation as Christ reveals it likewise means revealing an intersubjective truth, for this calling is to "sonship." All the works of service traditionally associated with the apostolate find their inner sense here. For the apostolic service is never simply an excuse, a ruse, to get the attention or the good will of a potential "hearer." Rather, the work of service is itself a revealing of what being "son of God" or "beloved of God" means. That is, the apostolic work is a way of expressing something essential to the apostolic message: namely, the dignity, the excellence, the loveableness which, by his calling, God gives to each and to all. Moreover, since "being-son" achieves rather than destroys "being-human," the Christian apostolate ought to be foremost among the forces promotive of genuine being-human for all people everywhere. The fact that, in modern times, the great social revolutions and reforms have largely occurred outside of, or in despite of, official Christianity invites our sober reflection.

The preceding sketch of the apostolate from an intersubjective viewpoint, though obviously incomplete, indicates the illumining power of this perspective. In the same way as apostolicity reveals better its reach and depth when it appears as both a revealing *in* and a revealing *of* "being with," the religious life will better reveal its inner meaning when it appears in the intersubjective light of "witnessing."

THE MEANING OF WITNESS

There is nothing particularly new in the notion that religious life is a form of witness. For many centuries now, there have been men and women in the Church whose public consecration, freely given and officially received, stands as a sign in the world. On the one hand, these consecrated virgins signify an eschatological reality: that is, the sacrifical love which consumes their holocaust testifies unequivocally that God is the Plenitude, the Totality, the All-sufficing. In the time of "in-between," the in-between of resurrection and parousia, even before the parousia reveals him as "all in all," these consecrated virgins proclaim him such to the whole world in an act of utter surrender which, if he were not "all in all," would be madness, the extreme of folly. On the other hand, they stand in the world as a sign of the Son, the servant who ministers to his brothers and who goes so far as to give his life for them. This two-fold witness, far from being a novelty in the Church, is one of her oldest and most precious jewels.[18]

And yet, after all, there is something new, for today the witnessing-act comes under our regard and reveals to us more fully than heretofore its inner structure. In so doing, it throws new and transformative light on the mystery of

[18]Soeur J. d'Arc, "Fonction de la vie religieuse dans l'Eglise et dans le monde," *Supplement de La Vie Spirituelle*, No. 66, Septembre 1963: pp. 359-60, 363-4.

religious life. Once again, and not unexpectedly, the revealing perspective is intersubjectivity.

For the witnessing-act appears as possible only in, and thanks to, a fundamental unity of situation between the one who gives witness and the one who receives it. This is but a way of saying that giver and receiver must be "with" one another in a like situation. But it is important to understand accurately their like situation. Unity of situation does not necessarily suppose having had like experiences—whether psychological, sociological, or historical. Common experiences do not assure the like situation intended here. Unity of situation here depends, not upon like experiences, but upon a like relationship: namely, a like relationship to the revealing Christ. Before the revealing Christ, both he who speaks and he who listens are in the same fundamental position. That is, each is drawn by him, each is questioned by him, and in like manner.[19]

What this implies for the witness is an utter, a radical, dispossession of himself in favor of the revealing Christ. The witness does not point to himself: neither to his holiness nor to his heroism. Rather, like John the Baptist, he points beyond himself to Another. There is, perhaps, no better image of the true witness than the pointing finger of the Baptist.

When we understand the self-dispossession implied in the "with" of witnessing, certain conceptions of the religious life and "personal sanctity" are unmasked as perversions: the idea that holiness is something which the religious must "have" in order to give; the notion that witnessing means pointing to our goodness or our virtues as an "example" of what Christian life really is; the persuasion, implicit or expressed, that religious are a privileged

[19]Roger Mehl, *De l'autorité des valeurs* (Presses Universitaires de France, Paris, 1957), pp. 21-2, 25-36.

"class" in the Church who deserve special marks of honor or preference on the part of "ordinary Christians." For the true witness does not possess the witnessed-to reality; he is rather possessed by it. He does not offer himself as an example to the world; he is rather altogether occupied with the revealing Christ and the revealing of Christ. He never considers himself a member of a privileged class; rather, he stands "with" all other persons before the revealing Christ deeply aware of their solidarity as called by him, questioned by him, saved by him, loved by him. Nothing more favors a genuine "with" than this awareness of being together "in the same boat." Need it be added that nothing so effectively destroys the "with" as pretentions to superiority, whether thinly or thickly dismissed, whereby the religious stands "apart from" or "above" others?

Yet, paradoxically, the true witness knows his witness, and he knows it as indispensable, even as worthy of esteem. In other words, the self-dispossession of the witness is strangely combined with an act of self-recovery. St. Paul admirably illustrates how self-recovery, though exceedingly delicate and fraught with dangers, can be accomplished without detriment to the "with." All important in this connection is the communal manner of this self-recovery: When the witness recovers himself, he is already and always "with" others before the revealing Christ whose transcendence he experiences as including himself exactly as it includes them. He discovers himself as called and questioned, as saved and loved "with" them and even as they. He recovers himself, in short, not as isolated but as integrated within the Christian community.

The reference to community suggests a further and highly significant truth. What establishes a community is the "with" or, equivalently, co-presence within a unity of situation. The bond of a community is not patterns of movement-in-unison, but awareness of standing together before a transcendent reality: the revealing Christ. Specifications of the bond in terms of a like form of dedication to the revealing Christ, as in the case of religious communities, effect more finely differentiated "withs" within one all-inclusive "with," namely, the Christian community. Two consequences follow for religious communities: (1) To confuse community with conformity would be disastrous; the test of community is not uniformity of patterned actions, but the depth and firmness of a felt solidarity. (2) To attenuate the bond of the specific religious community with the universal Christian community would likewise be disastrous, for the fundamental and final reference of the particular religious community is this all-inclusive community.

Traditionally the members of religious communities are distinguished by a three-fold vowed dedication whereby their witness takes the forms of evangelical poverty, chastity, and obedience. To complete this sketch of an inter-subjective interpretation of religious life, it therefore becomes necessary to take up briefly these specific expressions of the witnessing-act.

Ambiguity of the Vows

A striking anomaly which the intersubjective viewpoint makes immediately apparent concerns the names of the vows: poverty, chastity, and obedience. Not one of these names, I venture to say, is clearly and positively meaningful to the majority of our contemporaries. If the religious is indeed called to a life of witness according to the vows, then should we not expect the religious to be rather concerned over the unintelligibility of the vow names to most of the people in today's world? The fact that, on the whole, we religious seem relatively undisturbed by the difficulties which the vow names pose for our contemporaries strikes me as rather strange, even disquieting. For it seems to indicate, on the one hand, a certain indifference to the fate of our witness in the world of today; on the other hand, it suggests a satisfaction with definitions learned by rote and an evasion of the real difficulties which current linguistic problems imply. In any case, this anomalous state of affairs makes all the more urgent an interpretation of the vows in intersubjective terms.

There is hardly a better example of the problems raised by the vow names than "poverty." What this term immediately brings to mind for the majority of persons today is nothing positive. Rather, "poverty" says to them in the first place "misery" or "wretchedness." So destructive of human well-being and dignity is this misery or wretchedness that most of the humanitarian forces in our world are uniting to eliminate it. In the United States, for example, we are presently engaged in a declared war on poverty. Pope Paul and the Council Fathers have publicly urged a world-wide attack on the problem of world poverty. In view of these facts, the continued use of this term by religious invites reflection: Is it, after all, an indispensable term? Does it so accurately express the meaning of evangelical witness that, despite its pejorative sense in our world today, we must resolutely insist upon it?

The claim that "poverty" is a term irreplaceably apt for designating this aspect of evangelical dedication seems highly dubious. It is a well-known and frequently remarked fact that religious vowed to "poverty" are not usually poor in the customary sense. They are, by and large, not submitted to economic inconvenience, much less misery or wretchedness. Nor does this situation necessarily indicate a failure of evangelical spirit, a concession to "worldliness." The canonization of economic deprivation as such is not notably the spirit of the Good News, although the condemnation of economic injustice is.

Religious, not unaware of the literal inappropriateness of the term "poverty," usually explain their profession of it as meaning "poverty of spirit," this spirit being attested by the willingness to use economic goods only with permission. But, from the viewpoint of our contemporaries at least, the explanation is less than satisfactory. For one thing, the term "poverty" applied to "spirit" is confusing. The primary reference of the word "poor" is to economic deprivation. What, then, can a "poor spirit" be if not a spirit that is somehow lacking, somehow deprived? In itself, at any rate, the word "poor" suggests very poorly the intended positive meaning. Locating religious poverty in the willingness to ask permission hardly helps matters. The relation implied in "asking permission" is directly one of simple dependence. Not only does this relation fail to evoke directly the filial quality of evangelical truth, but it is likely to encourage misapprehensions. Among religious themselves, for example, an interpretation of poverty which emphasizes "permission" easily gives a foothold to the legalistic spirit, whereas to our contemporaries it suggests simple dependence or, worse still, servility.

But what is the positive meaning of evangelical "poverty"? It is precisely here, I believe, that an intersubjective interpretation shows its power. Viewed intersubjectively, "poverty of spirit" appears as that quality of "openness," of mutual trust and confidence, which kills at its root the vice of possessiveness. In its deepest sense, this openness is a sharing in the Sonship of Christ who exists in complete mutuality with the Father so that he can say: All that is Yours is Mine, and all that is Mine is Yours. As a result, the Son is "with" the Father in utter abandon, in complete confidence, in fullness of freedom. There is here no need to protect, to build defensive walls, to board up anxiously, to cling possessively. For the Father's love never falls away, and what is held in it is held so surely that it is not held at all. When this participation in sonship is reflected in the fraternal "with" of the religious community, it means living in like openness with others. There is then a true sharing of goods; possession is no more possessiveness, since it is mediated by the communal "we." What is for each is for all, that is, for the ministry: the service of the all-inclusive community of persons.

How, then, fitly express the eminently positive evangelical meaning? To be sure, there is no perfect formula. "Detachment," a negative term, passes over in silence the affirmative quality of loving mutuality whereby goods are held not in contempt but in common. The expression: "community of goods," suggested by Father Adrian Van Kaam, comes closer to this affirmative quality. One thing is certain: The religious witness ought not to be indifferent to the fate of evangelical truth in the world today. Is it not sadly ironic that, whereas this aspect of Christian truth answers to a deep and pervasive aspiration of our time—the success of Communism is not entirely due to chicanery and the evil spirit—its meaning appears to the many as hopelessly obscure or, perhaps, even as antagonistic to present hopes of world-wide economic betterment.

Like poverty, the term "obedience" poses difficulties. Insofar as it is used without qualification to designate a global virtue, ordinary usage refers it to childhood.[20] The child, whose experience is limited and whose powers of understanding are yet undeveloped, requires that adults

[20]Gabriel Marcel, *Homo Viator*, trans. Emma Craufurd (Harper Torchbooks, New York, 1962), p. 127.

substitute their judgment for his until the time when he can decide for himself. But such dependence in the adult, except in special and highly functionalized areas of his existence, strikes our contemporaries as infantile. Anything like a glorification of "dependence" in its own right, of living by the decision of others in all things, cannot but appear unintelligible to them. For they are persuaded that self-determination is a surpassing good, an essential excellence of adulthood. Moreover, the aspiration to adulthood, to the ever greater actualization of human powers of decision, is everywhere "in the air" today. In view of these circumstances, should religious continue to represent their evangelical life as a "life of obedience"?

Some will answer a decided "yes" on the grounds that contemporary usage merely reflects the moral decadence of our time: a breakdown of law and order inspired by prideful revolt. For these persons, clinging tenaciously to the term "obedience" would mean, on the one hand, opposing a widespread spirit of rebellion and, on the other, recalling our contemporaries to the truth of their creaturely condition.

But those who take this negative view overlook three important positive implications of the contemporary spirit: (1) The esteem of self-determination represents a genuine promotion of human dignity, for what gives an act its excellence is not only its content, but its manner of accomplishment. To act by self-determination is to act in a manner which befits a being called to "exist in the first person." (2) The aspiration to adulthood, far from opposing the gospel injunction to "become a child," greatly favors it because adulthood is a necessary condition of its fulfillment. One need not be especially acute to observe that "becoming" a child is possible only to an adult. The child cannot "become" a child; he *is* one. Evangelical childhood is, in fact, the achievement of adulthood. Its confidence and clearsightedness are not the naive simplicity of physical childhood, but a "second naiveté," a naiveté which has traversed a fully adult experience and is the hard-won fruit of a life-education. (3) The contemporary critique of obedience positively invites religious to evaluate honestly their interpretation of "religious obedience" in terms of observable effects: When obedience destroys genuine self-esteem, when it systematically weakens the powers of decision, when it conspires with tendencies to regression, infantilism, or passivity, it is highly suspect and hardly "religious."

Yet the contemporary critique of obedience remains negative in form. It valuably points out what religious obedience is not, but it leaves open the question: what is the positive meaning of this evangelical witness?

The root of the word "obedience" suggests an original meaning of "listening to." Thus understood, obedience points to that quality of the "with" which those who love know well: a careful, highly delicate attentiveness, a "waiting upon" which has nothing to do with servility because it is an expression of "openness," an openness that wants only to answer the other's appeal. In its fundamental sense, then, this attitude is a further characteristic of participated sonship: With Christ and by him, the religious witness vowed to the evangelical life would be attentive to every sign and responsive to every appeal of the Father. But, of course, the revelation of the Father and the response to him must take place within a human community. Hence, a second form of intersubjectivity, one whose quality derives from the "with" of sonship, is required: This is the community of those who seek together, who "listen" together, who "wait upon" together.

Emphasis upon the "together" is deliberate. Although the communal "with" is hierarchically structured, yet superiors and subordinates are together in a fundamental equality which their unity of situation assures, namely, their like relation of "listening to" the Father.[21] It may at first seem that hierarchy and equality cannot co-exist peacefully, but it is not so. For the paradoxical truth is that hierarchical structures are truly effective insofar as they operate within a fundamental equality. When those who govern refuse to acknowledge, not so much by words as by existential attitude, a fundamental equality between themselves and subordinates, they do not really "reach" subordinates; or, if they do, it is only to arouse their opposition or bitter resistance. Reversely, nothing more favors and furthers an openness of subordinates to those who govern than this felt fundamental equality.

The foregoing intersubjective interpretation of what has traditionally been called "religious obedience" makes abundantly plain its adult character: An attentive "listening in love," it draws upon the deepest personal resources and is anything but passive or childish. Accomplished in a fundamental equality of situation, it implies a dialogic attitude which is anything but servile or self-alienating. It would therefore seem inaccurate to designate this evangelical attitude by a term which, to our contemporaries and perhaps to ourselves, suggests first of all childhood and its dependence. In its stead I would propose a term that obviously refers to an adult dedication, namely, "fidelity." Two reasons in particular recommend this substitution: (1) The word "fidelity" allows a saving distinction between "obedience" as common usage today interprets it—that is, as the virtue of childhood or as a functional expedient for getting things done eficiently—and the evan-

21Mehl, *Op. Cit.*, pp. 12-9.

gelical attitude of "listening to." For religious themselves, no less than for contemporaries, this distinction is decisively important.[22] (2) The witness to fidelity is urgently needed in a world that is undoubtedly "coming of age." For, in a world whose citizens are impressed with their dignity and intent upon self-actualization, everything may finally depend upon the persuasiveness of the witnessing-act which anchors dignity and self-actualization in the capacity for fidelity.

Where "chastity" is concerned, agreement is rather general that the term is not notably exact. Chastity as "the installation of reason in the sexual sphere" or as "the refusal of unlawful sexual relations" is obviously not specific to celibates. To remedy the apparent inaccuracy, some suggest the term "virginity" as properly designating those who refrain from sexual enjoyment altogether. Yet, as Josef Pieper rightly observes, "virginity" popularly means nothing especially excellent: it signifies only "a condition of intactness or singleness."[23]

More serious, however, that the widespread failure to appreciate virginity as something excellent is the contemporary objection: In view of the newly developing awareness of human sexuality's great importance for the becoming and fulfilling of the person, virginity seems more than ever suspect. For, if it is true that the personality is awakened to itself in the sexual encounter, is not the voluntary rejection of sexual experience equivalent to the rejection of a personality deeply aware of itself? How is it possible to make a virtue of deliberately truncating one's

[22]This distinction should be very useful in achieving the "demystification" of obedience indicated by Karl Rahner: "Reflections on Obedience," *Cross Currents*, X (1960), 363-74.
[23]*Fortitude and Temperance*, trans. Daniel Coogan (Faber and Faber, Ltd., London, 1945), p. 91.

personal being? If deliberately and needlessly mutilating
the body is immoral, why not this deliberate and apparently needless mutilation of personality?

The force of the objection is plain; nor should there be
any diminishing of it. The contemporary revaluation of
human sexuality does indeed pose a searching question to
the virginal witness. Yet this searching question is truly a
"blessing in disguise." If it is met forthrightly, our understanding of what is customarily called "virginity" is newly
deepened, even transformed. For the contemporary question, posed in the name of a new appreciation of sexuality's
intersubjective meaning, elicits a response which sets in
sharp relief the pre-eminence of true virginity precisely
by virtue of its intersubjective meaning.

The benefit of the contemporary question is in fact
two-fold: (1) Negatively, it reveals how inadequate the
defense of virginity is which speaks only in terms of preserving the self "intact" or "inviolate" or "unsullied." Sexuality, as the objection rightly asserts, neither injures nor
violates nor sullies when it is truly human. On the contrary, when it is truly human, it "makes whole," it fecun-
dates and vivifies the deep sources of personal life. How
so? In a properly human sexual experience, separation is
overcome in a "with" which is as truly creative of personal
life as isolation is destructive of it. By thus bringing to
the fore this intersubjective and creative meaning of sexuality, the objection closes the door on a manner of conceiv-
ing Christian virginity that does justice neither to the
truly human sense of sexuality nor to the *co-esse* character
of self-being. (2) Positively, the contemporary question
suggests that any justification of Christian virginity ought
to be on intersubjective grounds and ought to show that,
on these grounds, it is at least as creative as the sexual encounter.

To arrive immediately at the intersubjective "secret" of evangelical virginity is nevertheless impossible. If the "with" of human sexuality is accomplished in secret, there is nothing surprising about an ultimate hiddenness of the Christian virginal "with." Yet, even as the wife radiates something of her "awaking in wonder" after the sleep of fruition, so too does the virgin-witness. Straightway, however, the precious quality of a truly Christian virgin-witness is felt as unique: Here is a presence that touches, opens, warms, and rejoices the heart in a manner of "giving" that is wholly devoted, though not at all possessive or clinging. In presence of an "openness" paradoxically open-to-all and utterly individual, warmly attentive though somehow "from elsewhere," two things appear certain: First, we are in presence of no truncated being; here personal powers are not only awakened, but operative in a kind of fullness. Secondly, there is no questioning the truth that this self-donative virginal presence reflects a "with" deeply mysterious: a fully evangelical "with" wherein an act of self-donation is given and received in a communion properly ineffable.

I am not suggesting, of course, that every factual virgin is a virgin-witness. If it is true that a significantly human sexual encounter is difficultly realized, it would be folly to imagine Christian virginal witness as simply or readily achieved—much less fully guaranteed by a public act. What I am claiming is rather that, when the Christian virginal encounter is genuinely realized, then the virgin-witness is present as a most precious sign in the world: a radiant and eminently persuasive sign of the human vocation to a love whose infinite exigence every self feels, but whose existence it hardly dares to believe.

A reality whose root and flower is so fully and deeply intersubjective is evidently poorly rendered by a term

primarily expressive of "singleness" or simple "intactness."
But how designate the quality of a presence so vibrant
and creative, so deeply mysterious? The poverty of our
language is hardly anywhere so embarrassing. Doubtless
this poverty of expression indicates the imperfection of
our awareness.

Yet I cannot agree with those who complain that the
modern world has lost its awareness of true virginity. It
seems to me rather that a newly emerging awareness is
still seeking itself. Paradoxically, the "finding" of this
awareness appears to coincide with the contemporary
"finding" of human sexuality as intersubjective creativity.
For, as the sexuality which the Christian foregoes is more
and more rightly valued as a good, virginity is more and
more disclosed as a "surpassing good." Thus, the contemporary revaluation of sexuality which some see as a
threat to Christian virginity is, in fact, nothing of the kind.

In concluding the second part of this paper, it is perhaps useful to tie threads together: The whole point of
Part II has been to offer evidence for the minor premise
of my argument, namely, that an apostolic religious life
is fundamentally and pre-eminently intersubjective. If the
minor premise holds, as I believe it does, and is conjoined
to the major premise of Part I, namely, that personal fulfillment is accomplished only in and through intersubjective communion, then the conclusion follows: Those dedicated to the apostolic task and living in religious community need not fear that they are excluded by their
calling from the personal fulfillment which intersubjective
communion alone assures. On the contrary, I hope to have
shown that the "with" which founds, sustains, and achieves
the apostolic task and religious life exceeds all others in
possibilities of depth and reach.

Yet the very neatness of the argument is misleading.
Things are not so simple. It is one thing to show that, in

their fundamental meaning, both apostolate and religious life are pre-eminently intersubjective and thus favorable to self-growth. It is quite another thing to question whether, in fact, the apostolate and religious life are currently interpreted in terms compatible with their intersubjective meaning or, equivalently, in terms compatible with self-growth. The whole task of renewal, a task far-reaching and exceedingly difficult, derives precisely from this difference. Such, in any case, is my belief. In the section which directly follows, I will offer what appears to me as sound reasons for it.

PART III: IMPLICATIONS OF INTERSUBJECTIVITY FOR APOSTOLIC RELIGIOUS

In a published report of conversations whose aim was to discover what others think of the American sister's task and performance in the Church today, two of three conclusions confirm strikingly the claim: Renewal for sisters is principally a matter of reinterpreting religious life and work in terms of intersubjectivity. These conclusions are: (1) Sisters are not known as persons: "Reserved, sweet, pleasant, genteel—all these adjectives are used to characterize sisters, but they make of the nun 'almost a minus sign as a person.'" [24] (2) Sisters are often looked upon as minors and, partly at least, it is their own fault. Placed in the context of this essay, the foregoing criticisms helpfully underline the gap between the intersubjective, hence self-actualizing, meaning of apostolic religious life and the everyday understanding of it which results, all too often, in anonymous personalities.

It is therefore not enough to have shown in a theoretical way that personal fulfillment in intersubjective communion is not only compatible with, but rigorously essen-

[24]"Priests, laymen in dialogue with nuns," in *The National Catholic Reporter* (Kansas City), December 16, 1964.

tial to, apostolic religious life. What must be shown, or at least indicated, are the major practical implications of this all-important truth. For, clearly, if these implications are not recognized and acted upon, the renewal effort will come to very little.

This discussion of implications is ordered according to three major and mutually related imperatives that follow directly from the "arguments" of Parts I and II: (1) An apostolic religious community should explicitly cultivate and significantly express an appreciation of what "being-human" means. (2) An apostolic religious community ought never to subordinate the service of persons, whether members or non-members, to a service of impersonal objectives. (3) An apostolic religious community should in every way promote an adult, truly human intersubjectivity not only among its members, but also in the larger human community. Obviously, these imperatives are not sharply distinguished from one another; rather, to some extent they imply one another. But I have chosen to discuss them singly because each does represent a sufficiently distinct aspect of the intersubjective situation, and I have placed them in this order because an appreciation of the human does serve to prepare the recognition of the person and, in turn, the recognition of the person does further and favor a genuine intersubjectivity.

Yet my choice of imperatives may conceivably raise questions for the apostolic religious: Why this pointed emphasis on the human? Is not the apostolic religious community in its aim and essence more than human? Why this apparent neglect of the essential reference of an apostolic religious community to the divine intersubjectivity?

It would be a mistake, certainly, to interpret my pointed insistence on the human throughout the following discussion as a repudiation of the "more than human." On the contrary, precisely a concern for the "more than human" counsels us to repair our past neglect of the human. What especially impedes our apostolic effectiveness, as the Loretto conversations indicate, is a failure to come to grips with the requirements of being-human. Hence, what may appear as an overemphasis on the human is a needed corrective of a past underemphasis, an underemphasis damaging not only to the success of apostolic works, but to the true well-being of religious themselves. Nor is "true well-being" exclusive of spiritual well-being. For the quality of a "spiritual life" is not normally independent of, or related to, the person's level of human development. If, then, these observations are accurate, a decision to emphasize the human is amply justified precisely from the viewpoint of the "more than human."

An appreciation of being-human, which I place first among the three imperatives, is an attitude not easily cornered. Paul Ricoeur observes, as I have noted in Part I, that a recognition of the person is more profound as it is more informed by meanings embodied in cultural works. For, since all these works are as so many signs of what humanness means, a true and full-bodied recognition of humanness supposes a careful attending to them. In sum, we arrive at an appreciation of being-human via its signs; we are not born with an esteem of the human.

When this appreciation exists, and to the degree that it exists, we know ourselves to be in the presence of a certain "tact," a certain "feel," for the rightly and really human. We are in presence of what has been aptly called "a cultivated human sensibility." Such a sensibility responds with an unerring grace, with the most finely differentiated affections, to the endless diversity of human meanings: nothing of the maudlin here, no lugubriousness, yet a deep and strong compassion, a sense of the tragic, a capacity to marvel, to look with wonder on the height and depth of being-human. But perhaps we know better this finely perceptive responsivity by its opposite: by the gross insensitivity of someone who "doesn't know when to laugh" or the depressing dullness of the one who "takes the joy out of everything."

That the valuing regard of others in their human truth is of basic importance for apostolic effectiveness goes without saying. In all our works of service—whether teaching or nursing, whether administering an institution or giving technical assistance—the affective and affecting act of recognition is at least as important as the work itself. For, indeed, this appreciating recognition is creative. Precisely, it is creative of the "self" insofar as it engenders genuine self-esteem.

If an appreciative recognition of being-human is creative in this fundamental sense, it would seem that every effort should be made to establish conditions promotive of it. But what are these conditions? A first point to notice is that, as an affective and affecting recognition, the "valuing regard" supposes a properly cultivated affectivity. In turn, a cultivated affectivity requires numerous, varied, significant, fully adult affective experiences. Now, among cultural works, the fine arts are foremost in providing opportunities of such experiences. It follows that, among the conditions which promote human recognition, the fine arts deserve a pre-eminent place.

Practical Recommendations

At least two practical recommendations would seem to follow from the foregoing "argument": (1) As many experiences as possible of fully adult expressions of the arts, not excluding "art films," should be made available to sisters. On no account should these experiences be regarded as a luxury or confused with amusement, for they are serious "works" which engage deeply our personal powers and advance significantly our becoming human. (2) Programs of "formation" should seriously attend to the requirements of affective maturation and should regard this phase of development as deserving a place alongside programs of theologico-spiritual instruction and academic or professional preparation. Possibilities of experiencing the arts should be abundantly provided, but such "temptations" as the following ought to be resisted: a) being academically systematic about these experiences and thereby giving them the air of classroom demonstrations, b) exercising forms of censorship with respect to the content of these experiences whereby what survives is indeed "pure" but also utterly trivial.

What the appreciation of being-human is meant to prepare is the more adequate recognition of concretely existing persons. It serves to hollow out and deepen, so to speak, the capacity to perceive and receive persons in their profound meaning and according to their inestimable dignity. But there are further problems centering on the actual recognition of, and response to, existing persons which must now be taken up more directly.

The first of these problems leads into the delicate matter of "religious obedience." Of first importance, it seems, is a critical revaluation of our interpretation and practice of obedience from the precise viewpoint of what is required by adult, personal dignity. Accordingly, the key distinction made in Part I between genuine self-esteem and egotistic self-love is basic to this discussion. For we can no longer afford to confuse self-esteem with self-love and, in declaring war upon self-love, risk the destruction of self-esteem. We cannot afford it because we now know, thanks to abundant clinical evidence and validating philosophic insights, that neither psychic health nor moral nor spiritual achievement is possible without genuine self-esteem. Then, too, we are not as naive as formerly: to love ourselves rightly, we are at last persuaded, is arduous indeed; to hate ourselves is perhaps all too easy.

In particular, the practice of what looks like "perfect obedience" may cloak subtle forms of self-hatred; that is, it may serve as excuse for evading the onerous responsibilities that derive from being-human and which are, in a way, the price of our dignity. To illustrate my meaning, I propose this sketch of a "pathology" of obedience:

1) Obedience can be an excuse for not coming to grips with the complexities of adult life. He who acts only by prescription has ready-made answers and need not trouble himself about responding creatively to the unedited demands of his concrete situation.

2) Obedience can be an excuse for evading responsibility. Not the one who obeys, but the one who commands is obliged to "answer for" an act.

3) Obedience can be a technique of innocence: that is, it can be used as a tool in the task of self-exoneration, a hopeless task imposed by a compulsive urge whose roots lie deep in archaic or neurotic guilt.

4) Obedience can be an expression of dependency. The infantile adult must lean, must cling; for him, therefore, obedience can easily serve as a technique of security. After all, authoritarian authorities look with special favor upon "docile" and cooperative subordinates.

5) Obedience can be a technique of holiness. In this case, it becomes a kind of magical solution for those who choose to regard sanctity as the prize of "technique." To be sure, when conceived and executed

literally, obedience is a very manageable device; it offers a "simple way" of avoiding authentic encounter with, and radical dependence upon, the Living God whose ways are not our ways.

If obedience can be the occasion of so many subtle forms of self-alienation and, thereby, a formidable obstacle to self-recognition, then it follows that a critical review of its current interpretation and practice is crucially important to the movement of renewal. Specifically, current interpretation and practice should be thoroughly reviewed in terms of the extent to which, as well as the ways in which, they offer a foothold to self-rejection. From this viewpoint, those ideals of obedience appear especially suspect which surround with a mystic aura the trivial details of daily living as "tests of obedience" or which multiply restrictions on decision-making to induce a sense of "humble dependence upon the divine will." For such interpretations lend themselves readily to childishly dependent modes of behavior and provide highly respectable escapes from the burdens of adult living.

Not that the truth of our dependence upon God is to be denied. On the contrary, it is all-important that it be felt and affirmed. But this truth, in the case of adult persons, is fittingly felt and affirmed under adult circumstances. Indeed, far more effectively than the artificially contrived circumstances of a "closed" and simplified environment, the hard facts of the exceedingly complicated contemporary situation elicit awareness of our utter need to rely upon God. Built into the apostolic task of our time, an immensely difficult and challenging task, are abundant occasions of feeling and affirming deeply our dependence upon God. Moreover, the unconditional engagement of the religious, the vow of fidelity, is a constant invitation to "the act of absolute recourse."[25] To remain faithful to such an unconditional promise is beyond the unaided power of any human being. Hence, the fully adult sense of dependence—that is, dependence upon God—is experienced more completely as the engagement is entered into more deeply.

There is, then, no need to fear that the deepening of what has traditionally been called "obedience" into the adult engagement called "fidelity" will mean a loss of genuine religious spirit. Everything indicates the contrary: Recognized in the dignity and truth of personal being, the religious becomes capable of more, not less, loving service.

Priority of Laws

If confusions relative to obedience can prevent religious from properly recognizing themselves as persons, confusions relative to "rules" can prevent them from properly recognizing others as persons. It is not uncommon, it seems, for religious to find themselves hampered in their response to other persons, non-members of the religious community in particular, by prescriptions referring to the schedule of religious exercises or to the requirements of enclosure. As apostolic service to persons becomes—rightly —more and more the major concern of religious, the conflict between the exigencies of "regularity" and the exigencies of apostolic service to persons is bound to become even more acute. For persons have a way of upsetting schedules and intruding on enclosures.

In view of this conflict-situation, foreseeable where it is not yet sharply felt, it may be useful to suggest a guideline, together with a few supporting arguments, for adaptative decision-making:

[25]The meaning of this phrase is richly developed in Marcel's essay: "Creative Fidelity" in *Creative Fidelity*, pp. 147-73.

1) The person should never be subordinated to our "laws," for the person is the true aim and intention of the law. Human law, rightly understood, is simply an attempt to express what is due to the person; as an attempt that is never completely successful, moreover, it is always open to completion and correction by due process. Nor does divine law subordinate the person to legal prescription. We are even expressly told that there is an equivalence between the service of the neighbor and the true service of God; that is to say, there is finally only one commandment. In this connection, how significant appears the action of Christ and his disciples: their plucking and eating the grain on the Sabbath. The Sabbath is indeed for man, not man for the Sabbath!

2) Contemporary psychology and philosophy strikingly confirm the personal reference of all law. Paul Ricoeur, for example, writes a very pertinent page on the opposing characteristics of the infantile and adult conscience. The conclusion of his analysis is to our point: to the extent that the other person in his personal value is not the reason of the guilt-experience, guilt may be called "infantile" or, in extreme cases, pathological; to the extent that the other in his personal value is at the center of the guilt-experience, guilt can be called "adult."[26] From this standpoint, it appears that the tendency to prefer rules to persons—when these conflict—reflects a childish moral sense.

3) Another reason for the tendency to place laws over persons is pharisaism. For the pharisee, indefinitely

[26]Ricoeur, "Morality without Sin or Sin without Moralism?" *Cross Currents,* V (1955), 339-52.

multiplied "laws" represent a "technique" of salvation whereby he hopes to save himself. And that is why pharisaism, the specific temptation of persons "professionally" religious, is so great an evil: it means a refusal of the Other who brings salvation as a gift.[27] Religious communities, precisely as highly organized and "officially" religious, should be especially sensitive to the slightest sign of this ever-threatening menace.

When the person, in his human dignity and supra-human destiny, is recognized as the true aim and intention of all rules, an essential condition of genuine intersubjectivity is already present. Yet, if the third of the imperatives is to be realized, a further condition must be met: the condition, namely, of "dialogue." What is essential to authentic co-presence is, above all, authentic speech.

The Importance of Dialogue

Why is this so? Dialogic therapy, as Part I shows, recognizes a curative and creative principle in speech: For both doctor and patient, the very act of speaking together is creative of a new and unforeseeable "with" whereby each comes to exist for himself in coming to exist for the other in a new and unforeseeable way. Contemporary philosophers validate in various ways the confirming insight: Not thought only, but persons come to be in language when they speak to each other "true words," that is, words truly expressive of the self.

But it would be a mistake to imagine the true word as easily found or readily spoken. Heidegger is fully right: passage to authentic speech is anything but automatic,

[27]Ricoeur, *La symbolique du mal,* pp. 134-44; this analysis of pharisaism deserves careful reading.

anything but a simple matter of "clear logic" or "good resolutions." A time inebriated with the wine of dialogue needs these sobering cautions. To trivialize dialogue is the specific menace of our time. The confusion of talk *about* dialogue with real engagement *in* dialogue would be an ironic confusion indeed. In any case, true dialogue imposes difficult conditions: an "openness" that implies freedom from the self-fascination which sees only its own reflection everywhere, a mutual trust that extends generous "credit" each to the other, a profound respect for each other as existing exigencies of a happiness that opens out onto the infinite of the Absolute Thou.

Such conditions resemble ideal limits and are therefore never fulfilled in a manner complete and total. To the extent that they are fulfilled, however, dialogue becomes "true" or "authentic." It goes without saying that a really notable realization of them is difficultly achieved.

In religious communities, moreover, existing structures and attitudes are apt to pose particular problems for the realization of these conditions. There is thus an urgent need to review communal forms and common attitudes from the precise viewpoint of their effect upon genuine community: the "being together" of persons in a "we."

I suggest that, where non-members of the community are concerned, the task of renewal could move along lines like these:

1) Basic to any fruitful association with non-members is a right appreciation of the all-inclusiveness of Christian community. Where members of religious institutes view non-members as "outsiders" and regard with suspicion fellow members who maintain friendship with non-members, a first requisite is the delicate matter of changing old, unwholesome attitudes.

2) Occasions of meaningful but informal association with non-members should be properly valued and promoted. In meetings that are strictly functional, role-playing is apt to defeat the chances of significant co-presence.

3) An unhampered and direct use of customary modes of communication should, of course, be regarded as the sacred right of the individual religious.

For establishing conditions conducive to intra-community "being-with," an important requirement is the careful re-examination of structures and attitudes in these general areas:

1) Rules of silence should be rethought in terms of our contemporary appreciation of dialogue as curative and creative. Literal or mutistic interpretations that bolster isolationist ideals of spirituality ought to be forthrightly rejected. But the dialogic viewpoint does not mean a denial of the true intention of rules of silence. On the contrary, it means the freeing of their true aim which is rather "recollection" than mutism. For recollection, rightly understood, is essentially related to dialogue. As Gabriel Marcel has incisively shown, true recollection never means a closing in of the self upon itself, but an opening of the "ingathered" self "in presence of . . ."[28] Thus, to be recollected in the presence of God, God entire, means to be open to his word—wherever and by whomever it is uttered.

2) The forms of community recreation should be rethought also in terms of conditions essential to "be-

[28]Gabriel Marcel, *The Mystery of Being: Reflection and Mystery*, trans. G.S. Fraser (Henry Regnery, Chicago, Gateway edition, 1960), pp. 162-3.

ing with." Highly formalized types lead to artificiality or triviality and, where they exist, ought to be discontinued. In general, it seems clear, "pressured" forms of recreation defeat their own purpose and scarcely aid "being with."

3) Finally, the meaning of "charitable speech" could be profitably examined. Too often it appears to mean a refusal to allow honest differences to emerge or a rejection of anything that is "controversial" or "critical." When charitable speech is so interpreted, a significant achieving of the "with" becomes impossible. For true co-presence supposes a "working through" of differences, not a repressing or evading of them. True "being with" is on the farther side, not the hither side, of honestly acknowledged differences. Religious, too, must accept the truth which Hegel saw so clearly: Any significant recognition of one person by another always involves something like a "battle." Unwillingness to engage in the "loving contest" may mean, in fact, the contrary of charity: it may mean unconcern for the other, disinterest in the other; or, more exactly, it may mean concern only for the self, interest only in the self.

The recognition that real charity lies on the farther side of oppositions raises a question: Is it possible that the oversimplifying interpretation of "charitable speech" is an aspect of a more general oversimplification? Can it be that many religious appear to our contemporaries as "not fully persons" or "colorless" because they have tried to arrive too easily and too quickly at "perfection" and have, in their haste and naiveté, refused or repressed the total truth of being-human? If this is so, as I suspect it is, then a fundamental aspect of renewal will be a coming to grips with the full-bodied truth of our human being.

To come to grips with the truth of our human being means, as this paper has tried to suggest, nothing glibly speculative; it means rather an existential, an arduous, "working through" of being-human. Indeed, like it or not, there is really no alternative. Only an oversimple juxta-posing of "natural" and "supernatural" allows the illusion that, existentially speaking, these are isolable realities and that choosing the "higher" absolves us from bothering about the "lower."

But there is something more here, and it is nothing negative. Coming to grips with our human truth means making available the mighty, the infathomable energies of our being. What is true of poetic images is true of hu-manlife generally: the more deeply we plunge into its primal sources, its architypal root, the more powerful is the thrust, the élan, toward an eschatological infinity. For it is precisely with these vital forces, these primal energies, that we love the Living God. Not to repress them, then, nor to accord them only a grudging recognition, but to encounter and assume them without destroying or di-minishing them—that is the immensely difficult task im-plied in becoming human. In the measure that we suc-ceed, the Good News will speak out in us its meaning of "life": life ever more abundant, ever more full and free.

The Influence of Scripture and Liturgy

SISTER JANE MARIE RICHARDSON, S.L.

Sisters, who happily profess to be, before all else, daughters of the Church, share in the general spirit of joy and expectancy pervading the entire Mystical Body today. As never before, the Spirit of Christ "presses us" to re-examine our consecration to the living God and to all men called to become one in Jesus Christ. This stimulating grace permeating the Church and therefore religious communities springs from a rediscovery of the pristine sources of her innermost life, the founts of sacred scripture and the sacred liturgy. Clearly, it is these same sources of life which can contribute most to the renewal of sisters.

The renovation of religious life is, therefore, simply one aspect of the overall renewal in faith and action to which the Holy Spirit calls all Christians today. To speak of Christian renewal is to recognize the Spirit of God at work in the Church to bring about her purity and perfection in Christ Jesus, to urge upon Christians the task of "restoring all things in Christ." Renewal is cooperation with the Spirit in his sanctifying mission which remains forever the same: "to renew the face of the earth." This rejuvenating work, of course, will never be concluded until the glorious day when Christ will come to establish the "new heaven and the new earth" spoken of in the Apocalypse. But the life-giving power of the Spirit surges through the Church in these days like a springtime of grace and warmth, finding concrete expression in that collective audience given by the Spirit to the entire Mystical Body of Christ, the Second Vatican Council.

Every new call of grace entails a new responsibility; every fresh summons to holiness implies a greater task to be accomplished in the world, here and now. In order to respond adequately, one must grasp what is happening throughout the Church in terms of an enlightened faith and a fortified spirit. It is thus that scriptural and liturgical studies become not only the origin of the renewal but also the privileged means to hasten its actuality. To estimate their influence on the renewal of sisters as such, it is necessary to see in what way these two channels of grace have affected the whole Church.

Therefore, the first part of this study will deal with the influence of Scripture and liturgy in the Church at large; secondly, we will investigate what new light they are shedding on the meaning and specific role of religious within the Church; and thirdly, an attempt will be made to show how the scriptural and liturgical sources offer illuminating insight into and effective guidance for practical aspects of the sisters' vocation in terms of renewal.

THE INFLUENCE OF SCRIPTURE AND LITURGY IN THE CHURCH

Penetration into the divinely inspired pages of scripture, those sacred books written by men of, in, and for the believing community, has brought to the Church today, more than anything else, a new understanding of her own nature and mission, a heightened sense of just what it means to be the people of God. The epochal *Constitution on the Church* radiates this joyous realization. Christians are being invited to grasp again what they never quite forgot, but still could not quite remember: that they are the holy people of God, called by the Father into the "household of the faith," fashioned by his love and grace into "a chosen race, a royal priesthood, a holy nation, a purchased people," destined to share his trinitarian life and joy forever. In both the Old and New Testaments, the sacred writers trace out this loving intention of God to make of all men one. Scripture focuses attention on this basic notion of the Church as a corporate person, the elect of God.

The origin of this election is the gratuitous choice of God: "It is you whom Yahweh your God has chosen" and not you who have chosen him. These words of Deuteronomy, charged with even greater force and fullness, are repeated in the heart of the New Testament revelation, the Last Supper discourse: "It is not you who have chosen me, but it is I who have chose you." The explanation for this choice remains simply love: neither merit nor worth justifies it. From now on there exists between God and his people a most intimate relationship, that of sonship, testifying to the transcendence of him who always "loves first." The story unfolds from Genesis to the Apocalypse.

It began with Abraham, less than forty centuries ago, when the venerable old man heard the Lord speak to him: "Leave your country and kinsfolk and go into the land that I will show you. . . . I will make a great nation of you." Already the characteristics of every Christian vocation, of every call to holiness are present: Leave . . . go . . . a community. . . .

So Abraham, the father of all believers, of all those who hear God's word and keep it, left his native land and journeyed forth under divine guidance. Little by little, the Lord prepares for himself a people who are to be more numerous than the stars of heaven, the spiritual progeny of the patriarch. Six hundred years pass, years of expansion and blessing; years of sin, too. And finally, slavery in Egypt.

But God's choice is always without repentance and, seeing the misery of his people, "with a mighty hand and an outstretched arm" he delivers them. Confirming his mercy in concrete form, God establishes through Moses an alliance with the children of Israel, a bond of fidelity and merciful power to love and save, which will henceforth command all the religious thought of his people. In establishing a covenant, God affirms his desire to bring men into communion with him; it is his means of setting aside a worshiping community for himself, one which will be able to respond fittingly to his overtures of love. In the New Testament, the covenant reaches a climactic plenitude: the whole mystery of Christ Jesus. Sealed in his blood, it will declare itself in every representation of his sacrifice, the sacred Eucharistic celebration, the source of man's communion with God and of man's communion with his fellowmen. Its consummation will be the nuptial feast of the lamb and the Church, his spouse.

All the myriad experiences of Israel—nomadic life, oppression and deliverance, wandering in the desert, battles to gain possession of a homeland, and internal strife—held a deep religious significance. In some respects they were a concrete experience of the ways of God. Through them, his gifts shone forth more forcefully, and step by step his secret intentions were revealed. In terms of these events, his people of the future will learn their own destiny; the new Israel will see itself typified in the old. Slavery, exodus, promised land— these are the foundation blocks which Christian faith translates in terms of sin, redemption in Christ, and communion with the Trinity. The very history of Israel becomes revelation, the vehicle by which God will teach his people who he is, who they are, and how much he loves them.

But this Old Testament revelation is only the stage setting for the appearance of him who would, in being lifted up, draw all men to himself; who would fashion for himself a perfect people, one no longer restricted to a single race or to observance of the Jewish law, one drawn "out of every tribe and tongue and people and nation." Jesus Christ, resplendent image of the Father, bursts forth in the full revelation of the New Testament. His coming shatters the distinction between Jew and Gentile and he gives to all those who welcome him the unifying Spirit of his own and the Father's love to form them into one body, a mystical prolongation of his own. It is in this illumination that the Church grasps what God meant when he promised Jeremia: "Behold the days are coming when I will make with the house of Israel a new alliance. Then I will be their God and they shall be my people."

So much will he be their God that he will send his Son to be one of them. And in that perfect humanity of Christ, God will accomplish and bring to glorious plenitude his marvelous plan woven through all the threads of revelation. Never again will God ask, as he did of Moses, that one make him a sanctuary in order that he might reside among them. No, his abiding presence throughout time reaches its climax when his Son "pitches his tent" in flesh and becomes the "firstborn of many brethren."

Thus across the whole sweep of sacred history is God's astonishing design made known. He will cleanse for himself an acceptable people and make them sons in his Son. Those thus chosen in Christ "before the foundation of the world" will form the society of the redeemed, called to be, as the *Constitution on the Church* reminds us, "a lasting and sure seed of unity, hope, and salvation for the whole human race."

This is what the Church means; this is what she really is: a people elected by the Father, redeemed by the Son, and sanctified and united in the Holy Spirit. In reflecting on this peoplehood, the beauty and dignity of the Church stand out in new clarity. First, there is the realization that the Christian community comes into being as the result of a free gift of God, of an act of predilection ("loving before") on his part, of a wholly gratuitous choice. Secondly, the Christian community must achieve and share its sonship by living the life of Christ, that is, by passing over from death to resurrection, from sin to selflessness, from slavish constraint to the freedom of the sons of God. In the Eucharistic sacrifice-banquet, she repeatedly pledges her fidelity and pursues her passover into her glorious, risen Lord. And thirdly, the community of Christ's Body, while never on earth finishing its paschal journey, is nevertheless holy and sacred, made one in mind and heart by the dynamic force of infinite personal Love slowly taking possession of it.

These three characteristics marking God's people—gratuity, task, and holy unity—are permanent features, enduring as long as the Church remains on pilgrimage. They are aspects of special significance now as the Church turns her attention to the modern world, not to judge it but to support it, not to decry it but to recognize its true values, not to shun it but to share its burdens. All this she will do, moved by unselfish love to serve and give, in fulfillment of a redemptive mission imposed on her by vocation, with a view to the total unification of all men in Christ. This is the relevancy the Church seeks today.

The awareness leading to this search for relevancy did not come about by accident. Rather, the Church has reached this better understanding of her nature, of her solidarity with all men, of her mission, as a result of profound theological study, based ultimately on biblical doctrine. The word of God penetrates the Church more powerfully than ever before.

The Family of God in Worship

But this word is not confined to a book, however beloved and sacred. God also speaks to his people in the dynamic dialogue of liturgy. These two sources of faith are so inseparably united, so intimately joined, that they share a common origin and serve a single end: the family of God in worship.

It is, in fact, this family at worship which has given its name to the people of God: those called together to be a worshiping assembly, the Church. This identification of what the Church is and what she does originated in God who, in forming a covenant with his children, has likewise given them the power to express their obedient love and total surrender in a liturgy summarizing their vocation. This divinely instituted cult becomes the perfect vehicle for expressing adequate praise and thanksgiving, both rendering glory to God in confessing his greatness. The "people acquired for the praise of his glory" focus now on his personal being and again, on his gifts, recognizing all the while their inseparability and ultimate identity. Because of sin, the praise will be sacrificial; because of redemption, the thanksgiving will be in Christ. These are the characteristics of the perfect worship offered to the Father by his children.

The most definitive feature of liturgy is its public character. The word itself signifies a work done by personally-involved members of a group for the good of the whole. The alliance of the Old Testament had already revealed the social structure of the plan of salvation: men will not find God in the solitude of a religious life cut off from others. Rather, they will relate to God by sharing in the life and destiny of the community chosen by God to be his people. Their cult will be a common praise and service of the living God by which they will find once again unity with the Creator and with one another and with all creation.

This social quality of worship is the necessary complementary aspect of scripture's emphasis on the solidarity established among those called by the Father to be his sons through Jesus Christ, in the Spirit. Liturgical worship follows as a consequence of being a people: the graced community assembles to meet the risen Lord and to allow him to take them to the Father. It is clearly not a private affair but a family feast. From this understanding there stands out in clear relief the right and obligation for all members to take part in the celebration.

The right to participate means that we are privileged to praise God together, that we are empowered to, that we deserve to. Such social homage, the gift of baptism's priesthood, is the prerogative of all those called to "worship the Father in spirit and in truth." Only the sons of God, only those who have received of Christ's fullness by becoming members of his one Body, are capable of offering the perfect sacrifice of praise and of partaking of the Bread that makes one. The early Fathers of the Church often drew attention to the profound unity between the Body of Christ made present through the words of consecration and the body of Christ gathered around the altar: "This is my Body." All those present have become the body of Christ even as the bread before them. They too are the sacrament of his presence.

Because Christians possess a family personality, because they enjoy the unity coming from having "one Lord, one faith, one baptism," they must travel to God together, firmly incorporated in his Son; this is a duty stemming from filial love and gratitude, an ecclesial homage by which, in the same Spirit, they cry out with one voice: "Father!" It is at this moment that they realize their brotherhood, their fraternal love and union. Filiation and fraternity are inseparable for the Christian and they grow simultaneously: becoming more and more sons of God, Christians are forged ever more surely into brothers and sisters who genuinely love and care for one another. In this way, fulfilling the obligation to honor God as a people carries with it the creative force which constantly fashions into one the many.

Both the right and the duty of communal worship come from the priestly character of the Christian vocation, by which the baptized family of God is able to do what Christ does. It is a power which belongs by heritage to those who have died and risen with Christ through sacramental grace. Not that each individual receives a special priesthood at his baptism, but rather that he is initiated into a priestly community, sharing the one royal priesthood of Christ. Priesthood is the power to bring God and men together in the closest possible intimacy.

This is why Christ is the great high priest, because God and man are so united in him that what is divine becomes human and what is human becomes divine, without any confusion or destruction of either. It is in this great reconciliation that his members take part.

The highest expression of this mediating occurs in the offering of sacrifice. Through incorporation into the Christian community, every baptized person is officially empowered to join with Christ in his redeeming act. His baptismal character means that he may and must do so.

Because he belongs to the society of the redeemed, the Christian also belongs to the society of the redeeming, those who associate themselves with the saving, sacrificial work of the Redeemer.

Liturgy is public and priestly, it is also requiring. Liturgy means doing something, it means celebrating; it engages all the human faculties. One may be learned about liturgical matters, but true understanding of worship must come from experience. Now, liturgy can only be experienced through total involvement. That is why active participation is not a matter of external conformity to prescribed rites. Participation, while including ritual, is something much more profound. It is doing what Christ does, choosing freely to give one's life for the redemption of others, deciding afresh at every sacramental event, especially that of the Eucharist, to carry out the Father's will in perfect obedience, moved by desire to share Christ's risen life with every man and woman alive. Inseparably linked with active surrender is thanksgiving, the irrepressible joy of those who in giving all are given all, and know it.

The power of living Christ's life that liturgy both requires and communicates plunges us into the heart of God's designs upon men, takes us to the core of his saving plan and brings it about here and now, through the sanctifying action of the Holy Spirit. Through liturgy, the people of God are able to act as people of God; to become ever more fully the company of the redeemed, since it is through liturgy, as the Secret of the ninth Sunday after Pentecost points out, that "the work of our redemption is accomplished."

Now the work of redemption is both immediate and gradual. Because the Church embraces both Christ and his members, it is at once holy and sinful, in "need of being purified and of following the way of penance and conversion." Redemption is, therefore, a slow process and one that is effected through repeated contact with Christ in his sacramental self-giving. Christians become sons insofar as they resemble the Son. It is the sacraments which bring this about, the God-given means whereby the believer, in the words of Edward Schillebeeckx, "reaches out in faith and love to take hold of Christ's redemption" in response to his taking hold of us. It is the arms of the Church which support us in this reaching out and it is the heart of the Church which welcomes us in Christ. Church here means flesh and blood members of Christ united in his name and sustained by his Spirit. A true Christian community knows this well. Meeting together in the sacrament of sacraments, their mutual love and support are strengthened and experienced anew. There is a wonderful sense of oneness which comes from acting as a group, not just in the spiritual order, but in the psychological as well. On the other hand, the Mass must ever be an expression of unity, even as it creates it. Abbot Marmion once declared that the greatest preparation for Mass was to be at peace with one's neighbor. A pastor in Latin America refused to celebrate Mass for his people until the two bitterly opposed factions in the parish resolved their anger. "Therefore, if you are offering your gift at the altar and there remember that your brother has anything against you. . . ."

Sacramental Action

It is the visible body of believers which forms the milieu of sacramental action: sacraments are social in nature. Through the sacraments Christ prolongs his redeeming work among men; these efficacious signs are the "social fingers" of Christ, whereby he continues to meet those in need of his power and presence. The hungry are fed by an ever-renewed multiplication of Bread that a world of baskets cannot gather up; the sick are cured by a healing strength that no disease can impair; the blind see, their eyes opened by the word of God proclaimed in his holy assembly; the naked find themselves clothed in a renewed likeness of Jesus Christ, through the transforming grace of penance. In the gospels our Lord is always seen at work in terms of human need and human conditions: a beggar, a leper, a befuddled apostle. So it is in the sacraments, yet here the need being met is at the deepest level of personal existence. Every man wants to live and to be, and this in an unlimited way. It is in God, in Christ, that "we live, move and are." The effect of meeting Christ in the sacraments is precisely greater life and being.

These things are familiar to Christian thinking. There is another aspect of sacramental significance which may not, however, be immediately apparent. It is the realization of what the existence of this sanctifying economy ("building up") has upon the whole created universe. Because of the sacraments, all events of human life somehow take on a different perspective, an almost transcendent character; they become, at least potentially, so much greater than they are in themselves—temporary happenings destined to fill time and then fade away. Things, too, receive new meaning and the possibility of becoming lasting in value.

How does this happen? It happens through the incarnation, the greatest sacrament. The Son of God in becoming man imparts to every aspect of human life, to every nook and cranny of man's nature a value that derives from his revolutionary coming. In taking on flesh, in assuming human nature, in becoming exactly like us in all things except sin, and in submitting to the full consequences of this type of living, Christ was able to recreate the very nature, not only of man, but of all the created universe and everything in it. The incarnation affects the totality of this world; there is nothing in creation that escapes its splendor and transforming energy. Hence, there is nothing that man can do or undergo that is unrelated to what Christ has done or suffered; everything that a man uses or needs, inasmuch as it serves his well-being and growth, has been blessed in Christ who also used and needed things.

Speaking concretely, birth and death, eating and working, water and books, persons and pain are not the same when seen by the Christian as when looked at without Christ. It is man who gives meaning to things, but it is Christ who gives meaning to man. Therefore, only in the incarnate Son of God does everything find its proper place and significance. It is he alone who gives ultimate meaning to everything that is; only in him does all that is make sense.

But more than this, because he has actually espoused all things human in becoming man, he has also redeemed them by virtue of having redeemed man. Yet as in the case of man, this redemption, while in one sense perfect, in another sense remains unfinished until each man reaches out to it in strong desire and persistent effort. And behind all men stands the whole universe, moaning in travail till its redemption be fulfilled, as Paul expresses it. The new heaven and the new earth of the Apocalypse must be built up by incorporating this world into the divine plan of salvation. Is that not contained in the familiar prayer of God's peole to the Holy Spirit: "Come . . . and thou shalt renew the face of the earth."

Completion of Redemption

The redemption of the whole creation is the purpose of the incarnation of the Son of God. Salvation is fulfilled in this world of reality, in this setting of time and space.

Christian faith is not some superstructure existing in an ungrounded atmosphere; it is not a religion placed along side of daily life, the life of factory and school and home and office, but it is a permeation of every aspect of man's existence, a transformation of it that does not destroy but fulfills. The man whom God loves and calls to communion with himself in trinitarian family life is a creature of flesh and blood, a being situated in history and in specific conditons; he is a temporally-rooted man. His action in time is his only means of achieving his destiny for eternity. In working for this world, the conscious Christian is laboring for the completion of Christ's redeeming activity. It is the task of the Church to help construct this world, to supply it with the inspiration and spirit of the gospel, to assume an active role in temporal affairs, persuaded that the incarnation of the Son of God leaves nothing untouched in its total penetration of reality.

A realization of this truth is the lesson that liturgy implicitly teaches the Christian people: because liturgical life is sacramental life, and because sacramental life is the redeeming activity of the Word made flesh, all those who live by this life must commit themselves to active participation in all that furthers the reign of incarnational grace, that is, to whatever will prosper the condition of man. Grace is never a flight from reality; Christianity is never an excuse for sidestepping the human. When one understands that grace imparts reality and that Christianity includes becoming truly human, then it becomes obvious that the redeeming task of the people of God has an incarnational dimension as well as an eschatological one.

Lastly, one can observe in liturgy the same accommodation of God to man which is reflected in scripture. By instituting sacred signs and choosing ordinary things to be channels of his divine energy, Christ, like the Father, adapted himself to what was meaningful to man and in so doing lifted it up to a new plane of dignity. The Christian, in adapting himself to the reality around him, likewise elevates it to a level of transcendent worth. God's capacity to adjust his ways to temporal situations and limitations must be similarly reflected in his children. Man's rhythm is not too much for God to cope with, but it can be a problem for other men. This is an important insight for one trying to live the God-life fully during days of renewal and adaptation. Accommodating to circumstances, to concrete situations, looking courageously at the demands of the present is really putting oneself in the way of truth. In facing reality, one always faces God. He who by the incarnation made our ways his, now by sacramental transformation makes his ways ours.

In summary, biblical and liturgical theology has stimulated a new awareness in the Church, an awareness which consists in the Church recognizing herself first, as the people of God, as a community of sons in Christ united by a given Spirit; and secondly, as a people in a plan of salvation, with a mission to continue Christ's work of redemption, which work consists in bringing all men and all creation to fulfillment. Thus, knowing themselves freely called and seriously missioned, Christians today face anew the task of cooperating with the Holy Spirit in bringing about the perfect unity of all men in Jesus Christ.

THE ROLE OF RELIGIOUS WITHIN THE CHURCH

Sisters share the common vocation of all those who have been baptized in Christ, the vocation to perfect communion with the Father through his Son in the Holy Spirit. They, like all Christians, have been singled out for the incomparable gift of grace which makes man capable of living the very life of God, of knowing and loving as God knows and loves. There is nothing greater in all creation than this wholly gratuitous, deifying presence and action of God which is called grace. It is the very seizure of man by God. To live in this presence and to cooperate in this action is life in the Spirit. This is the life uniting all the baptized, the one which religious share with all the faithful, the one whch makes them the people of God.

This understanding of the Church as the people of God, as a community of faith and love, helps religious to understand their own vocation to life in a religious society. Religious have been called by God to a particular ecclesial community of fraternal love and apostolic service, founded through a gift of the Spirit and sustained in its dynamic existence by this same Spirit. It is important here to stress God's action, for, as in the greater community of the Church, it is what he is doing in the group that is essential; what the group itself does is always by way of response.

Involved in this response is a two-fold activity which, while secondary to that of God, is primary to the human persons making up the community: sharing and communicating on all levels. This sharing and communicating are actually the building blocks of the religious household. Because religious life is intense Christian life lived together, that which joins all the members to one another will be the core of Christianity: the risen Lord. It is their belief in him, their commitment to him, their complete dedication to his redeeming activity that religious will share. This wanting to share seeks concrete expression in the liturgy of worship, the liturgy of prayer, and, in a broader sense, the liturgy of work oriented to a common goal. In some way, every aspect of the individual religious' life will reflect this sense of belonging to the family, which, far from setting her apart from the larger community of the Church, inserts her into it more deeply. Sharing time, interests, projects, material goods, is simply a humble extension of the shared faith and love, the unbreakable bond of the Spirit strengthened especially at every Eucharistic celebration.

Effective sharing depends, humanly speaking, on real communication between those who make up the community. In fact, communication brings about community: in Greek, the language of the New Testament, the same word signifies both. Communication, like sharing, exists on many levels; it is passing on to others what one has received—knowledge, gifts, opinions, ideas; it is establishing contact with others through words, gestures, even a glance; it is a putting in common what one has been given. How right, therefore, that "communicating" be the term used to signify partaking of the Lord's Supper, the supreme act of communion with the total Christ. Upon this fundamental union in Christ must be built the edifice of daily exchange and mutual giving. That means all the members of a religious community, both superiors and subjects, must dialogue with one another, must put in common their thoughts and plans, must share responsibility for the continuing existence of the community itself.

A community is created by the dual action of the triune God who calls and gives himself, and by those called who share and communicate constantly what they have been given. But scripture has more to teach us about being a community. A community is made up of persons. As Albert Gelin, that great exegete and spiritual master of the psalms, pointed out: "Person and community are inseparable in God's sight; each enriches the other by a kind of reciprocal causality; they cause each other to ascend to God in prayer." There is no development of person that does not take place in community; this is true not only on the sociological plane but even more on the religious. On the other hand, there is no community that is not made up of persons: one may have organizations which flourish on human endeavor, but man is more than his endeavor, and community requires the whole man. In the bible, God's approach to the men he calls is always personal. The old Israel never did quite understand this, but the new Israel, radiant in the light of the full revelation of three Persons in one God, grasped it well: Christ's teaching and example —the beatitudes, the new commandment, the miracles of compassion—drive home the truth. The very demand of faith (to go beyond oneself to rely on the one believed in) and of love (to give oneself totally to the other) expresses a movement which in the last analysis creates the person: someone utterly open— going out to all that is real. And faith and love, as pointed out earlier, are the brick and mortar of any Christian community. When God calls, it is persons he addresses; when man responds, it is three Persons to whom he is related. Only persons can share and communicate because this activity requires the free decision to love.

Community life then both forms and is formed by persons. God calls each of us by name. Jesus assures us that the very hairs of our head are numbered, signifying a concern that reaches to the minutest details of our life. In the Apocalypse God promises each of us a new name, the most personalizing of scriptural terms. The Dominican exegete Boismard explains that this new name signifies the perfect man in a perfect community. This constitutes the precise object of Christian hope.

Understanding this, religious are in a better position to evaluate their own community lives. The community life of religious should be a visible expression of the kind of love that is in God and a manifestation of harmony such as marked the life of the early Christian community: "And they continued steadfastly in the teaching of the apostles and in the communion of the breaking of the bread and in prayer. Now the multitude of the believers were of one heart and one soul." Like the great community of the Church, the smaller community of the religious family looks forward to the community life of heaven where there will be perfect happiness with the Father and with one another in his Son, Jesus. If an individual's personal experience of comunity life seems far removed from these ideal descriptions, let her ask herself sincerely if she is doing all she can to bring it about. The real inability to accomplish what one knows one ought to be doing is a part of Christian suffering. In this connection, Louis Lochet writes: "The perfection of fraternal charity which creates the climate of an evangelical community as witness of Christ cannot exist without trials and purifications which are deep and often painful. Why not expect this? Could there be a way of life which escapes the mystery of the cross, the paschal mystery?"

Prophetic Nature of Religious Vocation

A religious vocation has a profound resemblance to that of the prophets and apostles. It is clear in both the Old and New Testament that God reserves to himself the right to select certain persons from among his people who will belong to him in such a way that the normal pattern of their daily lives must be built upon a foundation that is determined by this new choice of them. Thus the prophets after God called them led lives radically different, humanly speaking, from those which they had led before. In other words, God intervened in their lives in such a way that life for them could no longer be structured except in terms of this specialized vocation. The apostles, the disciples and the crowds are clearly distinguished groups in the New Testament. To recognize this is in no way to undervalue the vocation common to them all: to enter into the kingdom of God. It is, however, to realize that within the Christian community there is a diversity of gifts and functions; there is for each member a particular way of fulfilling his call to holiness.

Historically, the emphasis put on the obligation of religious to strive for perfection suggested, implicitly at least, that other Christians were not so obligated. While the obligations of religious are spelled out in different terms, the fundamental necessity of seeking to be perfect as the heavenly Father is perfect rests upon every Christian. It belongs no less to the housewife than to the sister; no more to the bishop than to the bank clerk. For all, the consummation of vocation is perfect charity, total love of the Father and of the neighbor in Jesus Christ. Paul, in writing to his early converts, addresses Christians of every age and of every walk of life: "This is the will of God, your sanctification." Chapter five of the *Constitution on the Church* reminds the whole Church of her call to holiness in a beautiful meditation which realistically takes into account the concrete differences existing among her children, while insisting that "all the faithful of Christ, of whatever rank or status, are called to the fullness of the Christian life and to the perfection of holiness."

Religious life finds its primary justification in its relation to God, who is the all-holy. Fundamentally, it exists for his praise: he merits the total surrender involved even as he asks it. A task is imposed, a function is to be fulfilled; but prior to this is an election on the part of God who alone has the right to a perfect holocaust of self-giving adoration. No earthly function, not even of the highest charity, can explain religious life; to try to do so is to miss the point of the divine excellence to which the life is basically referred. Ultimately, one is a religious because God is God, just as a prophet was a prophet because God chose him to be so.

This fact in no way lessens the function of religious life. Religious are called to play a special, visible role in the Church. Because they share the common Christian task of communicating God's love and truth to all men and of restoring all things in Christ, religious have the same overall mission as that of all Christians. But because this task is complex and demanding, because it is easy for human beings to forget why they are doing what they are doing, then God selects from among his people certain persons who will serve as reminders to all (themselves included) of what the Christian life must ever be: a God-centered existence of love. This special function is needed since Christianity has a paradoxical nature that looks to the future while it comes to be only in the present. Theology says it is both eschatological and incarnational. One element may never substitute for the other; both are essential. The Christian knows that every man is called to perfect communion with the Father through the Son in the Holy Spirit, and therefore to perfect union with all other men. But to bring about this glorious destiny, he must collaborate earnestly with his fellow Christians and with all men of good will. He must take seriously this present life, the present moment, the present place, since only in time, only here and now does redemption occur. He knows this because Christ teaches him so. This is the way God chose to redeem, by becoming incarnate; hence, it is the only way the Christian people can cooperate in the redemption. All that was said before about the validity and enduring-ness of human activity is pertinent here. Nor does scripture apologize for the incarnation. Rather, it seems to imply, as many theologians in the Church have held, that even if man had not sinned, the incarnation would have taken place so that God might confer on all his creation, which he saw was good, a perfection and consummation that would more adequately reflect his own infinite splendor. Because of sin, the incarnation is redemptive; in being redemptive, however, it remains transforming, in fact, more so than ever before. The prophet Isaia proclaimed it long ago: "I am going to create new heavens and a new earth. . . . Let everyone be in jubilation and let all rejoice forever with what I am going to create, because I am going to create Jerusalem 'Joy' and its people 'Alleluia.'" This new creation, realized in Christ the Head must be realized in Christ's whole Body and catch up in its embrace the entire universe. This is the Church's situation. Therefore, it is the mission of sisters.

Working for the transformation of the universe is then an imperative, not an option for the Christian. But the work always receives its direction, its orientation from what is to come, from what has been promised. Because even Christians can miss the forecast for the trees, there must be among them those whose very meaning will be "I point beyond." This is the special function of the religious: she is to be a sign of the reality which lies ahead. She does not deny or argue what is immediately before her own eyes as well as before the eyes of others, but she seeks to point out its place in the total plan of salvation, simply by being a finger pointing to God. It is always difficult in modern life (and life is always modern to one truly living) to maintain a proper perspective in the face of daily minutiae. The religious, of course, experiences this difficulty like everyone else. So her witnessing is a reminder to herself as well as to the whole Church. Sisters can forget their eschatological role; this is why they must ever see themselves in the total plan of salvation. It seems superfluous to say, that in order to do this, they must have a clear grasp of that saving plan.

While their special function is one of witnessing to invisible reality possessed but still to come, sisters retain the obligation of contributing concretely to the building up of the kingdom of God on earth. Here especially the layman says to the religious: "The parousia has not yet come; there is much work to be done, there is much suffering to alleviate, much energy to be converted to God, many fields ripe for the harvest. This harvesting is hard work, back-bending labor. But it is a joyous thing, too, and noble, because it is the Lord's fields, the Lord's work, the Lord's crop."

Because of Christ, Christian love and concern must always be incarnate, visible, tangible, comprehensible to men. Charity is not the same as human love but it must be expressed through it. This is the complementary reminder the layman gives religious. "There is certainly, a diversity of spiritual gifts, but it is the same Spirit; a diversity of ministries, but the same Lord; a diversity of operations, but it is the same God who works all in all. To each one the manifestation of the Spirit is given in view of the common good."

How do religious carry out their function of witnessing? How do they become effective signs of God's absolute love and beauty, of his all-suffering goodness? By both accepting and striving for a charity so strong that it dares to renounce those human goods most dear to man. Accepting, because to be a religious is to be a receiver, someone to whom a gift has been given; striving, because charity knows no limits—it stretches out to infinite horizons.

This charity is rooted in sacrifice, the sacrifice of what is pleasing and attractive in order to dwell on what is more pleasing and attractive: God. For the religious, God is always the immediate point of reference. The renouncement of riches, marriage, and independent self-determination which forms the object of the three vows springs from the heart of the gospel, of which the rule is a reflection. The renouncement publicly announces a definitive embrace of the evangelical counsels, which to some degree rests on all Christians. One can see quite readily that, of the three vows, perfect chastity admits of least equivocation. Christ's teaching on riches, and on doing the Father's will as expressed in persons and events applies clearly to all who would follow him, but virginity for the kingdom's sake remains a teaching not understood by all: "Not all can accept this teaching; but those to whom it has been given. Let him accept it who can." This distinctive note of celibacy encloses a mystery of profound depths which, when consciously and positively lived, speaks most articulately, because most personally, to the observing world.

Theology of Vows

In the renewal now under way in the Church, the rich doctrinal fare flowing out from biblical and liturgical sources assures religious of a promising and positive theology of the vows, one not sidetracking their quality as voluntary renouncements but seeing this real sacrifice as point of departure for a fuller development of the entire religious life. Accent on the purpose and possibilities of the vows, on their Christian practice in a changing world flows intrinsically from a deeper knowledge and understanding of revelation: death is always for life. Thus a study of the evangelical counsels as woven through the seamless tapestry of the sacred writings can bring new awareness of their meaning. Since it is the Word of God himself who inspires the vows, it is he who can best unfold their meaning: a new consecration to him permeated with charity, beginning and end of all Christian life.

An illustration of a positive approach to the vows can be seen in a brief glance at the biblical notion of poverty. What is it?

It is certainly not misery. It is, fundamentally, not an economic question at all, but the spirit of the *anawim*, the poor of Yahweh. It is a detached disposition of heart and mind in regard to temporal goods. From the prophets to Jesus, the bible leans toward the suffering of the poor and interprets their meaning to us. There is a spiritual and blessed poverty, which is openness to the gift of God, in confident faith and patient humility. Actual poverty is a privileged road to this poverty of spirit. But its principle and its end is communion in the mystery of the liberality of our Lord Jesus Christ, "who, being rich, made himself poor for us, in order to enrich us by his poverty." It is this spirit of poverty and also a poverty of spirit that Christ counsels in the first beatitude and throughout the gospel. The first is in view of the second: to accept and use things with simple gratitude, honestly and joyously, and by this non-possessive dependence to proclaim a total surrender to the Father who knows his children have need of these things.

When one studies the life of Christ from the viewpoint of poverty there is added to his personal mode of living the concrete notions of the goodness of created things along with a healthy independence of them. For from the gospels it is clear that Christ both used and refrained from using material goods, that he appreciated as well as spurned them, that he was, in fact, willing to possess but never to be possessed by that which from the beginning was meant to be at the service of man. Without in any way condoning naivete, the gospel calls for a use of things which is free and unfettered, which is a recognition that everything comes from God. Religious, then, clinging to nothing and enjoying what modern technology makes available to them for God's service, are faced with a constant need to examine and purify their poverty of spirit, especially today, in its communal aspect. Since it is religious orders which render greatest testimony to the Church in her totality, it is important that the poverty witnessed there be seen as a service and not a possession of goods. The basic question put to religious in the matter of poverty is, in the words of Father Bernard Häring, "How can we transform the gifts of God's love into ways of loving, and means for serving?" Scripture study will not solve today's problems; that is not its purpose. But it will deepen and enlighten faith and direct our thinking along the lines of God's manifest spirit. This is the kind of testimony of Christ that religious seek to give.

The theology of the vows of religion as developed in the sacred writings is essential to the renewal of religious life, since only such a theology can direct the adaptations which the Church in Council asks religious to make today. The truths of faith are eternal and unchanging but the men to whom they are addressed learn only gradually and over a long period of time, never exhausting what by nature is infinite. What is true of the universal Church is proportionately true of every community within it: as understanding develops and builds on what has gone before, there must be changes commensurate with the new light. This is the normal way of progress. God never ceases to open up new dimensions of faith to all those who earnestly seek him, and he does so in every age by incorporating into his plan all the knowledge and skills that men have acquired in the past and are still acquiring in the present. There is evolution here rather than revolution. Einstein's remark applies here: "If I am anything today, it is because I am walking on the shoulders of giants." Right reverence for the past is authenticated by present work for the future. In consenting to the forward movement of history and actively contributing to it, one declares in substance that he believes in God's creative plan for the universe and that he wishes to be a part of it. Meditation on scripture develops this mentality. In the end, it is not isolated texts or teachings that open the mind and heart, but the overall impact of revealed truth, the fruit of intensive and extensive familiarity with the written word of God.

RENEWING VOCATIONS THROUGH
SCRIPTURE AND LITURGY

That scripture and liturgy are indispensable guides to the whole spiritual life of all Christians, including sisters, should by now be obvious. It may be useful to examine briefly just how a knowledge and love of scripture and liturgy can bring to greater fullness a sister's life of interior prayer and apostolic action. To bring to a greater fullness, because sisters are already leading lives of deep union with God and of dedicated service out of love for him. The special grace of today's renewal in the Church is seeing an added dimension to this prayer and service, namely, the social and communal. Sisters' union with Christ and desire to please him are beyond dispute. The Holy Spirit acting in the Church today is now asking for a flowering of this union to include others in a mutually conscious embrace. This is at present the consciousness every Christian community needs and is being offered: to know that we are united but also *to let one another know that we know.* It is not enough to pray for each other, to take the world to God in prayer. Something more is demanded if we would grow in genuine charity and that is prayer and work undertaken consciously together, each member impelled by a new awareness of his solidarity with the others. This is not a substitution for what has gone before, it is a further development. Belonging to the people of God and belonging to a group especially called to witness that God really is a family of Father, Son and Holy Spirit who have chosen us to share their community life, sisters continue to relate to God as deeply as ever before. But now they must add to that a relation to one another and to all men that is reflected in every attitude and gesture. To see this more clearly, a discussion of prayer and action is necessary.

Prayer is the concrete expression of piety. Piety has often been understood as private devotion, as solitary communion with God, as determining one's attitude before the Father. Notice that there is truth in this. The distortion consists not in falsehood but in not having *enough* truth. The concept is not false but incomplete. There is no Christian piety that is not personal, but personal piety expresses itself both publicly and privately. Piety is that gift of the Spirit whereby Christians recognize themselves as God's family, sons of the Father and brothers to one another. It is a filial and a fraternal loyalty, a gentle yet fierce pride in being able to call the Father's house "home." Through piety, sons worship well. Now this worship seeks all kinds of expression. Primarily, it reaches out to join hands with all members of the family in offering themselves in Christ to the Father; that is why liturgical worship has primacy in Christian prayer life. But this very public adoration leads naturally and inevitably to prolonged dialogue with the Father "in secret," which in its turn prepares for the great sacrificial banquet of thanksgiving and praise. Because piety has its origin in God, it is transcendent to man's nature; but because it also springs from the depth of the human heart, it is supremely intimate and immanent. Thus, in piety, the divine and the human mingle mysteriously.

Piety translated is true Christian prayer, a human and divine dialogue. Both God and man are truely present in it and bring to it their persons as they are. God can never engage himself except totally; to the extent that man brings all of himself into his prayer he approaches an analogous totality. Maurice Nedoncelle observes keenly that "the significant act of our calling upon God must preserve every one of the elements that go to make up our spontaneous life, and then, too, those that belong to the life of recollection." This involvement of one's whole being on the natural level must be matched with a comprehensive vision of the faith that takes in the full sweep of the Christian relationships set up at baptism: with God, yes, but also with one's fellow Christians and with all men whose only destiny is the family of the Trinity. To prayer, then, whether public or private, the religious must bring her whole human being and her whole Christian being.

While piety may be either private or public, it must always be both personal and communitarian. This means that sometimes one will be alone with the Father, with Christ, but never as an isolationist, and that sometimes one will pray with the whole assembly, but never as faceless man. The restrained dignity of liturgical worship, the loving embrace of the Church's rite, the offering of Christ and oneself made in union with the other members of his Body—all this forms our prayer in the true Christian spirit and saves us from an individualism or sentimentalism unworthy of a child of God. On the other hand, quiet and reflective prayer feeds the mind and nourishes the heart and, when coupled with "a warm and living love for scripture," preserves us from a legalistic devotion to cult or from an impersonal ritualism. In both, it is the Spirit in us who cries out "Father!"

Such an understanding of both private and public prayer or piety preserves us from a dangerous imbalance to which the human tendency to extremes constantly exposes us. There is a hierarchy of dignity, and it is for this reason that the liturgy is able to serve as a criterion for devotions, which remain essential to the Christian life. Devotions should be commended when, as the *Constitution on the Sacred Liturgy* says, "they accord with the laws and norms of the Church . . . (and) are so drawn up that they harmonize with the liturgical seasons, accord with the sacred liturgy, are in some fashion derived from it, and lead the people to it, since, in fact, the liturgy by its very nature far surpasses any of them." Devotions, then, have their place in Christian life; it is a matter of choosing them sanely, modestly, tastefully. The conciliar standard orients our thinking in regard to devotions, and assures the authenticity of our prayer life.

Contemplation and Action

Closely allied to the subject of prayer is that of action, in which what is within becomes visible without. There is one other question, often misunderstood, to which scriptural meditation offers great insight. It is the extremely important matter of the relation between contemplation and action. For a long time, contemplation and action, these two essential ingredients of the Christian life, were regarded in an "either-or" light; biblical theology makes clear their inseparability and harmony. Contemplation is being aware of God present in all reality; action is the normal response to this awareness. Just as contemplation is a wordless recognition and appreciation of God wherever he is found, so action is an effective desire to spread and strengthen that presence, an engagement of the whole man moved by faith to do something positive about restoring all things in Christ. Seeing and doing interpenetrate; one is unthinkable without the other. The more sisters see into the plan of God, the more fruitful will be their action. It is faith which gives direction; if it is missing, only sterile activism can result. Keeping busy is not necessarily apostolic. On the other hand, religious in communion with the living God cannot fail to act, for it is impossible to identify with Christ and the Father and not be fired with realistic love for men.

This realistic love for men is modeled on the action of Christ himself who sets the pattern for those who would come after him. His grasp of the situation around him and his interior alertness to the Father's will, made known by the Spirit within, formed but a single whole in the concrete existence of his life. It is a mistake to say that Christ lived a contemplative life for many years and an active life for only three or so. Rather, it is correct to say that Christ spent the greater part of his life in a private or hidden ministry and only a short time in the public ministry. Scripture says nothing about Christ retiring for years into the desert, like John the Baptist. Yet no one would ever doubt that Christ was a true contemplative. Some of the confusion is dispelled when the two basic forms of religious life are referred to as monastic and active, rather than as contemplative and active. All religious must contemplate God in revelation, in prayer, in persons and events. And all must cooperate concretely with the redeeming activity of Jesus Christ. Some religious will do this principally by a life of private and liturgical prayer;

others, the majority, by a life devoted to the spiritual and corporate works of mercy. Together, in the heart of the Church, they witness to Christ who said: "My Father works always, and I, I also work."

Religious, therefore, must enter as deeply as possible into their given apostolates. The greater their vision of faith, their grasp of God's plan of salvation, their awareness of the implications of the incarnation, the more completely will they give themselves for the salvation of men.

Every apostolate involves the cross, but this does not seem strange to those identified with Christ. The concrete nature of this cross varies in time and place. And it may well be that the process of becoming more relevant to the world of today will continue for sisters, as for the whole Church, their greatest share in the redemptive suffering of Christ.

Sisters today have the enviable and glorious possibility of standing in the forefront of the Church's renewal. Indeed, their vocation to be human, to be Christian, to be religious demands that they do so. Their wholehearted cooperation in the Church's mission to present to the world an intelligible and compassionate, a risen and relevant Christ depends on their willingness to enter fully into the springtime of grace of Vatican II, focal point of the Spirit's action in our time. Unless sisters are living in the Church of today, they are not living in the Church at all.

Just as an exploding theology of scripture and liturgy underlies what is happening in the whole Church, so these two founts of grace form the foundation upon which the renewal of everyone within the Church must take place. The renovation and adaptation of sisters must be seen in this context. Familiarity with God's word speaking to us in these living channels of power and love takes time and

requires effort and penetrates the inner man only gradually. Yet in God's Word is life—"He who hears my word
and believes in him who sent me has eternal life"—and in
listening to him we are able to answer joyfully in liturgical
prayer and song: "Come, Lord Jesus!"

6

Art and Beauty in the Life of the Sister

SISTER M. CORITA KENT, I.H.M.

A First-Rate Soup, Asparagus and Wineskins
"We shall love our time
  Our civilization
  Our technical science
  Our art
  Our sport
  Our world.
  We shall love with Christ's heart." Paul VI

Today is a question-making time for man, a time in which we have been forced to notice newly the uniqueness of people and things as they squirm out of categories and definitions. Perhaps some insights about the process of art may be illuminating for this time. The thing about art that delights and confounds us is that it never happens again. This delights us if we have learned how to look because the esthetic experince allows all of our human faculties to be absorbed in the environment of the present and for a while to be fully alive without reflecting, without turning back or looking ahead. Uniqueness confounds us because there are no rules for guides. There can be no science of the particular. In a sense this confounding is a delight because it puts us in touch with that aspect of reality which is described as uniqueness—the fact that nothing ever happens twice in the same way in every respect.

For that side of man which is tired of living with pat answers to problems which haven't been fully explored yet, art can be a kind of second wind—a breathing exercise. Both the rational and intuitive approaches to reality must be respected. Because man tended in our recent past to exaggerate the role of the rational to the neglect of the intuitive, it is now a relief to allow the intuitive to come into its own. Dealing with particulars, the here and now—not with abstractions or theories or concepts, man has a chance to look freshly and openly at a thing and ask questions:

This is. What do we know about it?

Where do we go from here?

etc.

Today man is impatient in many fields—in theology, as well as the other sciences—with too much definition that compartmentalizes before he knows what there is to be put into compartments. Maybe he wants to understand things better than he at the moment can. He must then take a creative leap that imagines or recognizes the possibility of things that haven't happened before, and then go on to make them come true in the area of making or understanding. The artist-scientist or artist-image-maker is exercising himself in leaping. Art means going in a direction that nobody has ever been before. The artist must possess a kind of endurance to keep it up, a willingness to take risks, to be always not sure (which seems quite reasonable because who is?). Frederico Fellini in an article entitled "9-1/2," which followed his film 8-1/2, says that uncertainty is a fundamental attribute for anyone who means to achieve progress. And John Cage, the composer, talks about error as the failure to adjust preconception to actuality. In this sense the artist, whether he be making in theology or in other sciences or in movies or anything, may have a better chance of getting ahead with fewer errors than the man who overindulges his rational faculties to the neglect of his intuition.

This uncertainty is the dirty, grubby, hard bone of the artist's life—this doing it new every time, this always taking the magic leap. There can be no rules about leaping into the new because nobody has ever been there, so who would know to make the rules about how to go. But there are basics about leaping in general which we have learned from watching men leap. Maybe the basics about leaping could be listed in this way—

First: The artist is always surrounded by specific persons and things.

Second: The artist notices from time to time new things—inventions, discoveries, attitudes, etc. and so he is forced to rearrange his views (adjust from preconception to actuality).

Third: These rearrangements we call his works, They are new.

Fourth: These rearrangements are in turn subject to the same process. They get rearranged and more works are produced. They are new (and the new works of the third basic are now old).

Fifth: People other than the artist notice his rearrangements and give them names. These are recorded and form a history of styles. Styles keep being replaced by new styles.

Sixth: Other people don't notice new inventions,
            changes of attitude, etc. They are not involved
            therefore with rearranging things and so are
            not very sympathetic with the process or the
            results of rearrangements. They would like
            things to stay as they were. They are made
            nervous by change. (This basic of art might
            be called the presence of un-art which is also
            a factor for the artist to reconsider in his re-
            arranging.)

Note of Warning

This chapter assumes a two-fold freedom. It cannot presume to provide it. One fold of the freedom comes from
having been exposed to great teachers and great works,
the former also performing the complicated process of
introducing the latter. The second fold of the freedom
comes from the student who after the exposure to greatness gives himself to the task of absorbing the greatness.
This is the essence of discipline: to know much, to follow
in the path of greatness and go on to new things. With this
two-fold freedom a person is able to discriminate between
what is great and what is trivial. He can delight in the
great as an end and in some of the trivial as raw material
for making. It is not easy and it is not always fun. But it
leads to increasing ease and delight. This freedom does
not come magically. If the person entering the religious
community has been deprived of this exposure to greatness, it ought to begin at entrance. For maturity in the
fine arts can mean a maturing in the related arts of contemplation, conversation, teaching and others of vital importance to a rich community life.

end of warning

Maybe what distinguishes the artist from the un-artist is un-nervousness or nervousness about change. We all have areas of un-artist and areas of artist in us. And some have so much artist in them that they can not only leap in their own rearranging but can get insights from watching leapers in fields other than their own. Only God is totally un-nervous. In this speedy world of ours when facts are multiplying rapidly and giant rearrangements are happening all around us, it seems dangerous to be made nervous by the new—to want what we can never have, to want things not to be rearranged. It would be better to be able to take the leap, which is to be able not only to live with change and newness but even to help make it.

To live constructively in such a time the sister needs to be an artist—to be a maker, which is simply to say that she must be beautiful and human and Christian. She must be artist not in the restricted sense of painting or writing or composing necessarily, but in the broader sense Maslow refers to in his book, *Toward a Psychology of Being:*

> Unconsciously I had assumed that creativeness was solely the prerogative of certain professionals. But then expectations were broken up by various of my subjects. For instance, one woman, uneducated, poor, a fulltime housewife and mother, did none of these conventionally creative things and yet was a marvelous cook, mother, wife and homemaker. With little money, her home was always beautiful. She was a perfect hostess. Her meals were banquets. Her taste in linens, silver, glass, crockery and furniture was impeccable. She was in all these areas original, novel, ingenious, unexpected, inventive. I just *had* to call her creative. I learned from her and others like her that a first-rate soup is more creative than a second-rate painting, and that, generally, cooking or parenthood or making a home could be creative while poetry need not be; it could be uncreative.[1]

[1]Abraham Maslow, *Toward a Psychology of Being* (D. Van Nostrand Co., Inc., Princeton, N.J., 1962), p. 128.

There is a wild booming joy resounding in many of the psalms which is a delight in the greatness of God and all he has made. And ever since the psalms set the tone, artists have carried on this tradition. Father Martindale says, "St. John of the Cross, supreme mystic and ascetic, and nicknamed Apostle of Nothingness so often did he insist that created things were nothing and must be discarded, was nevertheless a marvelous poet, drew with startling realism, loved the rocky landscape of Castile, and liked asparagus." In the process of making, of leaping, of building a first-rate soup, it is important that we like the asparagus which stands for all the stuff around us. In the I.B.M. film on the computer there is a good description of the creative process that has to do with liking asparagus and making soup. The narrator states that the artist is never bored. He looks at everything and stores it all up. He rejects nothing; he is completely uncritical. When a problem confronts him he goes through all the stuff he has accepted, sorts out what seems to be helpful in this situation and relates it in a new way, making a new solution. He prepares for leaps by taking in everything. Maslow says the creative process "can be, when the total objective situation calls for it, comfortably disorderly, sloppy, anarchic, chaotic, vague, doubtful, uncertain, indefinite, approximate, inexact, or inaccurate (all at certain moments in science, art, or life in general, quite desirable)."[2]

Along the time-line of history man has fallen many times and has been helped up after the falls, a little wiser. Often these falls resulted from his trying to act as if he were not human: trying to live without delight in the visible, tangible things of nature and art. Jansenism and puritanism are two instances. Sisters are affected as sisters by the

[2]Maslow, *ibid.*, p. 130.

former through reading and the spoken word ("spiritual" reading and "sermon" words), and as Americans they are influenced by the latter. American sisters are in double trouble. God picks up and so do men, in many mysterious ways. Everytime we sing the Little Office for Christmas we sing, "A marvelous mystery is revealed today: God becomes man and nature is redeemed. What he was, he still remains; what he was not, he now becomes without confusion or division." We are picked up and told that it's all right to be human; Christ did it and was not confused or divided. It isn't our human nature that causes us trouble, it's our lack of it. It is this difficulty that Robert Short in *The Gospel According to Peanuts* points out as Charlie Brown's trouble—original sin: "Original sin means that originally, in every individual, human nature just isn't what it ought to be."[3] To think material things are sinful is to misunderstand material things and the nature of sin. Material can be more and more alive. We are expressive material—alive. Sin is a death, a cutting off of life, settling for less than we are called to. In one of Charles Schulz's cartoon strips, Lucy draws a huge heart on a fence for Linus and shades in the left half of the heart saying, "This Linus is a picture of the human heart! One side is filled with hate and the other side is filled with love. These are the two forces which are constantly at war with each other . . ." Linus clutches at where his heart is, crosses his eyes, shakes his hair up and thrusts out his tongue and replies, "I think I know just what you mean . . . I can feel them fighting." Schulz is saying that it is hatred of people and things that is evil—not people and things themselves. It is good to see an American stamping out puritanism.

Earlier Americans who affirmed the positive value of things are Whitman and Dewey:

[3]Robert Short, *The Gospel According to Peanuts* (John Knox Press, Richmond, Va., 1965), pp. 39-40.

His [Whitman's] favorite occupation . . . seemed to be strolling or sauntering about outdoors by himself, looking at the grass, the trees, the flowers, the vistas of light, the varying aspects of the sky, and listening to the birds, the crickets, the tree frogs, and all the hundreds of natural sounds. It was evident that these things gave him a pleasure far beyond what they give to ordinary people. Until I knew the man . . . it had not occurred to me that any one could derive so much absolute happiness from these things as he did. He was very fond of flowers, either wild or cultivated; liked all sorts. I think he admired lilacs and sunflowers just as much as roses. Perhaps, indeed, no man who ever lived liked so many things and disliked so few as Walt Whitman. All natural objects seemed to have a charm for him. All sights and sounds seemed to please him. He appeared to like (and I believe he did like) all the men, women, and children he saw (though I never knew him to say that he liked any one), but each who knew him felt that he liked him or her, and that he liked others also.[4]

Walt Whitman is a glad psalmist. John Dewey is another. In his *Art as Experience* he gives recognition to the human in its connectedness with all things. He talks about works of art as "celebrations . . . of ordinary experience."

But total affirmation is not the only stance people take. Notice different people observing a couple in love. Some wonder in a questioning negative way, wonder what on earth he was able to see in her. Others wonder positively and say, "How great!" This wonder which sees greatness (which is in every human being) also sees the drawbacks and disadvantages connected with loving this not-perfect person; but viewing them from the perspective of love, wonder dwells rather on the good. And by this dwelling wonder makes it possible for the person to outgrow his defects. This kind of perceptive love empowers. Love is

[4] William James, *The Varieties of Religious Experience* (The New American Library, New York, 1961), p. 80.

not blind. It makes the lover see what no one else can. It makes the beloved able to do what no one thought him capable of. It is like the Eskimo mother who was asked if her baby could speak and answered that he could—she just couldn't understand him yet. The person who loves can already understand.

If we say there are no people who are not beautiful, perhaps we can say the same for things. Perhaps we need to be also in love with things to see their beauty. It has been said that the Western mind makes divisions between the beautiful and the ugly and tries to control nature and order it to certain ends, and that the Eastern way goes along with nature, to say that everything is beautiful. We might extend this to include many man-made things. For Western man it might be good exercise to put on an Eastern mind for a while and take a look at the world around him. With such a focus he could choose what he with his Western mind would label the ugliest street in his city and take another look and walk down this street telling himself that nothing was ugly.

If this Western-Eastern division is true, poets and artists have always been Eastern, have known that nothing was ugly, have delighted in the commonplace, the ordinary. They know the commonplace is not worthless; there is simply lots of it. Poets and artists—makers—look long and lovingly at commonplace things, rearrange them and put their rearrangements where others can notice them too. And when others notice them in these uncommon places, they appear uncommon, appear to be works of art, having the power to send people back among the ordinary things to notice for themselves. If art museums have a function, it may be to contain works which have the power to direct people to see.

Walking down the street the man with the Eastern focus on sees all the city-scape things and accepts them. (At this point it is well to remember that we are talking of the man as artist, maker, who sees from a loving perspective. And though, of course, he recognizes the disadvantages and dangers of the loved one—or things in this case—he looks at them with a positive wonder prevailing.) He would find it difficult to join the movement against billboards as blotters out of natural beauty because he finds the billboards beautiful too. And we suspect that the man who is able to find beauty in the billboards *and* the mauntains receives a deeper delight from the mountains than does the man who hates the billboards. The man who loves them sees them as a kind of communication from his fellow man. If in that area of his life where moral decisions are made he knows that very little of what he reads in the commercial hard or soft sell language is literally true, then he lives with a great kind of freedom, freed from pressures to want or buy. He can take the whole business on a fairy story or allegorical level and enjoy it immensely.

We have a pretty good understanding in our own day of the significance of fairy stories and myths. We know that "Little Red Riding Hood" is not factually true. It is artistically or poetically true. We are R.R.H.—we once were small children, we left childhood (mother's house) and entered the grown-up world (the forest with its wolf dangers); we work for our fellow man (taking food to grandmother); we do mess things up (picking flowers at the wrong time) because our human nature isn't what it ought to be (R.R.H. was very young and unformed when she went out); we do confront what seems to be the final tragedy (being eaten by the wolf), but we are saved by

Christ (the woodsman), and we do live happily ever after in heaven.

All the stories that were ever written operate on two levels—a literal level and an allegorical level. First these stories were told, then they were written, and now in our time they are filmed. All of them educate man. Christ told tales, saw to it that they also got into written form and he still operates through these stories of his own and through all the rest of the stories that have been told or written or filmed. Some people catch on to Christ's method of teaching faster than others. George Bernard Shaw, who said that the only way to educate without torture is through the arts, caught on faster than those who try to squeeze infinite truths into definitions.

Our time is a time of erasing the lines that divided things neatly. Today we find all the superlatives and the infinite fulfillment man hungers for portrayed not only in fairy stories or poems but also in billboards and magazine ads and T.V. commercials. We are doing an age old thing in new media. But when we learn (or teach) how to take fairy stories and myths and parables we must also learn (or teach) how to take billboards and magazine ads and T.V. commercials. In a sense this is simply to take signs as signs. Thank God for cityscapes—they have signs. Thank God for magazines—they have ads. We can take the following ad for Hunt's catsup and see how it operates on a myth level:

	And read it this way too:
"Hang on, little tomato	—little child
Stay on the vine.	—which is Christ
Keep growing until you're	—eat up all the good things
fat and juicy.	and people around you
	which add to your stature.

Get picked while you're fresh as dew.

—to give freshly in a particular job

Bubble in Hunt's seven spices until you're bursting with flavor.

—whole sacramental—7 for many—system which gives us divine flavor bursting out of our human nature

Sparkle and shine in a bright new bottle until some smart hamburger teams up with you.

—new challenges that come with new times

Then people will never forget you.

—marriage, or friends

You'll be catsup with the Big Tomato Taste.

—because we are beautiful and human and Christian

Hunt's

—promise of future greatness

The big tomatoes are ripened on the vine for 40 days and 40 nights and simmered with seven spices.
Not six, not four, not two.
Seven spices.

—all kinds of biblical resonances, food and periods of time and symbolic numbers.

Not tomorrow.
Not yesterday.

—Providence, all special plans for us that God has

But there's one certain day in the life of a tomato when it's rich and ripe and proud enough to go to a country fair."

—heaven, which has been given other names—banquet, fish net, etc.

This sign language is almost infinitely rich. Another person with a different background could read different things out of it, or into it. Nobody should believe ads and billboards. They are contemporary fairy tales and are the carriers, as fairy tales have always been, of man's loves and hopes and beliefs. Up and down the highways (good symbols too) we see words like "Cold, clear, well-water," "The best to you each morning," "Have a happy day," "Sunkist," "Del Monte's catsup makes meatballs sing," that read almost like contemporary translations of the psalms for us to be singing on our way. The game is endless which makes it a good symbol of eternity which will be a great endless game.

Ray Bradbury, who writes science-fiction now said that he was bitten by the space bug when he was 8, when Buck Rogers first appeared and that the most important thing in his life was the paper hitting the front porch. Fantastic then, many of those comic strips have now become scientific facts. These were *his* fairy stories. Men must dream or imagine or leap into what isn't yet. Fairy stories are food for the imagination. Playing around with signs and symbols helps us leap in the direction where there are no signs.

In an article on Jules Feiffer, Robert Short refers to his parables as new wineskins. "Truth will always need to be spoken in parables. This is because it is the nature of a parable to force us to ask seriously different kinds of questions; for only then can we come close to sincerely appreciating, or understanding, the suggested answer of the parable." Schulz and Feiffer and Salinger and the rest of our contemporary parable writers are consciously building new wineskins for the new wine of truth. We suspect that most of the copy writers of the commercial world are unconsciously building containers for the wine. It should not be too surprising that, along with all the other changes, wineskins are now built of glass. If we care enough about finding new containers for the wine we will use bottles—or *anything*—just so the wine doesn't get spilled out of old wineskins. The wisdom symbolized by the wine is needed to inspirit the men of our time.

Camus said that what non-Christians ask of Christians is that they speak out loud and clear so that even the simplest man could understand. Perhaps we could take lessons from contemporary publications which offer so much for so little. For 35¢ a week (or $4.74 for 34 weeks or $18 for 3 years or $25 for 5 years—the lowest cost per copy available anywhere) you can get parables according to *Time* magazine and can wander through the pages of ads and texts—free from any pressures to buy or believe— and make lots of relationships between *Time* and eternity:

> "Contac—expressly designed for the cold miseries aspirin can't reach." (What about that for getting in and making contact with the miseries—aren't all miseries cold ones—of others who are not reached by indirect helps?)

or

> "When you're a homely little lamp,
> You have to have lots of personality . . .
> and be very helpful
> . . . then people will take you home
> and love you!" (Do your own meaning making for this one.)

In the "Letter from the Publisher" section of *Time* for January 29, 1965 we read:

> "Time advertisers over the past 42 years have frequently been innovators—starting with the adventurous 15 who invested in Vol. 1, No. 1, and continuing with the first companies to use our color pages, gatefolds, inserts, regionals, and demographic editions. A sample of that spirit appears in the center of this issue: the Aluminum Company of

America prepared a seven-page, four-color gatefold insertion—the largest single advertising commitment ever made in any issue of TIME."

And when we turn to the insert we find it says good things like:

Change for the better . . .

The unfamiliar object . . . what it will do for you in the future is beyond the imagination. Right now, it is being transformed into thousands of things that are changing your life for the better . . .

The acceleration of change . . . and how you can benefit from it.

If you make new things, use new products or dream new dreams, see how in so many ways Alcoa is on the forward cutting edge of change.

And in the same issue an article on today's teenager closes with these sentences:

The first doubling of knowledge occurred in 1750, the second in 1900, the third in 1950, and the fourth only ten years later. The fifth and sixth, if the plot line holds its course, are close at hand. Teenagers today do not think of themselves as "knights in shining chinos" riding forth on rockets to save the universe. But even the coolest of them know that their careers could be almost that fantastic.

Sometimes its as simple as knowing when to stop reading, as in the ad with a magnificent photograph of tall trees which really needs no words. The first part of copy reads, "We think it's a wonderful way to look at life—lying on your back and gazing at treetops against the sky. Like these magnificent trees that were seedlings not too many years ago, etc." The etc. tells about a lumber company and we stop here if lumber is not our immediate concern. We have already had our fun.

The more obvious goods in the low priced weekly magazines (even beautifully named *Look* and *Life*) are the photographs which richly move us in two ways as any good work of art does: *to* the work in a contemplative viewing for its own sake and *through* the work in a symbolic action that couples the here and now with eternity. The photograph in its still or moving state is our own art, one that has great power to move us. It does the moving in a much less obvious (and perhaps for that reason better) way than those works which have carried the label of art for a longer time.

Time, Life, Look are in this sense real and contemporary manuals of contemplation. Nor should their more elegant European sisters be ignored—*Realities* and *Magnum,* etc. They also have good names. And these are manuals of contemplation for the common man, who if he learned to use them rightly would become more and more contemplative.

Admitting all this asparagus into our lives, storing up things from around us, we have material to work with when we are confronted with the need for solving new problems. The human being cannot act fully without expressing visibly and audibly; or rather because he has this potential as an essential of his humanity, he cannot afford to stash it under a bushel basket. The beautiful and the human seem inseparable. "We want to be beautiful," Ugo Betti put it. Jacqueline Kennedy, for example, made a beautiful wineskin, the funeral of her husband. She took drums and flags and salutes and cannons and a small son and daughter and heads of states and bells and voices and uniforms and wonderful processions of words and of people and of memories and of promises for the future. This was an artful thing. She had been all along gathering in from the world around her—love of past and present things, care for past and present acts of human concern for God and man and divine concern for man. Out of all this as raw material, she made a new thing which was a human way of acting. She made a beautiful new thing and it was possible for all of us to share in this, in large part because it was visible and tangible though it encompassed much more that was not visible or tangible. And in the center of all this there was a feast, a banquet (the Mass) which was greatly disguised for many people (it was in an old wineskin) and remained for them only mysterious and removed from them. This banquet is that which prevents John Kennedy's death from being tragic. It is the great promise of life without death but life through death. The meaning of this banquet was hidden from most people and this was a lack of artistry, a lack of humanity, a lack of Christianity. The world expects of Christians that they speak up loud and clear so that the simplest man can understand. Why was the Mass so disguised and the rest of the celebration so clear to all? Perhaps because not enough artistry—or humanity—or Christianity has been expended yet on wineskins. If all the material things were taken away from the rest of the celebration how little of greatness man would have expressed or understood. Man needs to move his body in the beautiful ways only a human can. He needs to sing, to blow bugles and to frame great longings and loves into audible prose. Even Christ didn't try to live out his life on earth without lilies and stories and wedding feasts and singing with his friends and poetry and bread and wine (the best wine).

Cardinal Suenens says, "To be separated from the world and yet to be present in it to inspire and save it, is a situation paradoxical enough for all Christians but particularly so for nuns." Today we are recovering from the false notion that "separate from the world" means to avoid the beautiful and the human and thereby be more Christian. Yet there is a kind of separation that the sister senses is necessary—at least for as long as sisters are necessary at all—which is akin to the separation Camus speaks of as being necessary for artists. He says that:

> The artist of today becomes unreal if he remains in his ivory tower or sterilized if he spends his time galloping around the political arena. Yet between the two lies the arduous way of true art. It seems to me that the writer must be fully aware of the dramas of his time and that he must take sides every time he can or knows how to do so. But he must also maintain or resume from time to time a certain distance in relation to our history. Every work presupposes a content of reality and a creator who shapes the container. Consequently, the artist, if he must share the misfortune of his time, must also tear himself away in order to consider that misfortune and give it form. This continual shuttling, this tension that gradually becomes increasingly dangerous, is the task of the artist today. Perhaps this means that in a short time there will be no more artists. And perhaps not.[5]

Part of the being in the world is to understand the language people are using and the experiments they are engaged in so that we from another way of life may see the same problems and be able to cooperate in the ongoing work. Part of understanding the language and experiments comes from knowing about art and artists. Artists make pictures (or books or music or buildings) with stuff that comes out of their own time. They see today, the today we are all working in and with, and their special insights can give us hints about what's needed in our time. They sense what is real, they see what is new, they are quick to drop what is phony or no longer meaningful. They make new wineskins. And if our business is to put the always new truth into new wineskins, we need to know the very latest about wineskin making. This means we should be

[5] Albert Camus, *Resistance, Rebellion, and Death* (Alfred A. Knopf, Inc., New York, 1961), p. 238.

listening to the most experimental (or avant garde or whatever) music, seeing the newest plays and films, reading the latest poems and novels (with the freedom and the discipline referred to in the warning note on page 212). We need to be hungry for new insights.

Earlier we showed what could happen if we took a fresh view of the ad world. This is a playing around with what in itself may not be the greatest art but makes good symbols. When we talk about good films, music, etc. we are on a different level, and we remember that great art can be contemplated for its own sake and this would be sufficient. To contact beauty is enough for it to exercise its magic on us and transform us. But in addition these arts may be read in a symbolic way which differs from art to art. All works of art are symbols in themselves of the greatness and order that exists in the cosmos. Music and painting are this kind of symbol. Literature and film are this kind of symbol *and* the other kind as well. We contemplate the story of the film but we can also, after that, study it to find other meanings in it. Enjoyed for themselves, literature and film strengthen and beautify and christianize us. They can also be parables. Though in fact we have been able for some time to work with literature in these ways, we may not be aware that our newest art, the film, has these great potentials. They are our wineskins.

If we separate ourselves from the great arts of our time, we cannot be leaven enriching our society from within. We may well be peripheral to our society—unaware of its pains and joys, unable to communicate with it, to benefit from it or to help it. We will be refusing to care about the fight to free man that James Baldwin speaks of: "The war of an artist with his society is a lover's war. And he does at his best, what lovers do, which is to reveal the beloved to himself, and with that revelation, make freedom real."

A sister is the same as any other woman. She wants to be beautiful and human and Christian—not less beautiful, less human, less Christian than other women. A sister is only different in the job she chooses to do. And to do this job she has promised to enjoy things fully and not to possess them for herself, to love people greatly and not to possess them, to unite with a group of people who want to do the same job which is too big for an individual or an individual family to do alone. To the extent that her community prevents her from being beautiful and human and Christian, that community must be remade and remade over and over again. For this job the sister needs to be an artist—a maker. Perhaps the words of Paul VI to artists could then be descriptive also of sisters: ". . . creators, vivacious people and stimulators of a thousand ideas and of a thousand inventions." And

> Our ministry has need of your help because, as you know, our ministry is that of preaching and of making accessible and understandable, and even stirring, the world of the spirit, the invisible world of God, the unexpressible. And in this operation of expressing the invisible world in accessible and understandable formulas you are the masters. It is your profession, and your art is precisely that snatching of the treasures of heaven and of the spirit and clothing them in understandable words, colors and forms.

Not only must the sister be active in making new her own immediate community, she must be able to see it as an integral part in the making of the whole new world community. With great creativeness she will grasp at least some of the complex relations that exist among all peoples and all times as they move forward to the great party with the best wine (saved till last) toward which Christ's first sign pointed. As a maker, she will rejoice to share in the making of the new creation.

7

The Sister in the New City

Sister M. Angelica Seng, O.S.F.

A prophet is a man of God in dialogue with his own time. His function is to interpret the scriptures to the men of his time in relation to the needs of his time. Obviously, every Christian must, to some extent, assume the role of prophet. Obviously too, it is necessary that a few Christians assume the prophetic role more conscientiously, more publicly, with greater awareness of the responsibilities involved in evidencing that role in and to the world. Let us assert at once that sisters must be numbered among those few; that they must not function as "ancestral voices prophesying war," but as voices "crying in the wilderness; make ready the way of the Lord." The fact that the *wilderness* today is urbanized, mechanized, rapidly changing, only increases the challenge to make ready the way for the fulfillment of Christ.

So the sister must be a woman in dialogue with her own times if she is to fulfill her sacramental prophetic commitment. The role which any Christian assumes in a given period of history must be determined on the basis of her knowledge of the word *Christian* and her knowledge of her own time. Only on this basis can effective and relevant dialogue be established.

To enter into a full discussion of *role* would indeed consume more than a chapter, and such is not our purpose. Let it suffice to say that it is impossible to come to an understanding of one's own role apart from the understanding of the role of others. A role is only recognizable in relation to another role or position. Likewise, it is impossible to understand *role* apart from some grasp of the culture and values of a particular people in a particular period of history. Thus, to talk about the role of the sister in our ever more urbanized society, one cannot escape such questions as the meaning of the human person, of Christian, of being a woman, and finally of being a sister in this decade of this century in this country in this city in this profession. The sister is, must be, a woman in dialogue with her time.

Today we are witnessing massive urbanization, continual and rapid change. The fact of rapid societal change is one of the most significant considerations in any discussion of the role of the sister in the modern world. Our response to continual change must be that of continual experimentation and creativity. Therefore, we must build a structure in religious life which fosters experimentation and change. The religious woman must be adaptable, courageous, and creative. As we will attempt to prove later, perhaps the most stable structure of religious life in our own time will be the stability of the adaptable personality.

Even the most cursory examination of the United States today will alert us to the rapid growth of metropolitan areas. Whole sections of our country may properly be called metropolitan regions, where one metropolitan area, composed of inner city and suburbia, juxtaposes another area, composed of inner city and suburbia. Both the inner city and the suburb pose a unique challenge to modern man, to the Christian, and to the sister.

As our cities grow and grow at the periphery, they are rotting at the core. The inner city is a mission land for the Church, but a mission land unlike other mission territories which provide virgin soil for the seed of faith. This mission land bears the traces of a previous generation which was called Christian, but whose Christianity has left only a surface image with no message for the alien minds which live in that area. It is an area spotted with massive structures of churches and schools, old and empty and irrelevant. To the people of the inner city today, these are artifacts of another culture and a different people. The church steeple does not tower over this community but is lost amid the tall, arrogant highrisers of the verticle slums.

In many ways the Church has been a dying institution in the inner city. There are nearly eighty parishes in the city of Chicago where parish lists have dwindled tremendously. These parishes can properly be called mission territories with, unfortunately, far too few missionaries.

More than a mission land, the highriser world has been almost a wasteland for the Church. All we have offered to the people of this world are the middle class institutions which we have confusedly but consistently identified with the Christian message. Practically all the analyses of the needs of the inner city have been made within a middle class orientation and against a middle class value system. The attitude of the Church has too often been one of "I come as a bearer of gifts." And, too often, these gifts have been, not gifts of scripture, sacrament, and life, but middle class gifts of respectability, thrift, cleanliness, legality, and morality.

Perhaps we have labored too much the "problem" of the inner city; perhaps we ought simply to examine the needs of people everywhere, though these needs are probably more dramatically evident in the inner city. These needs may be categorized under three headings: the need for

Needs

human community, the need for respect and understanding of person, and the need for freedom-response. And are these not the heart of the Christian message? What is the role, the response, of the sister to the people of the inner city? Where is the sister in the inner city? How can she become a witness to community, to person, to freedom? These are values which transcend any particular period in history and any section of the city. But how we give witness to these values depends upon the particular period of history and the particular people to whom we are sent.

As these needs are so apparent among the people of the inner city, so too are they evident among religious women today. There is irony in this. Is it to be recommended that the blind lead the blind? Only when we see a need dramatically illustrated in another will we be able to recognize that same need in ourselves. The sisters have much to learn from the people of the inner city. They must first of all learn that they, the sisters, are middle class. How can they, then, witness to community, to freedom, to person, among the poor? They will have to learn the answer to this question as they experiment. And experiments of this nature have only just begun in any significant way.

THE SISTERS' WORK IN THE INNER CITY

The real work that has been done deserves recognition and encouragement. There have been positive and successful attempts on the part of sisters to meet the challenge of their time in dialogue and action. What are some of the ways in which sisters have responded to the urban challenge? What follows by way of specific example concern largely the Chicago area, since the author is most familiar with that particular city. No doubt there are similar projects in operation in other metropolitan areas.

Among sisters in Chicago there has grown up a movement known as the Urban Apostolate of the Sisters. The movement started in the winter of 1961, when a group of sisters from the near west side of Chicago (a depressed area) joined forces to discover how they might meet more effectively the needs of the people they serve. The sisters were discouraged in the face of the tremendous obstacles to running their schools and other institutions in this underprivileged area. Through the initiative of a few leaders, they began to realize how much they could learn from one another, as well as how much they could do to serve the needs of the community. Plainly, nothing could be done without unified effort. They sought assistance from the Office of Urban Affairs of the Chicago Archdiocese. Sister Mary William, D.C., a social worker, was released from her other duties on one day a week in order to assist the sisters. Through her stimulation as well as through the efforts of Msgr. John J. Egan of the urban affairs office, the movement spread to other inner city neighborhoods. As the movement grew, a Central Committee of Sisters was elected to coordinate its activities. The sisters worked with other Church and civic groups as well as with the Office of Urban Affairs, sponsored by the Cardinal Archbishop of Chicago. Several sisters met with the Cardinal to inform him of the growth of the movement and to receive his approval.

In August, 1963, a three-day seminar for all the sisters involved in this Urban Apostolate movement was held at Xavier College. In May, 1964, a Weekend of Intensification was held for approximately twenty sisters who had exerted leadership in the Urban Apostolate. Now there are four hundred sisters active in the movement, from five different areas of the city and from approximately ten religious communities.

The importance of the movement lies precisely in this: that the movement sprang up as the sisters' response to their needs in attempting to be relevant and effective in the inner city. The vitality of the movement depends on the initiative, creativity, and efforts of the sisters in the field.

A quotation from the Constitution will clarify the aims and work of the movement:

> THE URBAN APOSTOLATE OF THE SISTERS is a voluntary association of sisters working in the Chicago Archdiocese which commits itself to
>
> 1. *Program of education* whereby the sisters become aware of the many dimensions of the work of the Church and needs of human society.
>
> 2. *Program of communication* whereby the sisters learn from the thinking, the successes and the failures of others, and are encouraged and strengthened by them.
>
> 3. *Program of action* whereby the sisters, as a result of study and planning, take appropriate steps to aid in the solution of the problems of the people.

The movement has been structured as follows:

Areas   Areas are simply the grouping of contiguous convents within the same geographical neighborhood. The boundaries of the areas are determined on the basis of convenience for the Sisters as well as of mutual interests and concerns.

The Area Program Committee   This committee consists of two or three Sisters selected by the Sisters in their area to be responsible for the meetings and activities of the area for a period of one year.

The Coordinating Committee   This committee is composed primarily of representatives from each area. It is to serve as a vehicle of communication between the areas, to coordinate any city-wide activities of the movement, and to respond to the requests from the sisters in the area.

The Advisory Committee The advisory committee meets several times a year to evaluate the work of the sisters and to make recommendations to the sisters. Members of this committee represent different fields of competency: Mrs. Carmen Mendoza of the Cardinal's Committee for the Spanish Speaking; Mrs. Dorothy Drisch, one of the originators of the Christian Family Movement in Chicago; Mrs. Marcella Meyer, vice-president of the Organization of the Southwest Community; Mr. Edward Marciniak, Director of the Chicago Commission on Human Relations; Dr. Paul Mundy, Chairman of the Department of Sociology of Loyola University; Rev. Arthur Brazier, first president of the Woodlawn Organization; Rev. Douglas Still, director of Social Welfare for the Church Federation of Greater Chicago; Sister Mary Ann Ida, B.V.M., president of Mundelein College; Sister Maureen, S.S.N.D., author of *The Convent in the Modern World;* Rev. Robert Clark of the Catholic School Board; and Rev. John McKenzie, S.J., of Loyola University, author of *Two-Edged Sword.*

There is no ready-made program of action in the movement, since the needs of the neighborhoods differ. The sisters within each area determine the program for their area. The success of the movement depends upon the initiative of the sisters in the field. Some of the area activities already engaged in are the following:

—meetings with teen-age gangs in the neighborhood.

—visits to the homes of students and neighbors.

✓   —meetings with Protestant, Catholic, and Jewish clergymen in the community.

✓   —making known the agencies within the neighborhood
and the services which are available to the people of
the area.

—cooperation in the activities and projects of the community organizations in the neighborhood.

—meetings with civic, welfare, and political officials.

Periodically, the Urban Apostolate of the Sisters pub-
lishes a newsletter called *Encounter, the Sisters' Approach
to Metropolitan Challenge.*

Orientation days are held for the sisters who are newly
assigned to the inner city, and several new areas are now
being started. Although this movement has begun in the
inner city, there is no reason that it be limited to the inner
city. Sisters in our middle class and suburban neighborhood have much to profit from increased local communication and collective action. The Urban Apostolate of the
Sisters does not focus primarily on the formation of the
sisters. It is concerned with how the sisters can meet more
effectively the needs of the people with whom they work.
However, in the sisters' effective Christian response to
these needs, they will be formed experientially as religious
and as apostles.

Home Visiting

The Urban Apostolate of the Sisters represents an inter-
community venture. However, there are examples of responses of individual religious communities to the challenge of the inner city. One such example is the Cabrini
program of the School Sisters of St. Francis. This program
began in April of 1962 when one of the priests from a
parish in the Cabrini public housing area of Chicago saw

a picture in the diocesan newspaper of two sisters visiting the home of a Negro couple as part of an educational workshop for teachers sponsored by Friendship House. Father thought immediately of his elderly, lonely poor, who would welcome such visits. There were so many within the highrise public housing buildings in need of interest, companionship, respect, and love, and he knew the sisters could give them these things. There were no sisters stationed in the parish in which Father worked because the school had been condemned and torn down as a fire hazard. So he called two sisters who are teachers at Alvernia High School, one of the more than thirty schools conducted by this community in the Chicago Archdiocese. This was an unusual request, for members of this teaching community to receive in view of the fact that the sisters at that time were not allowed to visit in homes, not even those of the students they taught.

The two sisters discussed Father's request with their Mother General and received permission to make a few home visits for Father. That was all they had to do to know that they had to respond to these needs of the people in this area and to know that they could respond with no injustice to their teaching commitments. Indeed, these visits were, in every respect, an enrichment of their professional commitment.

The two sisters drew together a volunteer committee of eight sisters who would work on a program whereby they could extend this volunteer home visiting program to all of the five hundred School Sisters of St. Francis in the Chicago archdiocese. From September through December, the committee made four or five visits to the Cabrini area; they met with the priests working there; they sought the advice of professional sociologists and social workers; they met with personnel from the various social and welfare agencies in the Cabrini neighborhood; and they contacted Protestant clergymen in the area.

It very quickly became apparent that the sisters were not to visit the poor in the capacity of teachers or social workers, but simply as fellow human beings extending their interest, love, and friendship. This was not to be a proselytizing venture either. It was and is one more means of bearing Christian witness. This is especially true and necessary in view of the needs of our time. Ought not the sisters to be the first to meet these needs? This is surely part of their apostolate and it may also lead others to find time to serve the poor. If religious women will not find the time, who will?

The professional teacher, in a special way, has the need to meet the poor, to cross economic class lines, to participate in the activities of the human race, and thus to become more human, more informed, and more Christian. This is not at all to say that the only way to become Christian is to visit the homes of the poor. However, person to person contact with the poor, although it takes time (maybe because it takes time) is more likely to enrich the professional competence of the teacher than to detract from it, simply because it enriches us as human beings and as Christians. There is so much that a teacher can do to bring others to help in serving the poor and in developing a sense of social responsibility. But first the teacher must have this sense herself: it cannot be gleaned from books; she must serve the needs of Christ in this city in this century. Students and parents do become interested and committed through the teacher's interest and commitment.

Training Programs

Home visiting of the poor is a new experience for most religious, especially for the teacher, Therefore, is was necessary that some special preparation be given to those who wished to engage in this project. Keeping this in mind, the committee of eight sisters launched a new program. On a volunteer basis the sisters could commit themselves to four visits per semester, provided that they first participate in the short training program.

Two days of formal preparation were required for the sisters volunteering to do this work. One day of preparation was a workshop on race relations conducted by the staff of Friendship House. It is very important that sisters who begin to work with the poor in a Negro neighborhood do not simply reinforce certain stereotyped images which they have of the Negro. Therefore, the sisters must have contact with middle class Negroes before they begin such a program with the poor. As part of the Friendship House workshop the sisters were taken to visit in the homes of middle class Negroes.

The second day of preparation consisted in acquiring a knowledge of the Cabrini area, some sociological explanation of the causes of poverty, and some practical suggestions for the home visit.

No lesson plan in hand, no role of teacher to play, the religious will generally feel very insecure on her first home visit to the poor. The last phase of preparation was a guided home visit for the sisters. Their guides were leaders among the people in the community who had worked hard to plan this program with the committee of eight sisters. This program belonged to the people of Cabrini as well as to the School Sisters of St. Francis.

By February of 1963, eighty sisters were visiting in the homes of the poor in the Cabrini area. The results of the Cabrini program of the School Sisters of St. Francis are intangible, but nonetheless real. The people of Cabrini welcomed them and taught them much; they know the sisters now.

The sisters engaged in the visiting are teachers from
about fifteen middle class parishes in the Chicago metropolitan area. Wherever possible, the sisters have tried to
make the students and adults in their parishes aware of
the Cabrini needs and, with lay teachers, students, and
their parents, have worked on a variety of special projects
with the people of Cabrini. In some instances the people
of Cabrini have made return visits to the convents and
schools of "their" sisters.

The stated goal of the Cabrini Program is fourfold:

1) To enrich the teaching of the sister by a better
   understanding of the psychological, economical, and
   political forces in our society which have created
   Chicago's poor.

2) To develop the person of the sister by direct personal contact and communication with individuals
   who are culturally different.

3) To provide the opportunity for the sisters to participate in a directly evangelical and missionary work
   as another means of fulfilling their baptismal com-
   mitement.

4) To allow the sisters to come to a better appreciation
   of their Franciscan vocation by dedication to those
   who are especially and visibly poor.

The sisters doing the visiting work in teams of six or
eight, electing their own team chairman. Each team
focuses its attention on one highrise building within the
Cabrini area. The chairmen form a central committee to
work with the sister who is designated as coordinator of
the program. Flowing from this involvement of Sisters in
the Cabrini area, junior professed sisters who are completing their college training participate in a two-day
seminar on race and poverty. As part of this seminar, the

young sisters spend a Sunday afternoon visiting the friends of the sisters in the Cabrini area. The people of Cabrini are most eager to help teach the young sisters.

Protest Activities

An incident which received wide public attention, the incident of the picketing sisters, is linked directly to the Cabrini program of the School Sisters of St. Francis. Six of the seven sisters who demonstrated are members of this community, and all six had visited in the Cabrini area. These sisters were requested by their fellow students to participate in the demonstration against the segregated policy of the Illinois Club for Catholic Women. The sisters, with their fellow students, attempted to negotiate a change in the policy of the club before demonstrating, and they warned the administration of the club that they would take a public stand against such a policy, which was a public scandal both within and without the Loyola University community. Much of the controversy centered around the use of the Club swimming pool facilities by the Loyola coeds. Although the club announced a change in policy after the demonstration by the sisters and other students, there has not been water in the swimming pool since the incident. Perhaps it is the first Catholic integrated empty swimming pool in the nation.

But the real significance of the sisters' demonstrating has little to do with the Illinois Club for Catholic Women and much to do with the people of Cabrini and the Negro people of Mississippi and the people of the slums in St. Louis. They were the people who read well the meaning of the action, which was told to them through a picture of sisters on that picket line. No bishop's statement or joint declaration of the National Conference of Religion and Race will reach them as effectively as that picture of the sisters. Somehow sisters must reach the people of the inner city, and this was an effective method. At the same time, it is true that this action alienated from the sisters some of those whom people consider decent, respectable, middle class Catholics. Opposition to the action came largely from the ranks of Catholics. But a simple note, hardly legible, from the people in Cabrini to the sisters who demonstrated told the sisters where the real victory lay.

Adult Education Program

Another experimental project in the city of Chicago has shown the creativity and interest of sisters in the problem of urban renewal (using the term in the broad sense and not referring to the governmental program). The religious community involved in this example is the Institute of the Blessed Virgin Mary. These sisters conduct Loretto Academy in the Woodlawn area in Chicago. This area has about a fifty percent unemployment rate. Therefore, the sisters at the Academy, in order to respond to the needs of their neighborhood, began to offer adult evening education classes so that the adults could have a better opportunity of securing a job. This program was conducted on a volunteer basis for both teacher and student during the school year 1963-64. Eighty adults enrolled in the program. Classes were offered in sewing, typing, reading, and so on; in effect, the program was a basic education or literacy program which attempted to bring all students up to at least a sixth grade reading level, since this is minimal for vocational training and jobs.

Through the curriculum for basic education which the sisters developed, they were able to secure a Federal grant from the Manpower Development Training Office under which they were contracted to conduct a twelve-week day-time adult education program. This was a pilot project in the state of Illinois, and all expenses were covered by the government. The students were sent to the program from the Illinois Employment Bureau, and they were given a financial allotment by the government, with job placement service available to them after the course.

The program began in July, 1964. There were many co-operating agencies working with the program, including the Woodlawn Organization. However, the program was initiated and directed by Mother Peter Claver, I.B.V.M. DePaul University and the University of Illinois were co-operating schools in this program. The sisters are now beginning another volunteer evening course with an accelerated curriculum for adults who have completed eight years of grammar school. By means of this course they hope to enable the students to pass the State GED (Government Educational Development) test and thereby secure a high school diploma. Again, eighty students are enrolled in the course.

The sisters at Loretto Academy in Chicago have been an example of how effective, creative, and relevant the sisters can be to fulfill the needs of the people in the inner city. They were charter members of the Woodlawn Organization, active in the building of its constitution, and present at its first Constituent Assembly in the spring of 1961. The sisters have attended meetings of the organization and have offered the use of their facilities to the organization. The sisters rode with their people in the bus registration campaign.

Preparing for Housing Project

A discussion of the sisters in Chicago's inner city would not be complete without a reference to the work of the Daughters of Charity. Marillac House is a settlement house on the near west side of Chicago. In 1957 the Chicago Housing Authority planned to erect a highrise public housing unit in a section of the neighborhood which was only about two blocks from Marillac House. The people already living in the neighborhood feared the demolition and resented the project. In order not to have a community divided between the project dwellers and the inhabitants of the area, as has often been the case in other sections of the city, the Daughters of Charity initiated a plan to prepare the neighborhood for the public housing units, as well as an orientation program for the public housing dwellers. They consulted the Chicago Housing Authority, which enthusiastically endorsed such a plan. They also conferred with the many public and private service agencies working in public housing areas throughout the city. They wanted to build a preventive and positive program in the neighborhood. The sisters tried to get a private grant to sponsor their sixteen-point program, but without success. One of the points of the plan even necessitated renting a storefront nearer to the public housing buildings—an interesting twist on the storefront churches in the area.

Because the Chicago Housing Authority was eager to have the program of the sisters put into effect, it secured permission from Washington to offer the sisters an apartment in the highrise building to serve as their social service center. This was the first time that an apartment in public housing was leased for a function other than family living. Because the sisters were responsible for staffing the center, it became the full time assignment of one sister with a lay staff. The center is called Rendu House, named after a Daughter of Charity who worked in the slums of Paris.

One of the most recent experiments of the Daughters of Charity at Marillac House is to have one of their sisters

act as liaison betwen tenants and owner of one of the
tenement houses in their neighborhood. The tenants now
have acquired hope of securing their rights through sister
and through their own united efforts, for they have
learned to trust one another through her. Even the land-
lord has come to regard the building as "Sister Louisa's
building."

Experimental Programs

Some things, certainly, have already been done; many
more are being done now. But in proportion to the needs
we have scarcely begun. In proportion to the number of
sisters working within our large metropolitan areas we
are poorly represented in the inner city. Our Lord did
not say, "Blessed are you for when I was hungry, thirsty,
and naked, you formed a discussion club for me in your
middle class ghetto." We must move from an awareness
of the problems to practical solutions which we can ourselves effect. We must be willing to make more and more
far reaching experiments to cope with the problems before
us.

Following are some suggestions for such experimentation: We must approach the inner city as a missionary
team rather than as a hierarchical institution. Since most
religious communities are committed to staffing different
types of instiutions within a city, it is asking too much of
any one community to suggest that four or five sisters be
released to form an experimental missionary team in the
inner city. Yet the creation of such a team is feasible on
an inter-community basis. Could not several communities
which staff many institutions within a particular city free
two sisters to serve on this team? The team could be run
democratically, with no especially designated superior. In
this way, the sisters' own experience of responsibility,

freedom, and corresponding initiative will enable them better to impart these characteristics to the people of the inner city. (There is another advantage to this inter-community team work, an advantage which is not mere fringe benefit, either: the sisters will have much to learn from the shared heritages and spirits of their respective communities, and this sharing will certainly help to create an ecumenical atmosphere both within and without the Church.)

The sisters will be only a part of a larger team composed of priests and laymen working out of some type of missionary center in the neighborhood. It is important that the team make no institutional commitment as they *begin* their work in the inner city neighborhood. It will sometime be necessary that the team does not identify itself with any particular parish or school in the neighborhood. This is especially true where the parish has, in the past, rejected the newcomer and now remains in the Negro's mind simply a relic of the white man's world.

The team must come to know the people of the inner city neighborhood. This is their first step. Any program they attempt to build *into* the neighborhood will not long endure. The people must build their own program, their own community, and their own Church. The team is there to *believe* in the people, to be itself convinced and committed to a group capable of solving its own problems in a Christian.

However, this is not to say that the inner city will lift itself up by its own bootstraps and solve all its own problems. Its own problems have not been made by the people who inhabit the inner city today; they are simply the inheritors. The problems of the inner city are the problems of the people of the metropolitan area. The class isolation which city life has permitted and intensified is the greatest obstacle to solving the problems of the inner city—and the suburb too, for that matter.

This missionary team will be in an ideal position to help build the bridge between the middle class world and the poor. We must consider this aspect as a very important corollary to their role in the inner city. Most religious communities working in our larger cities have schools in many different types of socio-economic neighborhoods of the city. The structure of the religious community in this regard could facilitate contact and communication between classes and neighborhoods. Although the needs of the inner city are overwhelming, the team must not limit itself to responding to these immediate needs and possibly, thereby, simply improving ghetto existence. Its vision must be broader, more far reaching, embracing more than the highriser world. It must, in fact, recognize the obligation of education and communication with the middle class world.

Some of this education cannot take place without what some would call an exploitation of the poor. We must ask humbly that the poor be patient with us until we come to respect them. But first we must come to know them. This team ought to provide opportunities for their postulants, novices, and scholastics to assist them in the inner city. They could participate in a tutorial program, in organized recreational activities, in a program of home visitation to the elderly, in an adult literacy program. Actually, the significance of their work will not be so much in what they accomplish or give to the people of the inner city, but rather in what they themselves learn. Their most striking understanding must be that they, the sisters, are middle class, and to be a middle class must not be confused with being Christian. We are not here to give a middle class world to the poor but to build a Christian world with the poor.

Besides such an educational program for those in the formation program of religious communities, it is important that there be some type of in-service program for the many sisters staffing the schools and hospitals throughout the city. If the sisters teaching or serving the people of middle class neighborhoods come to recognize that a great need of their people is an awareness and understanding of the poor and that they must lead their parishioners and students to their responsibility to the poor, the inner city team will have a vast resource of people, time, and money to assist and collaborate in the growth of a Christian community in the inner city.

The Person to Person Encounter

For too long now even the responsible middle class citizen has been content with a donation mentality, which is anonymous, cold, and unavailing. While no one denies the value of money in easing physical situations, one cannot consider that his Christian obligation can be fulfilled in only that way. Christianity must be a person to person encounter. Here the team must lead the way—but *lead*, in such a way that all classes will want to enter into dialogue with each other.

It seems strange that in a Catholic city, such as Chicago, for instance, there can be such utter need for help. So many are so busy, too busy to see; or, too busy to want to see the needs of Christ in the poor. How many people, good respectable Catholic people, ride by or through the slums every day to and from work or school, but feel no obligation to the people living there? Can Christ be recognized in such a response?

So often, consciences can be dulled with the attitude, "Let the welfare department do it; they're professionals; we're not social workers." But that is merely a convenient argument. The poor do not need that welfare check as much as they need someone to restore their self-respect, of which, in too many cases, they have been robbed. They have a need to be more than numbers on a case worker's list. They need the security of being loved by man, by God, and by his Church. They have a need to be served, and the fulfillment of that need doesn't come through the mail. It will come through personal contact with every individual.

Professional specialization does not justify our failures to respond to the needs, the human needs, we cannot help but see. But everyone is too busy with other obligations—the secretary, the factory worker, the business executive, the teacher—too busy to give time to the poor (and this means *poor* in the literal sense of the word). The sister can lead the way so that baptized, confirmed members of the Church in this particular city in this particular period of history will be able to meet the unique needs of the Church in this day.

Probably the most important function of the inner city missionary team will be one of coordination rather than of direct service to the poor. There is here, of course, the danger of bureaucratization, and this danger must be recognized by the team. Therefore, it is most important that the team identify as much as possible with the people of their neighborhood. They must live in the inner city and not in a fenced-off monastic convent. There has been so little experimentation on the part of the Church in the public housing areas of our cities. It is quite possible that in such an area the missionary team of sisters will be able to live in an apartment within the highrise building. There they can be identified as neighbor, and not as teacher, nurse, social worker, or agency staff member. From this vantage point they will be ideally situated to participate in the building of community organizations and the discovery of community leaders. The slum area is not a leaderless area; we simply do not know how to identify the leaders.

The sister working in community organizational work will be doing what has been called pre-evangelization. But this type of work will provide unlimited opportunities for that type of evangelization which is always a person to person effort. The type of community organization referred to here is one which is based on the belief in the democratic process, the dignity of each person and his ability to join with others in meeting his own needs and the needs of the group. It will be that type of organization which is based on the needs and interests of the people as they see them, and not as middle class sociologies, city planners, welfare workers, and housing authorities analyze them. It will be an organization which will give hope to the people to rise to meet their own needs and to feel the power of their self-determined collective action. Examples of this type of organization are the Woodlawn Organization and the Northwest Community Organization in Chicago.

An experimental missionary team of this nature would be well suited to participate in many interfaith efforts to assist the people of the neighborhood. The missionary team, not being bound to any parochial structure, would be fluid enough to relate better to the many small sects and storefront churches found in such an area. Joint scripture services, hymn fests, and welfare projects could be launched by religious leaders in the area.

Contact with these religious sects could prove to be an invaluable course in methodology. There is no question of their influence on the poor and, more, of their identification with them. In all humility we must be willing to admit that they have succeeded where we have failed. Working with these people will help us to see once more that to be effective in the highrise world we must be the Church of the Poor.

After the team has lived in the area long enough and has come to know the people and the leaders in this neighborhood, they may see the need for making some institutional commitment in response to the needs as they judge them. Government financial help is available for the launching of adult educational programs. Programs for high school dropouts could be set up. Educational opportunities for unwed mothers is a need in these neighborhoods.

The team attempting to identify with the people of the community will, by that very identification, be better able to relate to the often absentee power structure in the inner city. The team should not hesitate to negotiate with the welfare officials, the housing authorities, and the political bosses on behalf of the people. The people whom the team represents will not simply be a "company union" of the power structure; rather they will be a people having power because they have hope and because they believe in th democratic process and in the power of their collective action.

The picture presented above is an ideal, not in the sense that it is unreal or unworkable, but in the sense that it has not yet been put into practice. That such teams will operate in the future in this and in many as yet unforeseen ways is more than conjecture; it is an absolute need which must be realized and made practicable as soon as possible.

THE SUBURBAN APOSTOLATE

Preoccupation with the needs of the inner city ought not to blind us to the problems of suburbia. There the sister's role must be vastly different but no less important.

Official religion in every period of history has both a conserving and a dissenting role. There seems little question that Catholicism has performed well its conserving function. To many it appears to be a citadel of traditionalism. Today, if the Church is to remain faithful to her mission, a dissenting voice must be heard in the middle class world of the United States. This author believes that the sister in our suburban communities must become a *disturbing* leaven. She ought not to "fit in" well, to feel too secure. This may seem to be a negative approach, but it is not. Rather it is in this manner that the sister will exercise her critical faculties; and real criticism is never merely negative. The best critic is one who sees good and evil; encourages the good and offers solutions for the evil. In the very act of criticism, the sister is thus forced to be creative in initiating solutions to existing conditions.

Perhaps the very evangelical vocation of the religious woman is a dissent from the values of our middle class society. But that voice in the person of the sister must be recognized as the *Word*. Then the dissenting voice will gather to itself a Christian community, and the cry of that community will no longer only be a *dissenting* one, but a *becoming* One.

A necessary first step is that sisters question and challenge their role in the middle clas community in an effort, not to deny the good, but to seek the better. We will not attempt to enter the controversy over the value of our parochial school system and the sisters' place within that system. But let us look at the opportunities for greater effectiveness within the institutional structure of the sisters' present work. No doubt some of the recommendations which follow are already being tried in some of our middle class parishes. If they are, good; if not, "let us begin."

The goals of the Urban Apostolate Movement of the Sisters, cited earlier in this chapter, are necessary to the suburbs as well as to the inner city. We suggest that sisters of different communities working within one suburb meet regularly and thereby participate in a joint program of education, communication, and action. Perhaps the most difficult task of the sisters of suburbia is that, while they identify with the people of suburbia, they must at the same time be able to stand back from that society and exercise the judgmental role of religion. The sisters must not become members of "the one, holy, U.S., middle class religion."

Rectory Relations

To establish communication between the sisters of different convents in suburbia is often easier than building the bridge to the rectory. Basic to this difficulty is the fact of the social conditioning to which we have been subjected concerning the role of woman. To further complicate the matter, within strains of our Catholic sub-culture we have strong "Victorian lady" concepts of the sister.

Many sisters have been conditioned in the name of a pseudo-reverence and obedience, to regard their relations with priests and especially with the pastor as one of silence, obedience, and dependence. Perhaps it is something akin to a father-daughter relationship, in which the daughter never even reaches the adolescent stage. In some circumstances it appears, in fact, to be closer to a shepherd-sheep relationship.

First the sisters have to face the fact of the conditioning within themselves. Then they must have the courage to reject it by taking the initiative in breaking this image. We recognize that there are many priests only too eager to help the sisters emerge from the shadow of nineteenth century concepts of "Be good, sweet maid, and let who will be clever." The sisters must seek means of adult communication and discussion with the pastor. They must show that their concern and responsibility is not confined to the school but goes out to all of the parish. Priests and sisters, in practice as well as in theory, must form a team in which each member is recognized as an adult, responsible member.

Working with Parish Groups

There are innumerable opportunities for the sisters to work with adults within the present parish structure. The significance of the CCD program has frequently been emphasized. A greater percentage of Catholic children will be excluded from our private school system each year. This is especially true of suburban areas and of high school students. Sisters ought to become vital parts of the CCD program. Likewise, they must feel it their responsibility to make the CCD program dynamic and effective. The private high schools in the suburbs could be opened after regular school hours to provide a convenient and suitable location for catechetical instructions. The sisters' task might very well be not only to teach the student, but to teach and prepare the instructors of the students.

Young people, who are too old for the parish school and too young for adult parish organizations, are often a neglected group, or worse, a maligned group. About the only effort many parishes make to satisfy the needs of this group is to offer an occasional social function. A sister who takes the initiative in organizing YCS and YCW groups would indeed be witnessing to Christian zeal.

The sister could lead or participate in scripture discussion groups; she could assist the priests in moderating CFM groups. Both new and traditional parish organizations ought to know the power of the sister's love and commitment. They ought to experience the stimulation of her thinking and the generosity of her labor. The sister in turn will not only lead these adults but will have the opportunity to grow with them. The benefit of such contact is always reciprocal.

Sisters could participate in the planning and directing of weekend retreats or days of recollection for women of the parish. Two sisters from Chicago recently directed a weekend retreat for a group of Methodist ladies at Wesley Woods, Lake Geneva, Wisconsin. The theme for the retreat was "The Role of the Christian Woman in the Twentieth Century." That theme, discussed under the direction of sisters, would hardly be unsuitable for Catholic women in suburbia.

Communication with adults of the parish could be facilitated if the sisters would make themselves available to the parishioners as they come and go for Sunday worship. Certainly the sisters ought to be free (and if not, ought continually to seek permission) to visit the homes of their students, when this is judged helpful to the student and to his family. These visits to homes ought not be limited only to the parents of students, however. The sisters in suburbia must give witness to virginity in a familial society. Probably their first task again will be to break down the image of a Victorian lady afraid of love and sex. When that image has been shattered, then the sister who is a woman fulfilled in love and free to love will testify to the beauty and fruitfulness of virginity in every contact she has with the adults of the parish. This witness can only be made to the degree that she opens herself to these adults to build with them the ties of friendship.

Much in the way of religious life as it is constituted today militates against the witness to love and this extending of friendship. If the religious is to be more relevant to the suburban community, then the structure of her life, and often the schedule of her day, will have to be altered. If the sister avails herself of the hospitality of the parishioners, her convent home also must have an open door. The aura of mystery surrounding the sister must go. Hers is not a monastic vocation.

Sisters could witness to poverty in this affluent society by making every effort to prevent the parish from being captured by the fund-raising urge and drive. Her voice ought to be the first voice of protest against the listing of contributions and the lack of them in the parish bulletin.

We do not expect sisters to live in shacks amid the beautiful houses of suburbia; neither, however, do suburbanites expect them to live in palaces. We must distinguish luxuries from convenience, beauty from cost. This distinction becomes a double necessity if the sisters are going to bring the needs of the inner city to the suburban minds and awaken social responsibility for the good of the physically and visibly poor, as recommended earlier in this chapter.

The sisters' witness to obedience must simply be a witness to the freedom of the life of the Church, in the parish and in the lives of the people of God. The concept of obedience and authority cannot be divorced from our understanding of the nature of human community. With all the organizations and clubs spattering suburbia, we must still question the suburbanites' grasp of the profundity of community. The religious community within the parish community must give witness to the full dimension of community through the joy and friendship of its members as well as through the strength of its team approach in the work of the apostolate. Competitive individualism stands pale next to the strength of a community of friends. Thus a team of educated Catholics (laity and sisters, neither of whom are lacking in our suburbs) will serve as Christian leaven in this middle class world.

Sisters in suburbia have an obligation not only to the Catholics of the suburbs but also to their Protestant and Jewish neighbors. As educational leaders in the community, they ought to work closely with civic organizations. Through sisters trained in these matters, programs promoting art and culture could the planned for the area. Parish facilities are often excellently suited for programs of this nature. Political lectures, debates, and discussions could be arranged through the initiative of the sisters in cooperation with neighborhood organizations and other churches or synagogues in the area. Working together on common projects for the good will of all will certainly foster an ecumenical open-mindedness which will help to make a community of an area. Communication and cooperation with public school leaders is essential to the sisters' educational commitment in the suburbs.

There is yet to be considered the role of our Catholic suburban high schools and colleges. What impact have they made on their neighborhood? Are they simply institutional ghettoes and structures of clay and sand within a "saved" society? They need not be; indeed, they dare not be. These institutions have enormous potential for Christian witness. The material facilities of these institutions should be open at all times for lay retreats, for lectures, for conferences on any topic pertinent to twentieth century living. Far more important, there is the personnel of these institutions, well educated, dedicated, and conven-

iently *there*, easily available to share experiences and
knowledge, to assist in developing and enlivening with intellectual ferment the spiritual life of the parishes which
call upon them for assistance in carrying out projects such
as those mentioned above.

The task of this author has been a comparatively easy
one in listing general suggestions which, in application,
must be interpreted according to the uniqueness of each
individual situation. But the problems must be solved by
the sisters engaged in their respective works in the different areas of the city. They are problems of preparation,
of time, of rule, and of attitude.

In our attempt to be practical and specific concerning
the work of the sister in these times of rapid change and
urban renewal, we run the risk of being utterly irrelevant
five or even two years from now. The only safe and lasting
recommendation to make is to encourage continual experimentation.

SHARING IN COMMUNITY LIFE

Those who work in creating community organization
within certain neighborhoods of our cities know the importance of what they call "citizen participation." This
means generally that the rank and file citizen within the
neighborhood has a sense of responsibility for the organization; he feels responsible for dreaming, planning, and
working; he recognizes his power within the organization
and knows that he participates in some fashion in the decision making process within the community organization.

If religious communities are going to be vital and dynamic structures in our time, they must build this type of
"sister participation." Every sister must feel responsible
for her community (and I do not mean by this respon-

sible to her superior—good as that may be). She must dream, plan, and act. She must have the power to initiate. She must feel herself a part of the decision-making process of her community.

The word *community* may be a very misleading one because it is used in so many different ways today. In regard to religious life, it often seems to refer to some nonentity like "the Order." This is not the community about which we are talking. Nor are we identifying community with the power structure of religious groups, as is often the connotation religious give when they speak of their community. Also, it must be clear that we are not talking about these organizational mechanisms which are geared to producing efficient work.

Sometimes religious speak of their community in terms of a family. General reference to family spirit may be warranted and justified. But there is danger that we accept a certain maternalism which fosters childishness in sisters and stultifies the maturing process. In fact, religious communities are not families.

By community as used here we mean a human, Christian community, perhaps best characterized by calling it a community of friends. We are referring to that type of community and communication which is essential to the development of the person, essential to the redemption of the person and society. An individual cannot even find her own identity apart from community. This is the type of community which will encourage that I-thou relationship necessary to personal and Christian growth. This is the type of community which frees the individual to be herself. This is the type of community which will lead the sister to understand what it means to identify with another and unltimately to identify with the Other. This type of community life will be the best type of preparation and formation for the sister who is to do God's work in our rapidly changing urban society.

Change must ferment and be initiated at the bottom of the hierarchical structure of religious communities as well as at the top of these structures. Unless the sisters actively and immediately engaged in apostolic work are dreaming, planning, and initiating, the type of continual, creative adaptation which is necessary to respond to the needs of our time cannot take place. No one will deny that we need enlightened leadership in major religious superiors. But changes which are simply legislated from the top without initiation, ferment, and even agitation at the bottom are unduly susceptible to failure. If the structure, organization and atmosphere or religious institutes do not permit and encourage freedom and initiative in the sisters, then the structure must be changed in view of the needs of our time. This principle is basic to any of the practical suggestions made in this chapter.

Earlier it was suggested that perhaps the only stable structure which religious communities must work toward is the stability of the very adaptable personality. This is the person needed to participate in the continual experimentation demanded by our time. If, however, this experimentation becomes bogged down in the bureaucratic structure of religious communities and changes become practically institutionalized before they can go into effect, the adaptation to the needs of the time will be antiquated before they are begun. The purpose of the structure of religious communities must be to free the person to respond to the needs of the time. The purpose of the organization within religious life is to encourage community.

Formation Programs

If we expect to find a fulfilled, creative, and adaptable personality in the sister of today, we must look at the formation program of our religious communities. A zealous, generous, and professionally competent religious could be formed in a program which this author judges detrimental to the formation of the type of personality needed in twentieth century urban society. We need zeal, generosity, and professional competency, yes. But even more we need a sister who prizes her freedom, a freedom which has been enhanced rather than limited by religious commitment; a sister who responds to Christ with all her powers and in all the manifestations of his will; a sister who does not find her security in her efficiency, her work, or her profession, but simply in her grasp of the meaning of creaturehood and of divine sonship; a sister who dares to dream and to hope; a sister who does not fear to experiment, courageous in failure, determined in effort; a sister who loves deeply, passionately, and freely, and through that love gives birth to Christ in every human encounter.

The formation of this sister calls for a general liberal art education with heavy portions of psychology, sociology, and theology, as well as the fine arts.

However, even more important than academic and professional preparation is the provision in the years of training for growth in responsibility (which is not to be equated with the ability to do what one is told to do), for growth in the powers of communication, for growth in leadership, creativity, and initiative, for growth in the ability to respond with a warm, free, and sincere love to her fellow sisters as well as to the laity.

Therefore the young novices and scholastics must have the opportunity to work not only with children but with adults. They must gradually assume more and more apostolic responsibility during the formation period (which may mean that academic programs will have to be lightened). Initiative must be welcomed and mistakes expected.

The building of friendships among the young sisters is to be encouraged, as well as many opportunities for group discussions and questioning. The specifics of how this could be accomplished in the formation period is not the purpose of this chapter. But if the sisters are to be prepared to meet the challenge of urban change and renewal, the training period must foster initiative, creativity, and adaptability.

Maternalism during the sisters' formation is detrimental to the development of the mature personality. The enthroning of the superior as a substitute god is an injustice both to the sisters and to their future superiors. Sisters must see their superiors as fellow human persons, fallible, subject to mistakes, and members of humanity. Then only will they be able to respond to their superiors with love. Then only will they be able to grow in a Christian understanding of authority compatible with theology as well as with the needs of the people of God today.

The people of God today are crying in the wilderness of our crowded, caged slums, in the wilderness of our complacent but respectable suburbs. The voice of God's prophet must be heard. This is the role of the sister in our urban world. She is a woman of God in dialogue with her own times. From that dialogue may the Word be formed.

8

The Sister
in Secular Life

SISTER JANE MARIE LUECKE, O.S.B.

In an address to a group of sisters on September 8, 1964, Pope Paul VI expressed the hope that the religious women in the Catholic Church might "get back a more direct and full participation in the life of the Church," and enumerated four general categories of such direct participation: the liturgy, social welfare, the modern apostolate, and the service of the brethren.[1] In doing so, Paul was probably only making somewhat more specific the direction suggested to nuns by both his recent predecessors. Pius XII began this—what seemed then a new—turn in religious direction in 1951 with his address to teaching sisters. But he made his most compelling statement about the importance of apostolic works in his 1958 radio addresses to contemplative nuns. In those addresses he suggested that even those orders destined by their constitutions exclusively to contemplation but who actually practiced certain forms of the external apostolate should continue to do so; orders which had performed these activities in ancient times should return to the practice, with adaptation to the present circumstances. His final words can perhaps be

[1]"New Horizons for the Woman Religious," *The Pope Speaks*, X (Autumn 1964), p. 17.

understood fully only today after our experience of Vatican II:

> Lifting yourselves always higher, always nearer to God, broaden your horizons and become ever more capable of orientating yourselves *on this earth*. Far from drawing you within yourselves and behind the walls of your convent, your union with God broadens your mind and heart *according to the dimensions of the world and the redeeming work of Christ*, which is perpetuated in the Church. This is what guides you, supports your undertakings and render them fruitful for every good purpose.[2] (Emphasis mine.)

Thus, while never denying the primacy of prayer and the necessity for the right kind of discipline and detachment implicit in the evangelical vows,[3] Pius XII and his two successors have made it increasingly evident that religious women are to share in the Church's burden of bringing Christ to every creature, and that their doing so can be only an aid to their contemplative life as religious.

Pius XII did not begin until 1951 to spell out new directions to religious women. But he began as early as 1939 to lay the foundation for this new direction in his challenging statements on the position of women in society. It is perhaps in these talks to Catholic laywomen, which continued through the forties and fifties, that we can find some guidelines for implementing Paul's challenge that we participate directly in "social welfare, the modern apostolate, and the service of the brethren." At the same time that Pius XII insisted on woman's awesome responsibility as wife and mother in a home, he insisted equally that she could not limit herself to this role, but must 'col-

[2]"The Contemplative Life," *The Pope Speaks*, V (Summer 1958), p. 80.
[3]See especially John XXIII, "The Contribution of Nuns to the Success of the Ecumenical Council," *The Pope Speaks*, VIII (Autumn 1962), pp. 153-162; and Pius XII, "An Instruction to Religious Superiors," *The Pope Speaks*, V (Spring 1959), pp. 201-208.

laborate with man toward the good of the State." However, he always made the distinction that, as a woman in the spheres of social and political activities or in labor situations, "she apply herself especially to those matters" which call for her specifically feminine qualifications: "tact, delicacy and maternal instinct rather than administrative rigidity." She should expound and safeguard the rights and duties of women and their interests through civic institutions and legislation. She should mold public opinion and initiate effective apostolates in the professions open to women and in cultural, socal, and political organizations. Finally in 1957, he told a congress of women that "your help is needed on behalf of the world's needy people in three fields: spiritual, cultural, material;" and added: Charity will "help you to sense instinctively the needs of your neighbor. It will make you aware of the call of the Kingdom of God and will indicate to you those critical areas in which your intervention is most needed."[4]

John XXIII gave a further insight on woman's activity or occupation outside her home when he said that her choice of activity should provide her "some means for continuously developing a maternal spirit." In this way her most valuable qualification—motherhood, which is "so much a part of her nature that it is operative even when actual generation of offspring does not occur"—would be utilized for the total good of society. He suggested that "the fields of education, social work, and religious and apostolic activity," offered the best opportunities for transforming occupations into "spiritual motherhood."[5]

[4]"The Mission of the Catholic Woman," *The Pope Speaks,* IV (Spring 1958), pp. 421-422. See also: "The Dignity of Woman," *The Pope Speaks,* III (Spring 1957), pp. 367-375, and six addresses to women included in *The Unwearied Advocate,* II, ed. Rev. Vincent A. Yzerman (St. Cloud, Minn., 1956), pp. 22-51.
[5]"Woman and Society," *The Pope Speaks,* VII (Spring 1962), p. 345.

It is not difficult to transfer the above quotations—directed to laywomen—to the religious woman. She is a woman and any perfection in her particular state will be achieved in her only if it is built on her nature as a woman. Besides, she is a modern woman and—if the correlation which I sense in reading the popes' messages to laywomen and those to religious women is at all valid— she should assume her title of "*modern* religious woman" and be true to all of its implications and responsibilities. Doing so may seem a betrayal of the role of "religious" women only because we cannot seem to find a precedent for it in the last one thousand years. But a thousand years is too short a time in this case for a judgment from history, since women as such exercised no public role in our society during this time until this century. The fact is, however, that in the Anglo-Saxon and Germanic societies of the seventh to tenth centuries, which are so much our particular heritage, women did exert a position of influence and leadership in public life. Concomitantly then there were nuns like Hilda of Whitby who not only governed a double monastery of men and women but was hostess to, and a participant in, a Synod that affected the entire history of the Roman Church.[6] And Hilda was not unique; she was a product of her times. The Church, far from taking a

[6] F. M. Stenton, *Anglo-Saxon England* (Oxford, 1947) p., 172, comments that the distinctive feature of Boniface's work in Germany "is the extent to which it depended on the help of women," and adds pointedly: "He had been trained in a church which allowed them [women] unusual influence." Interesting also is the statement made by Dom Stephen Hilspisch, *History of Benedictine Nuns* (Liturgical Press, Collegeville, 1958), p. 40, that when the Church imposed strict enclosure on nuns it "was not accepted at first by the nuns of the Anglo-Saxon island. For one thing, it had no basis in the Rule of St. Benedict; and moreover it was not compatible with the position held by a woman in Germanic society, especially a woman of noble family."

dubious step in suggesting that sisters today begin to play a more public apostolic role, has been if anything slow in making the suggestion—if indeed the sisters themselves should have had to wait for the Church to so suggest.

In an effort then to envision ways that sisters might participate in "social welfare, the modern apostolate, and the service of the brethren," it may be well to ask sincerely apostolic lay women how they envision their own role in public or secular life. Just such a question, along with many others, was asked of ten such women last year, and their answers were published in a series of articles in a Catholic magazine.[7] Giving both general directives about the role of women and making specific suggestions for areas of activity or fields of work, these women said that many new fields are now open to women: theology, medicine, law, psychiatry, psychology, pathology, journalism, and politics. Women can make a special contribution to society through these provided they consider "professional excellence" as a "primary obligation." With this prospect of almost limitless openings, the panelists noted that society needs especially from women specialists, educational specialists, and social specialists. For in today's technological surge, women might work most effectively with the humanizing process, since the special feminine qualities they can bring to their public service are the "humanistic" and "personalistic" ones. Thus, women should contribute a "resourcefulness to peace keeping," a "devotion to healing," and an "ethically restraining power to politics." One commented that a responsible approach to the population explosion may mean that the "maternity of women may cease to be concerned exclusively with her

[7]"The New Catholic Woman," *Ave Maria*, C (Sept. 19 to Nov. 21, 1964), 10 articles. I refer to the last three only as being appropos of the subject of this chapter.

own children, and may embrace the children of the world, including the children to come." Recognizing "non-involvement" as one of today's social sicknesses, women then "must maintain a full awareness, of today's problems, opportunities, and responsibilities to her fellow human beings," and become involved in such "temporal" and "social" issues as housing, employment, education, urban renewal, and civil rights.

Of the welter of observations made in the articles, one seemed to me particularly significant: "Nothing has prepared us to take our place in the secular community. This is really new ground and, *if* we decide we can spare the time, we'll just have to dig in." Sisters might sympathize with the feeling expressed, for if they are to widen their apostolate many of them can say the same, "Nothing has prepared us for this!" Or sisters may find in the statement a challenge. Have we not been called on to provide women with direction? The reaction to the comment that I find most shattering is the realization that the woman who made the statement was probably "prepared" for her life's work in one of our institutions. For what such a realization shatters is the defensive attitude that we are already engaged full time in apostolic work, in serving society through out institutions; that we have "medical, educational, and social specialists" working and over-working in these institutions for the good of society; and that the diversity of institutions operated by sisters is as broad as the spectrum of activity suggested above.

Indeed, even a cursory glance through the pages of the Catholic Directory will bear out the defense. For sisters operate schools and resident institutions not only for every age level, but for such special persons as the blind, the deaf, the emotionally disturbed, the mentally retarded, the socially delinquent, and the homeless. They train for business, for nursing, as well as for general living. Sisters in the medical fields care not only for general patients but also for incurables, convalescents, the aged and infirm, for foundlings and unwed mothers, and for psychiatric patients. Sisters also operate settlement houses and other houses for giving religious instruction and supervised recreation and club work; homes or hotels for transients, for working girls and students, for immigrants, for friendless women. They operate summer camps for children; retreat houses for girls, women, and married couples; and clinics—medical, psychological, and educational.

But if in the face of all this evidence of our "service of the brethren" the popes persist in asking us to "get back a more direct and full participation" in the Church's mission, it might be suggested that our *institutional apostolate* has either failed to be apostolic or is not *per se* sufficient for today's needs.

INSTITUTIONAL–PERSONAL

The words "institutional apostolate" have been italicized above because it seems to me that an appropriation and delineation of terms may be helpful in clarifying this suggested failure or insufficiency. Hence, I propose making a distinction, for the purposes of this chapter, between *personal apostolate* of religious women, and their *institutional apostolate*. Such a distinction of course may be valid only for the purposes of analysis. In practice the two must always somehow and somewhere be synthesized. Religious women, in witnessing to the *person* who is Christ, are also witnessing to the community that is his mysical body—to the *institution* that is his Church. It becomes a matter of emphasis; but this makes all the difference, for it is precisely the matter of emphasis that is changing the entire character of the Church since Vatican II.

Traditionally, religious women have worked within institutions belonging to their own order or congregation, or belonging to the parish or diocesan structure. The apostolic value of these institutions accrues both from their "presence" in society and from the impact made by them on the persons who make the effort of "going to" them. This value cannot be underestimated for it represents a service in many cases that could not be widely or successsfully provided in our complex society without the institutional framework. At the same time, however, few would hesitate to say that the apostolic character of such institutions depends ultimately on the personally apostolic character of the individuals working in them. And it is here that the matter of emphasis can account perhaps for significant failures. A negative example many provide the strongest illustration. A religious congregation assigns a "staff" of sisters to run a hospital or school or any other institution. Both because of professional requirements and because there are more and more people in the world to be served by this institution, the work is multiplied to the extent that finally it cannot be done as "persons serving persons." Indeed, the congregation is happy enough if the staff can "run the place," can get its "work" done, which usually means manipulating things. For if "it" does succeed in getting "it" done, the institution will somehow be successful!

In this negative example the emphasis is on institution as "institution" rather than on institution as made up of individual, apostolic, religious persons united in a common apostolate. Shifting the emphasis to the latter will be a slow and difficult process in many religious institutions. The difficulty has been seen in the Vatican Council where the process of de-emphasizing the hierarchically infallible structure of the Church and of emphasizing pastoral and personal responsibility has finally only been initiated. It is now necessarily left to be implemented by the individual bishops and Christians in their own milieus. The shift will be slow because it depends first of all on a change in mentality—in that mentality which somehow consecrated an unthinking doing of an assigned job and staying within its limits, waiting for the answers and directions from above; a mentality which held at least somewhat suspect any personal assumption of responsibility toward serving the persons encountered in and through that job.

The right interpretation of personal responsibility may well provide the key to the evolvement of a new mentality. For no one, least of all a superior, would deny that a sense of personal responsibility has always been expected and respected in each sister who was assigned to a job in any one institution. However, one wonders if the kind of responsibility expected was not simply the responsibility to do what she was told; to do the job only as the superior saw it; to think "institution" first, and personal apostolate second—if any time or energy was left for it. Of course, a superior must have a great deal of courage and faith in order to foster and respect in her subjects the kind of responsibility that requires of each individual sister the maturity to weigh both the common good and her apostolic role. This is so whether that superior is overseeing the work of twenty, or two hundred, or two thousand sisters. It is necessary first of all to establish a flexible or liberating psychological framework for the exercise of such individual responsibility—and the kind of subjects who can justify their superior's faith in them. This, incidentally, is the courage and faith Pope Paul is evincing in loosening his "infallibility" to the "collegiality" of some 2500 bishops scattered over the face of the earth. Such courage is not however to be admired only in those superiors who hap-

pen to possess it; it can and must be demanded of all superiors if even the *institutional apostolates* operated by
their congregations are to be worth the effort of maintain-
ing them.

A sense of individual and apostolic responsibility within
the common apostolate of the institution affects radically
not so much what work is done, but how it is done. The
woman who commented that she was not at all prepared
for assuming an apostolic role in the secular community is
a case in point. If she had received her education in an
institution where individual sisters not only gave her the
warmth and riches of their personal apostolic approach to
to their teaching, but who also radiated (both in their
classes and in whatever other contacts they had with
their students) their mature awareness of woman's role
both in the home and in public life, and their own awareness of and dedication to the needs of the Church and the
world, our young woman would have been prepared to
find her place in the secular community. She would not
have learned it in any one class; it would have resulted
from how the totality of her educational experience (the
sisters themselves especially) was geared.

Religious sisters can and do have an *institutional apostolate*. But in the final analysis this is not something different from a *personal apostolate*, for we may make our institutions apostolic only by shifting the emphasis so as to
signify that we exercise *personal apostolates within our
institutions*.

PERSONAL APOSTOLATES OUTSIDE THE INSTITUTION

We suggested some pages above that the popes' per-
sistence in asking sisters to "get back a more direct and
full participation" in the Church's apostolic mission might

indicate that our institutional apostolate (in spite of the multiplicity and diversity it exhibits) is not *per se* sufficient for today's needs. The tenor of our post-Vatican II-Church makes this more than a suggestion. Pope Paul himself, for example, in his short reign has made two history-shattering flights into foreign countries and has immersed himself while there in the non-Roman-Church elements he met. Paul, and the thousands of bishops and priests who are moving more and more in non-Catholic circles, is setting the example of a *personal apostolate in secular life* —in the world outside the pale of our Catholic institution. This is the new—the renewed—Church. A religious order or institute then, by virtue of its prerogative to witness "by community" to the "community" that is the Church, must be a "new, a renewed" congregation or institute if it is to be true to the image to which it is witnessing. The rest of this chapter, then, will deal precisely with the question of how religious communities can implement and effect personal apostolates by their sisters in secular life.

An Extension of Present Roles in Institutions

Probably the most assimilable and practical method for a religious (and her community) to begin effecting a personal apostolate in secular life is by extending outside her institution aspects of her present professional work. This sort of apostolate has actually been practiced by many sisters for many years. The value of discussing its possibilities here, then, is not to suggest a new apostolate, but only to stimulate individual sisters to exploit possibilities and, more important, to suggest that such an extension of her work outside the institution be properly valued, encouraged, and provided for in each sister's overall workload by both her major and her local superiors.

In general, what a sister's work within an institution
may provide her with are contacts outside, and these contacts may be grouped for the sake of clarity under such
labels as *personal-professional, civic-professional,* and *professional-professional.* All of them depend on the professional competence of the sister within the institution; that
is, any one of them will be successfully apostolic only if
the sister is first of all both highly competent and apostolically oriented in the performance of her work within
the institution itself.

An outside contact that I call personal-professional is
one that is made through or because of a person encountered in one's work within an institution. Thus, a sister-
teacher has contact with the parents of her pupils; a sister-
nurse with the family of her patients; a sister in charge of
specialized groups—such as delinquent girls, the blind,
deaf, or mentally retarded—again with parents or families
of these persons. Such a contact is begun as pupil- or
patient-oriented; that is, the contact may be made first
of all in order to understand the needs of that person, or
to inform the parents or families of these needs and thus
to contribute to a better solution of them. However, the
contact need not stop there—should not, if the sister is a
mature Christian. This contact can become an adult-ori-
ented association in which conversation may only begin
with "John has been so apathetic lately; I've wondered if
there is something you could tell me so that I can help
him?" Topics may then range from the "new breed" to the
"old breed"; to keeping up with the Church and with
society; to urban renewal and civil rights; to the State of
the Union message and birth control, and to a hundred
others.

Everything depends, of course, on whether the sister
knows enough about human relations, and about these

subjects, to listen and to respond, as well as to initiate ideas intelligently. For the first step of a personal apostolate of this kind is perhaps on the affective level rather than on the idea level. Its fruitfulness may be in the sister's opening of herself for communication, in a sharing of feelings and a diffusing of the love that is Christ, rather than in a meeting of intellects. Ideally the two levels are concomitant and prompt each other. Thus a sister and parent encounter over a pupil's lack of discipline may be most effective if it is begun as a sharing of attitudes toward discipline in terms of today's society and needs. However, a resultant discussion could embrace the whole area of human creativity and productivity as well as freedom and responsibility, or responsible parent-child love and teacher-pupil love. It might, on the other hand, become a round-table discussion among a group of parents and sisters and eventuate in a real growth on the part of all in their task of building the right kind of discipline both in their children and in themselves.

Leading or participating in group discussions, being members of panels or lecturing for groups or parents, are more formalized ways for a sister to extend her professional work within an institution over into the secular milieu in which her pupil or charge lives. Such activity takes time and energy, of course; hence, if it is considered an important extension of a sister's personal apostolate, both have to be given consideration.

Where and when a sister exercises this apostolic role with the parents of her pupils or patients, if that is to mean "in secular life," must also be considered. Does she wait for them to come to her at her convenience either in the classroom or in the convent? Probably not, or at least not always. Most effectively she would go to them in their homes, or at least meet them half-way—such as serving

with them in parish or civic movements. Visiting them in
their homes is one answer, and is considered potentially
effective enough for the good of pupils that many schools
require their sister-teachers to visit the home of each of
their students during the first few weeks of school each
fall. However, this kind of 15-minute formalized visit is
completely pupil-oriented and usually remains so. I think
sisters might explore the possibilities of less brief and less
patterned home visiting to the end of serving (of loving
and relating to) these adult persons as well as of serving
the young person who is their common responsibility.

The second kind of contact a sister might utilize for a
personal apostolate that flows from her profession within
a Catholic institution may be viewed as a widening of the
first, since she may be working side by side with these
same parents and others like them. This is the civic-professional contact, or the matter of using one's professional
know-how as an entry into such civic endeavors as interracial and civil rights movements, political meetings
especially regarding legislation affecting social welfare in
any one of its multiple aspects, and programs on anti-
poverty, urban renewal, and urban *mores*. All of these are
outgrowths of social problems; hence they would be
served knowledgeably best by sisters trained in sociology
and social work, in some of the medical fields, perhaps,
and by teachers in the social and political sciences and related areas. There is perhaps as broad an area for serving
cultural needs open to sisters whose professional know-
how is in the fine arts. Is it conceivable that a sister who
teaches drama might work in some way with a secular
theater group in her city, just as some sisters who teach
audio-visual arts work with the local TV studio in making
films? Certainly fine sister-musicians, -artists, -poets and
-dramatists, through their professional status within their

own institutions could effectively contribute to the cultural needs of their city and state by personally entering the arena of civic organizations that work to raise the cultural tone of society. As more and more sisters are trained professionally in theology and philosophy, are they not equipped to participate effectively in minister-level interfaith dialogue.

Since in this particular section we are limiting ourselves to the use of sisters' professional know-how in the service of civic betterment, one practical suggestion might be that religious congregations or institutions maintain a Speakers Bureau. This would involve only the preparing each fall of a list of sisters and the topics of talks they are ready to give, and sending it to all the civic organizations, schools, and church groups in the locality. Even if a half-dozen sisters prepare one talk each for the year (well enough to adapt it to different age and interest groups) the spread of such an endeavor could become incalculable within a few years.

The third and last kind of contact a sister's professional work gives her is what we facetiously labeled as the "professional-professional." While this is the most refined and demanding level of secular professional contact for a sister, it is nevertheless probably the one that the largest numbers of sisters have moved in. The reason for this is curiously selfish: a sister could justify attending professional meetings, or joining professional societies, on the grounds that doing so would benefit her. While there is nothing wrong with this reason, it is not sufficient. I suggest that sisters who are well-equipped professionally and personally should feel an obligation to participate in and contribute to their secular professional societies and to work with their secular professional peers in their own locale. And I suggest that doing so might constitute a very fruitful personal apostolate in secular life especially for a sister whose full time work within the institution is not conducive to more diversified apostolates. Furthermore, it is in their area that it is easiest to address all sisters—whether they are medical, social, or educational specialists in any type of institution—in the same general terms, for each can apply the example to her own professional group.

While many sisters do belong to secular professional societies, not enough of them serve as officers, speak at their conferences, or publish in their journals. There are variances, however. For example, in my state (Oklahoma) it is not unusual to find a Catholic sister elected to the presidency or chairmanship of a state hospital association or sub-group. On the other hand, it would be noteworthy to find her teacher-confrere an officer in a state educational group. No one is pleasantly *shocked* to see a sister's by-line in the highest professional journal; however, one is usually pleasantly *pleased* to find it there, indicating that this does not happen frequently enough to pass by unnoticed. For example, when one sister's article appeared in one of the finer, long-established English journals, I checked and discovered that this was the first by a sister in that journal's sixty-one years of publishing.

There are at least two reasons for this state of affairs: the first is that such "outside" activities are not considered part of a sister's workload when she receives her institutional assignment. Thus, for example, the time her professional counterpart in a secular university spends in writing articles and giving lectures, the sister-professor in a Catholic college probably spends in her second and third jobs—prefecting a dormitory *and* moderating the school publications. The fact is, of course, that the standards for scholarship and the competition for placement in a journal or on a program are high. Therefore, even in those national

secular associations with heavy sister-memberships, who
of these gifted sisters has been assigned the time and given
the motivation to do the kind of original scholarship that
can surmount such competition? I remember being impressed in this connection by the large numbers of sisters
at the meetings of the Modern Language Association and
by the fact that it has been a number of years since one
of their names has appeared on the program as giving a
paper.

A second reason why sisters do not contribute to secular
professional societies in proportion to their numbers may
be that many of those sisters who do make tremendous
contributions to professional organizations as such are
limited to Catholic organizations composed (until the recent influx of lay persons among Catholic institutional
personnel) almost entirely of religious. In this connection,
it may be time to pose the question: why duplicate these
organizations? Why maintain and underwrite an NCEA
when perhaps the most telling effect it may have in one
year at least is to keep Catholic educational specialists
from contributing toward the good of the NEA? It certainly was responsible for the absence from the NEA conventions of thousands of voters who might have changed
the outcome of some of the dubious resolutions passed
there. At the same time, the specifically Catholic values
the NCEA provides might still be given at a one-day conference held in connection with the NEA conventions.

Sisters have also a professional contact with their peers
in their own locale. A good example of how such a contact may become a continuing personal apostolate in secular life may be drawn from the story of the Good Shepherd
Sister which appeared in the January, 1965 issue of *The
Catholic Digest*. Sister Mary Philip spent a summer as a
probation officer working out of the City-Hall-Court-

House of St. Paul, Minnesota, in order to gain the on-the-job training required for a master's degree in social welfare work. In her capacity as a badge-carrying officer, Sister sat in on juvenile court staff meetings, ate in the cafeteria, and in general rubbed social and professional shoulders with the personnel of the probation office, the police and sheriff's office, and the welfare office. The real example to be drawn from the story, it seems to me, is only a hope that sister will be allowed and encouraged to use her familiarity with these offices in the city of any one of the homes operated by her order she is assigned to. There is also the hope that she might become sufficiently esteemed there to be asked to sit in on staff meetings, or to contribute in any other way that fits and benefits the social welfare and penal aspects of our society.

Examples of sisters who are doing a great deal in this direction are actually numerous. One that comes to mind is that of a sister-psychologist, who is a counselor in a private girls' academy. Sister not only maintains a close professional relationship with individual psychologists in her city, but she also meets with them in their professional groups, shares cases, takes and sends referrals, and is generally accepted and esteemed as one of them. Another example may be that of a sister-teacher of journalism in a high school who, because she handles the school publicity, has made herself part of her city newspaper offices, to the extent that city editors call her when they need a lead for tracking down some "Catholic" information, or some advice on how to approach the sister-administrators in other Catholic institutions. They do this, however, not because sister is apostolic, but first of all because she knows their business as well as they do.

And knowing their profession as well or better than "they" do is the first indispensable qualification for all

the personal apostolates in secular life suggested in this
section of our chapter. It is not the only one. If she is to
be effectively apostolic as a religious woman in this capacity, she must be equally well qualified as a woman and as a
religious. Briefly this may mean that she brings into her
work the special qualities of a woman—"tact, delicacy, and
the maternal instinct"—and the special aptitudes of a religious: total commitment to the love of God expressing
itself in love and service to others. In the final analysis,
of course, only the religious woman who is effectively personal and apostolic in her professional role within an institution will be so in this type of apostolate outside that institution. However, apostolic action may beget its own
grace; and a sister who has lost (if she ever had) the
spark in her institutional role may find it ignited through
the challenge of witnessing to Christ's redeeming love as
an individual person in a secular situation, especially in
one where she is knowledgeable or capable enough to
sense (and thus generously to donate again) her personal
worth.

Part Time Apostolates in Secular Life

The distinction between the kinds of apostolic activity,
and the time involved in them, in this section and those of
the previous section is less apparent than it is real. For
this reason there is value in emphasizing the distinction.
In this section we will recognize or suggest some apostolic
activities sisters may undertake in secular situations which
are more diversified in character, and which require perhaps only more general training or qualifications. Furthermore, the emphasis here is on the fact that this is work
taken on in addition to the full time job held by the sister
within an institution, while the emphasis above was on
the fact that the exercise of her professional role outside

the walls of her institution is part and parcel of a sister's work inside that institution and, hence, should be recognized and provided for as such by those who determine her workload.

The report of the program inaugurated by the Sisters of Charity of New York in the summer of 1964, even the brief one given in the *National Catholic Reporter*,[8] offers a wealth of suggestions for diversified apostolic work. I can only repeat some of them and then suggest a few others that may follow the needs of other areas of the country.

In general, the kind of activities sisters might "go out" to engage in fall into such categories as the following: visiting—in homes, in hospitals and social welfare institutions, in jails and other penal institutions;[9] teaching religion to children who cannot attend Catholic schools or classes in religion, and teaching other subjects to those in depressed areas who cannot receive adequate instruction in general; supervising, in depressed areas, recreational activities, crafts, and cultural activities, including taking children on trips to culture centers—museums, zoos and parks, fairs, and entertainment events; leading discussions with groups of adults or young adults and giving adult education lectures to the spiritually and culturally needy as well as to the materially needy; meeting personally the diversified needs of persons in such centers as Newman Clubs on secular campuses, charities offices, and information officers; bringing medical care to such places as the migrant workers' camps by means of mobile clinics; training lay persons for CCD work; and collaborating with existing civic and church groups such as the interracial

[8]Nov. 13, 1964, p. 7.
[9]There is a sister in Chicago who for seventeen years has carried on an apostolate of visiting jails every Sunday.

councils, Christian Family Movement, dialogue groups, the National Council of Christians and Jews, and others.

If such apostolic activities as the above do not require specialized professional training, many of them nevertheless can be carried on most successfully only by sisters with some training as teachers, or social workers, or in the medical professions. At the same time, what all of them require more than anything else are the human qualities of understanding and resourcefulness that come from life experience coupled with good general educational background, and more specifically they need the precisely feminine human qualities that have been fused with a total religious commitment. And some activities require only these human and religious qualities. However, given these qualifications, sisters will need to have studied or learned in some way about such things as today's social problems, group dynamics, apostolic opportunities and methods (plus a good deal of biblical and liturgical theology) if their part time work in these secular situations is to be effectively and successfully apostolic.

Sisters can engage in other part time works that reach into secular life in an apostolic way, but which are more particularized both as to qualifications and to area of influence. Such is the writing and publishing done by sisters for the general market; the letter-writing apostolate of some shut-in sisters, and the writing of letters to newspapers and congressmen on important issues. Such also includes part time teaching in a secular university, or over educational TV, both of which are more and more commonly being done by religious women; and it may extend to the part time employment of a sister-musician in a philharmonic orchestra.

Since all of these apostolic endeavors constitute part time work for the sister who engages in any one or more of them, the important issue is the allotment of time for them. When do sisters carry on such personal apostolates in secular life? The Sisters of Charity of New York took on theirs as summer employment (or for a week of the summer) when their schools were closed. However, they and hundreds of sisters throughout the country are somehow trying to sandwich something of this work into their full time schedules within their institutions. Doing so without a serious re-thinking and re-planning of their total workloads may eventuate in physical, spiritual, and psychological havoc for individual sisters; or in institutional havoc where sisters are so taken up with their outside activities that they do not perform their work justly within the institution. And either havoc may eventuate in ecenomic problems for the community or congregation.

The economics of any human situation somehow influences, and may effect real control over, other elements in that situation. And yet one has a certain hesitancy about admitting the economics of the apostolate—perhaps that is why the basic problem of sisters engaging in it more fully has not been faced and solved. We want to work for nothing—that was part of giving oneself to God. And the effort to keep this spirit of generosity alive in sisters perhaps accounts for the administrative reluctance to talk about this aspect of the situation. Furthermore, the differences in situations makes it impossible to generalize. Some religious institutions are financially affluent enough to underwrite a program of extra apostolic work by their sisters. Others, especially in the less dense and less affluent Catholic population centers, are caught in a dilemma. Some, in giving themselves generously and without remuneration to the extra apostolic work while carrying on herculean tasks within their institutions in order to support themselves, now have the added expense of medical aids for sisters whose health has thereby been broken; others, in showing reluctance to make this kind of sacrifice, have been condemned as selfish and non-apostolic. However, sisters who have given themselves wholeheartedly and then found themselves financially straitened have been equally condemned (and their generosity quickly forgotten) for not being able to support themselves.

The subject then is important enough to demand our discussing it before completing our survey of apostolic works religious women may undertake. However, our doing so at this point is not to indicate that economics does not influence the choice and implementation of the suggestions in the previous and the following sections of this chapter. For in the final analysis, the reason a sister cannot exert leadership in her professional associations is that the congregation cannot (or will not) afford to provide (or hire) someone else "to prefect that dormitory!" Such an attitude is basically due to poor judgment about how we fulfill our present roles, not only in a full and apostolic way, but also economically most advantageously. In the works described in this section something else comes into play, and that is the whole matter of our assimilating new roles to fit the needs and the image of our Vatican II Church. Hence, administrative heads of religious congregations must do some creative thinking about insuring a sound economy in their shifting structures; They deserve not only sympathy in this task, but also some positive suggestions.

But as we have already suggested above, the economics of religious houses as it affects workloads differs so widely not only over the country but also within one small area, and even within the various branch houses of one community in a small area, that it is impossible to give any one example as applying to all. Making a division between working in an institution that belongs to the congregation and in one that does not (such as the parish or diocesan school) is perhaps a practical device, but it is far from being universally justified. Hence, each reader will have to apply one or other principle of evaluation to her own situation. With this in mind, I suggest that there are sisters in this country who are overworking. They are perhaps assigned to jobs that should require two persons; hence, in order to do the second person's job, they sacrifice those activities especially geared to cultivating their persons in relation to God and to the other persons with whom they create "com-unity"—prayer time, reading and spiritual study time, common meal time, and time for communication and recreation. Now if all these jobs are essential to the common good and there are no more sisters available to do them, the obvious answer would seem to be that lay help should be hired, first of all for the less costly and less apostolically fruitful labor.[10] In some cases, however, a religious institute will not consider hiring more lay help regardless of their financial state simply because there is a traditional mentality opposed to hiring anyone so long as there is a sister still able to maintain a vertical posture. In other cases there is genuine financial inadequacy because the complex building demands and wage scale of today's institutions make it difficult to operate a non-profit organization out of the red.

[10]At the risk of being simplistic, I might comment that the incongruity of sisters doing the work of two persons in the light of today's problem of unemployment deserves some thought. It might be suggested, indeed, that religious congregations could make their first contribution to social welfare by giving employment to some of the unemployed and thereby make it possible for their sisters to be sufficiently whole women that they can truly witness as religious women.

Many of those congregations, then, who have generously responded to the Church by taking on part time apostolates in the secular community in addition to their institutional apostolate have only amplified the workload-economics problem. For sisters have been allowed and even encouraged by their superiors to take on such work, and have done so enthusiastically, but there has been no concomitant balancing of their workload within the institution. And the reason is so obvious it is usually ignored: the congregation that is barely making financial ends meet cannot pay out today's salaries to additional personnel who will replace sisters so that they can take on extra work *for nothing.* And the majority (there are exceptions) of the part-time apostolic activities suggested for sisters are non-remunerative.

In spite of all this, the complexity of the economic situation will no longer excuse sisters from taking on at least part time apostolic works in secular life. My concern in elaborating on the economic element is only to emphasize the need for creative thinking on all levels of religious life and work, lest having somehow produced a "biblically-liturgically-apostolically-centered" community of religious women, they find themselves made inoperative by emonomics. Religious today are expected (and have been exhorted by the popes) to earn their own living. And why not? Even St. Paul stopped preaching to make tents to support himself when the preaching itself did not.[11]

The thinking then must be creative. If to fit the image of the Vatican II Church religious congregations come to administer fewer and less complex institutions and enter diversified personal apostolates outside, a more flexible economy must (and can) be devised. A balance of some

[11] See Acts 18.

high-paying outside work against other donated services is one suggestion. Efficiency studies on use of personnel to their highest apostolic effectiveness is another. Such studies, however, can only be valuable if the ones making them begin with an understanding of the theology of the religious life and the value of the religious woman as a witness to Christ and his Church in the world. With this understanding, they will probably gauge first what a woman needs—for example, the time for praying, reading, relaxing, and working—in order to have and to radiate that extra dimension required if she is to "be" a *religious* woman. From here then our creative economists can begin to blue-print suggestions for an economy that will support (and this includes the training of the young and the caring for the retired and the sick) a community in different kinds of apostolates.

Full Time Work in Secular Situations

In this third and last section on personal apostolates for sisters outside Church institutions, no new kinds will be suggested; some of those given in the two previous sections will simply be re-drawn as full time employment for individuals or groups of sisters. Since the works themselves are the same, all of the personal qualifications and the community aspects concerning them pointed out above will hold, if anything to a greater degree, when the sister is spending all her working hours in a secular situation.

An individual sister may (has in some cases; could in others) fill a professional position in a secular university or school, in a secular hospital either on general or on special duty, in a research center (either academic or professional), in a psychological testing or counseling center, in a social welfare agency, or in association with a more particularized specialization such as the fine arts or the practical arts. If she does so, it may be assumed that she has been hired or appointed to it first of all because she is professionally qualified—and probably better qualified than her peers in order to offset the unusual aspect of her being a religious. On the other hand, if she is to achieve an effective apostolate worthy of her community's faith in placing her in such a position, she must also qualify exceptionally well as a woman, and as a religious woman. And the three are designedly given in that order: professional-woman-religious.

Sister Mary William, the Daughter of Charity of St. Vincent de Paul who directs a social service agency in a public housing project for Chicago's' poor, as reported in the May, 1964, issue of *Today*, is a good example. She was placed in her position by her superiors fundamentally because she is "a tough-minded professional," not because she was burning up with religious apostolic zeal to serve God's' poor. And this in spite of the fact that it is certainly the latter qualities that have given her work its special grace and effectiveness. The balance of emphasis is especially important in the "social" type of apostolate; for there are sisters, sitting perhaps in their classrooms feeling apostolically frustrated, convinced that they would be transformed into wonder-working apostles if their communities would only allow them to attempt something equivalent to Sister Mary William's Rendu House, where they could serve out counsel and love along with a friendly cup of coffee.

Fewer apostolic day-dreamers would take on professorships in secular university, or special-duty nursing in a secular hospital, without the required degrees, of course. The professional competence needed in these positions is not greater than that of Sister Mary William in her job; but it is as great. The president of the Rhode Island col-

lege that hired the Grey Nun, Sister St. Jean de Milan, to
their psychology department explained to the press that
she was simply "the best applicant for the position." The
sister-psychologist mentioned previously would be hired in
a minute to a medical center staff she associates with if
her congregation would see fit to release her for such full
time employment. I am reminded also of a sister who
worked in her doctoral research toward determining and
regulating the ovulation cycle in mice and who was invited as a result to work with a secular research team on
scientific investigation that will bring more light and more
reliance on the rhythm method for controlling human
fertility. One can only be thrilled by the apostolic dimensions which that gifted sister could bring to such an assignment, working as she would be with the top-level
minds who will influence the outcome of the human and
social problem of overpopulation.

As in this last example, the appointment of sisters to
secular positions has come about in many cases naturally,
as well as by Church encouragement, through their having
worked closely with their peers through graduate or other
research programs in their special fields, and even through
their having continued their association through professional channels.

Sisters who are assigned full time to work in Newman
Centers on secular campuses need not in every case be
highly specialized. At the same time, some of them should
be (and be recognized as such on the university faculty)
in order that their work in the Newman Center will be
esteemed in relation to its academic environment. These
sisters need also more general qualifications: the understanding and gift for counseling young people, women
especially; the ability to lead discussions on a variety of
topics; and the talent for organizing and administering
programs of various kinds.

The other types of part time apostolic work requiring more general training of the kind usually signified under CCD courses (theological and methodological) may also become full time employment. It is difficult to maintain a strict separation here between what is a Catholic-institutional apostolate and what is done outside an institutional framework. For how is a well-organized, full time catechical and parish worker program in a parish (or a diocese) not "institutional"? Or an adult education program administered in a given place or operated by a given group? The need for a distinction is only technical, however, and need not be labored. In practice, the work fits our discussion if it is highly personalized and requires to some extent at least the sisters' working off of the parish or diocesan community property; that is, it requires their going to the people rather than waiting in every case for people to come to them. A mixture of the two will remain in any full time program.

A description of one example will suffice to suggest the varying possibilities latent in such full time apostolic endeavors. A group of sisters may work out from a parish house or school facility, or out from their motherhouse, in diversified capacities. They, or some of them, may hold catechetical classes for children in public schools at those times and in those places convenient to the children. They will also conduct discussion and lecture programs with adults. Some of them will spend most of their time going to homes and to individuals in welfare institutions to offer to these people what constitutes the spiritual and corporal works of mercy—the love that shows itself in comfort, counsel, instruction; in caring for the sick, the hungry, the poorly clothed, the bored, and the depressed. And they will make themselves known as always being available for such services in the center from which the work.

Perhaps the value, the extent, and the reason for involving sisters in such work can be grasped more readily if it is called by the generic name under which it most truly falls: this is "pastoral" work. And the Church in calling on women religious to perform it (whereas she also calls on the laity to do so) is seeking to enlist the special prerogative of "religious-woman-witness" to the sharing of a pastor's work. The priests who are most ardently advocating such a sharing will describe its need as concerning women especially, who cannot get from priests the help they need (or the particular kind of sympathy) in many of their problems and situations, but who could do so, and might be prone to seek it, more readily from a "woman of God." Such service might also be made effectively available by individual sisters in secular or state, as well as Catholic, charity offices, welfare offices, and information centers. It should take on also the dimension of a sister's giving lectures and individual counselling to women during retreats and recollection days, and all in all answering the needs and the call of the Church to be a woman of God in the diaspora which is our modern society.

The practical implementation of a response to this call requires sane as well as zealously creative thinking. In addition to all that has been said or implied previously in this tone, it might be suggested that the value in a sister's full time employment in a secular situation will be most fully realized if the initiative for taking on the work comes from her rather than from the administrative level of her religious congregation. For if she has the professional qualifications to understand the nature and demands as well as the apostolic potential of the work, and the womanly and religious enthusiasm to respond to that potential, she is probably the only one in a position to judge

whether it should be undertaken at all. This is assuming
also that she is sensitive to the truest ideals and the common good of her congregation. However, such a sister will
not be able to make such a judgment unless she has had
some experience in the work, either in her institutional
role or part time outside that role. In other words, that
sister is probably one who has demonstrated her ability to
exercise a *personal* apostolate within her present *institutional* framework, and thereby her ability to do so in another kind of institutional framework, or what will become so if it begins to involve numbers of persons.

There are exceptions. Some sisters have had both the
personal and the apostolic sense killed in them by their
institutions; for any highly stylized or formalized process
is dehumanizing—in persons as it is in art forms. Some of
these sisters will revive in a personally responsible role
outside that institution, but few if any will do so without
a concomitant renewal of their humanity and spirituality
in "com-unity" in the best Vatican II sense. And all of
them will do so best, in the full time sense, initially within
their institutions supplemented by apostolic contacts outside.

I am suggesting then that, concomitantly with entering
diversified personal apostolates, congregations of religious
see to personalizing their institutional apostolates in such
a way that sisters sense some of the same value in their
service in them as they do in ventures outside, and that
simultaneously the recipients of their service feel the impact of this personal love. Thus, by each sister's cooperating in a personal and, hence, responsible way toward the
common good and goal, the institution which is their
"communal self" will be of the caliber to witness worthily
to the "com-unity" which is the Church and the people
of God. And such a witnessing is needed and will continue

to be needed in a society that portends to become more rather than less complex and institutionalized as it grows denser and more urbanized.

In another sense, the institutional apostolate will remain with us, even if more and more sisters are placed in work outside it, certainly as long as it takes to train and re-train sisters for other types of work; and also as long as it will take to make a change-over from an institutionally-framed economy to an individually-salaried and non-salaried economy. And there is reason to think that many congregations of religious sisters will always maintain both kinds of apostolates to the advantage of both—but both.

For an apostolate in the secular life outside our institutions is also essential if we are to be true to our renewed image, the Church, and to the exhortation of her pre-eminent servant, Pope Paul, who said, "It is not a privilege to remain on the fringes of the life of the Church and to build a spirituality of your own that has nothing to do with sharing of words,of grace and of charity that is proper to the Catholic comunity of the brethren in Christ"— that Christ who "went about doing good and healing all."

9

The American Sister Today

Sister M. Daniel Turner, S.N.D. de Namur

The American sister—strictly speaking, there is neither precedent nor parallel in the long history of the Church for the contemporary American sister. True, she reflects the western cultural tradition to which she belongs, and, in particular, the Western monastic tradition. In the structure of religious life which she has inherited and in many usages of American communities, these influences prevail. But the sisters in the United States differ profoundly, even within a given congregation, from their colleagues abroad because of the milieu in which they live and in which most communities have been developing for many years —the new world of United States Catholicism.

This new world evolved in the middle years of the last century. Separation of Church and state as Americans then conceived it meant that the state felt no responsibility for religious education. At the same time it provided for compulsory schooling and set up a system of its own, secular in theory, but for the greater part of the nineteenth century, militantly Protestant in practice. For the children of the immigrant majority in the Catholic population, situated at the bottom of the social scale, these schools represented a spiritual peril of the first magnitude.

Catholic schools were imperative. Into this breach stepped the religious communities of women. It seems sometimes, reviewing their history, as if they must have sprung up out of the prairies so rapid and so difficult to explain was their early growth. They came, however, from France, Western Germany and Belgium, from countries of a far different cultural and political milieux from that of the American prairies. By the standards of the day, many of these religious were well educated women. Few indeed were less so than the parents of the children who thronged their classrooms. They were in a strong position, needed, respected, cherished even; vocations multiplied.

A century later, on the whole still needed, respected and generally popular among Catholics, the United States communities of religious women took a thoughtful look at themselves. Though the contemporary criticism of Catholic education was then hardly begun, the religious communities realized from self-examination that they were not responding adequately to the needs of their time. Stimulated by the directives of Pope Pius XII and the challenges of a pluralist society, the sisters resolved to grow in stature—spiritually, professionally, apostolically. They set about the task with feminine realism.

At the NCEA meeting in Kansas City, 1952, a little group under the energetic leadership of Sister Mary Emil, I.H.M., decided that something should be done about the education of sisters. By 1955 they were holding their first regional Sister Formation meetings; in 1956, supported by the Ford Foundation, a representative group met to devise the Everett Curriculum. In the same year the Holy See established formally the Conference of Major Superiors. In its organization a notable departure from European precedent occurred. Expected to follow this pattern of accepting a priest as president of the Con-

ference of Major Superiors of *Women,* the American
Mothers General and Provincials sturdily declined, choosing instead Mother M. Gerald, the able mother general of
the Adrian Dominicans.

Meanwhile the sister Formation Conference went from
success to success. One community after another adopted
the policy of keeping young sisters in training until their
professional preparation was completed. Under the imagi-
native editorship of Sister Ritamary, C.H.M., the Sister
Formation *Bulletin* acquired more and more influence.
When she retired from the editorship, in the fall of 1964,
the circulation had reached 11,000, including nearly all
American sisters in formation work, and many abroad.
In 1960 Sister Annette, C.S.J., already distinguished for
her work in psychology, succeeded Sister Mary Emil as
executive secretary. She inaugurated a close and fruitful
association with Anglican sisters, sponsored innumerable
conferences and workshops; steadily she broadened the
horizons of the sisterhoods in the United States.

In August, 1964, the Sister Formation Conference was
placed under the direction of a new Committee of the
Conference of Major Superiors, thus bringing the two
organizations into a clearly defined relationship. Together
they express the dynamic, or if you will charismatic, spirit
that pulsates within the religious sisterhoods today.

It is the American sister, considered precisely as the
personification of this spirit, that is my subject—the American sister *today.* More keenly than ever before in our history, we American sisters are conscious of our responsibility to our today: the present moment, that moment (the
Kairos) which Bernard Häring describes "as the whisperings of grace and the external circumstances of our lives;
those especially which relate to the needs of our neighbor
and the community." Indeed the essays in this book have

so amplified the whisperings and so concretized the circumstances of the present moment that the whisperings have become for the thoughtful reader mighty roars, and the circumstances unprecedented challenges. If, however, the whisperings and the circumstances of our day are also graces, then our response will indicate how meaningful the present moment, *the Kairos,* is for us, and conversely how meaningful is our *being* to the present moment. We cannot therefore reply to the whisperings and meet the circumstances with phrases and attitudes that were significant for another historical-socio-cultural period. No. We must communicate in terms that speak to our today, and the search for such terms constitutes for us an immediate responsibility.

Before responding to the many and varied problems, doubts, and proposals that this book has presented, can we not discern among the whisperings certain basic questions that are being asked of the American Sister today? I think we can. They are, I submit, no different from the fundamental questions being asked of every man in an existentially-oriented world: Who are you? What meaning have you for me?

Specific Nature of the Religious

It is, therefore, the very *person* of the religious, not the validity of her work, that the world is questioning today. The work is recognized as valid; non-religious are engaged in it. Why, then, is the religious necessary if any Christian can carry out the work she is doing? Is she giving to that work something other than a non-religious worker is able to give? These questions, focused on the apostolate, shift emphasis to the wrong areas of investigation. It would be better for the Christian community if the religious herself would take a long look at the questions of identity and apostolate. If she herself has no satisfactory sense of identity *as* religious she will never be able to clear the focus trained on her by the world around her— a world which will continue to ask: Who are you? What meaning have you for me? If these questions are not acknowledged, the conclusion will inevitably be: You *are* irrelevant.

However, if these fundamental questions are, I will not say answered, but respected, and respected within the context of the gospel imperatives, then our *Kairos,* our today, will be relevant for tomorrow. We shall respect these questions if we realize that they are not the restive queries of an adolescent world. Rather man, becoming more keenly aware of the saving acts of God in and through history, understands now as never before that "nothing finite or determinate can be final." Precisely because salvation history is mystery, precisely because God, in the words of Father Thomas Barrosse, "enables man to experience his Person more fully through so many successive divine irruptions into the world of man," man realizes poignantly he must never stop questioning who he is and what is his meaning for other men. The questions must be asked anew each day—*today.* God is revealing himself through man today. By facing and honestly trying to answer the questions erupting from our milieu, we can come to a greater sense of our own identity and a consequent understanding of our mission.

What then is the part of religious in this "saving divine self-revelation"? What is the truth of our vocation? Unequivocally the Council Fathers affirm: "It is evident to everyone that all the faithful of Christ, whatever their rank or status, are called to the fullness of the Christian life and the perfection of charity" (chap. V, sec. 40). By the vows of baptism all persons are committed to perfection. In the Christian economy there is no compromise.

To a great multitude, not to an exceptional few, Christ challenged: "None of you can be my disciple if he does not take leave of all that he possesses" (Luke 14:33). Can we then in seeking to answer this query "who are you" reply with conventional phrases? Can we say without qualification that the religious are those who live in a state of perfection? Can we affirm that religious within the Christian community serve God directly, that is, with undivided heart, with greater love? I think not. It is not that these conventional phrases are invalid, much less meaningless. But often these very phrases imply for many persons a denial of the radical transformation that becomes every Christian. Against the background of the gospel, these phrases appear to be not only a misconstruction of the truth of our religious profession but also a depreciation of the beauty and grandeur of our Christian vocation.

For if we maintain that by religious vows we love God directly, the implication is that others, non-religious, love him indirectly. How can we reconcile this dictum with that glorious truth of Christianity, applicable to all Christians, that each act of love unites us directly to God, that ontologically we are transformed, Christified by grace?

Moreover, how can we in any valid way conclude that we love God more than non-religious? To reply that this is so because we serve him with undivided hearts is to speak as if the vows worked automatically—*ex opere operato!* Such an operation might prove inviting, but only to those who forget that the greatness and fecundity of love lie not in passivity, but in the daily, active surrender of self to another. Would it not be more realistic, and thus more Christian, to insist that *each* person, religious and non-religious, must love God with an undivided heart, and only in this way—by striving for a total and unconditioned surrender of self to God— does the individual, whatever form his Christian existence may take, fulfill his baptismal commitment and thus have positive meaning for his brother?

Unity of All Christians

To answer the questions concerning the truth of our calling, we religious must follow the leadership of St. Paul. We must appreciate more deeply that divine simplicity which unifies and harmonizes the various modes of being within the Church. To respond to the Christian vocation is to encounter Christ; to experience the Christian vocation is to be in Christ. There is no other calling: "You are one body, with a single spirit; each of you, when he was called, called in the same hope; with the same Lord, the same faith, the same baptism. . . . But each of us has received his own special grace, dealt out to him by Christ's gift" (Eph 4:4-8).

If we ponder this truth—You are one body—we cannot but conclude that the religious profession, which we have traditionally called a second baptism, in no way separates us from the people of God, in no way supplants the responsibilities, the exigencies of first baptism. Rather we must maintain that every response made in perfect love to the Spirit's call—whatever its specificity—produces anew the effects of our first baptism. Through the various modes of being, as a Christian, each person must incarnate Christ, die and rise again with Christ. Each must re-live this paschal mystery. Each Christian, religious and non-religious, must, if he takes his baptismal commitment seriously, live a new kind of existence (Rom 6:5).

What ever the form in which they live out their baptismal vows, all Christians must bear witness to this truth: the paschal mystery is the only reality. Each Christian's relation to the secular world, that is, the world inasmuch as it is opposed to and alienated from God, is fundamentally the same: like Christ, the Christian must die and rise in order that this world may be restored, integrated, transformed. Possession through renunciation, growth through diminishment, life through death—this is the radical position of every committed Christian, religious and lay. If this be so, it follows that the answers we religious conventionally offer to the crucial question "who are you" are not answers at all because they are not directed to the clarification of identity which we need. If all Christians, by virtue of their baptism, are committed to love God directly, with undivided hearts, then what makes the religious a necessary person in salvation history? We must probe further.

There are some who would make the distinction between religious and non-religious one of orientation and perspective. Christ—God and man, God-with-us and God transcendent, who pitched his tent among us and whose kingdom is not of this world—this is the Christ that all Christians are committed to be by virtue of their baptismal incorporation. It is concluded that the apparent dichotomy which is at one in Christ and in the Mystical Body as a whole can be worked out in the individual Christian only by a dominance of one of the terms. Such reasoning makes the non-religious Christ in this world, in the flesh, united to humanity, and the religious a witness to Christ's otherness, his transcendence of this world of the flesh. But if in Christ immanence and transcendence are not separated, and if by baptism every Christian is in Christ, does it not follow that each is in the whole Christ, and that each must bear witness to the whole of his reality? If the world is to see Christ in the Christian, must not the Christian be so integrated that the world sees the same apparent dichotomy that is in Christ mirrored in his members? Otherwise we miss the "many-splendored thing" our baptism has made of us: Christ, wholly other and yet Emmanuel.

What distinguishes the members of the Body, it seems to me, then, is not that the non-religious is this-world, immanent, incarnational in his orientation, and the religious other-world, transcendent, eschatological in his perspective. To make these the specifying characteristics of the two states is, I submit, to negate what has happened to us all in Christ. As *Christians* we must all be in the world, but yet not of it. Presence to the world and other-worldliness are not antithetical; they are paradoxical, if you will, but, more precisely, within the Christian vocation they are complementary. Any other position is simply non-Christian. In the sacrament of initiation all Christians pass over from death to life; all are incorporated into the body of Christ. In passing through the waters of baptism all Christians "suffer a sea-change into something rich and strange." The plunging into the paschal mystery is thus accomplished at baptism; by it our whole life is oriented toward living out the death-resurrection mystery.

But it is not for every Christian to use the same means in the living out of the paschal mystery. This can be accomplished in distinctive ways. Each way, however, involves the incarnation: the wedding of the human and the divine through the kenosis of Christ—a kenosis not of destruction but of transformation (Phil 2:5). Christ's kenosis, the giving of self through self-emptying, was realized by a total dispossession of himself—his divinity and his humanity.

Both in baptism and in life, transforming union follows this incarnational archetype. The kenosis of the suffering Servant, Christ, is common to all life; but the fulfillment, the living out of the kenosis, admits of more or less radical means. What does identify the Christian within the Mystical Body is, I suggest, the "special grace dealt out to him by Christ's gift"—the *means* he uses to realize his baptismal vows.

Some Christians choose to live out their baptismal commitment through the baptismal vows alone. These are the non-religious, non-married Christians in whom the wedding of the human and the divine effected at baptism is perpetuated and perfected in their realizing the death-resurrection mystery in their daily choices—choices continually involving an emptying of self and a consequent intensification of union with God. Thus their living out of the kenosis is accomplished by means which are intrinsic to their baptismal identity.

Those who realize their baptismal vows in and through marital union express symbolically the wedding of the human and the divine through selfless loves, through personal kenosis. Yet the *means* they choose to incarnate this union are the natural means man uses for self-giving, for self-transcendence.

Distinguishing Mark of the Religious

Thus, I conclude that what distinguishes the religious within the Christian community is the *radical means,* the vows of poverty and chastity which she chooses to guarantee her participation in the paschal mystery; her sharing in the world's transformation. Moreover, I suggest that the religious by the vow of obedience is totally, unreservedly, and irrevocably at the disposition of the Church. She wills to follow the Lamb wherever he may go, not only in eternity, but also in time. Realizing the good invested in the basic human powers of generativity, proprietorship and independence the religious lays these radical life forces at the disposal of the Church. She thus gives visible and unique witness to that virginal quality which must characterize every Christian's relation to God. She incarnates the truth that this virginization is only possible to the degree that the Christian life is a sharing in the death-resurrection mystery of Christ. She makes no less present in her person the incarnational dimension of Christ's life—his saving action among men in and through a life of uncompromising obedience. But she does this through *radical means*.

For us religious, then, the really critical questions will always concern the vows, the radical means we have taken to realize our baptismal commitment. Do the vows as we live them *today* effect what they signify? Do these radical means, in our hands, recover for the Church, make available to the Church, as Teilhard de Chardin thought they should, "the power invested in love, in gold, and in independence"?

Yet in stating that the really critical questions concerning religious identity pertain to the vows, we must remember, too, the uderlying supposition that the use of radical means presupposes radical integration in the person wielding such means. For the Christian community the ultimately crucial question is always going to be: what is the *quality* of the person who elects a religious life, who chooses the way of the vows. To call attention to this basic presupposition no doubt appears trite. Yet we religious cannot afford to forget that to be vowed to Christ through poverty, chastity, and obedience demands a fully integrated person. Total surrender implies total possession of self. And having said this, I think we have the *key* to our original questions—Who are you? What meaning have you for me? For if a person chooses radical means for realizing her selfhood within the Christian community, in fact within the world, she indicates that,

for her, *to be* is to be for others. For her, integrity, freedom, responsibility are realized most fully in communion
with others. The radical means ensure for her the maxi-
mum of liberty for charity.

If religious are totally integrated persons, then I would
like to think that, of all Christians, they are the most open,
the most responsive to the charismatic spirit that envigo-
rates the Mystical Body to guarantee its continuing
growth. If religious have *in fact* risked all, surrendered all;
if they have, not merely metaphorically but really, uprooted themselves, then I would hope that they would be
the instruments for the Holy Spirit's constant renewal of
the face of the earth. For, I submit, that by choosing the
vows of poverty, chastity, and obedience, we religious
realistically affirm that all finite expressions of the divine
are precisely that—finite. The religious cannot confine or
limit Christ's creative presence or power to any human
mode of being and action, no matter how exalted.

Thus, made aware by their very profession of the responsibility to question, to evaluate existing patterns of
thought and life, religious are not defensive or hostile to
the reality of change. Religious accept change as a positive
force within the Christian life. I would like to think that
Father Robert Johann's words are best verified in religious: "Man no longer sees himself as being responsible
merely for bringing his conduct into conformity with pre-
existing patterns. . .; he feels himself now responsible for
the very patterns themselves. . . . They (the patterns)
must be measured . . . for their shortcomings against the
very (transcendent) values they try to express."

Is this not an option for instability? Is this not a cham-
pioning of change for novelty's sake, for sensationalism?
No, for "perpetual renovators" are not iconoclasts—de-
stroyers. They are discoverers. Their discovery reveals that

the Christian vocation, and thus the religious vocation, is a call, a call to love from Love—a love that is infinite, a love that "seeks an ever fuller presence" among men. It is an openness to this ever fuller Presence which precludes hardness or opacity on the one side and rebellion or chaos on the other. "Perpetual renovators" are not seeking change *per se;* they are seeking a fullness of love. Love, the most stabilizing reality, grounds man not in narcissistic infantilism, but in the fullness of being. Questions then are never raised and decisions are never made in isolation, in separateness, in alienation from God or others. Questions are asked, decisions are made in communion with others.

THE CONCEPT OF COMMUNITY

Fundamental then to any questions we may propose concerning the vows, those radical means we have chosen for realizing our part within the Mystical Body, is our understanding of the concept of community. The vows are means. They exist for the religious; the religious does not exist for them. I maintain, however, that this truth can be distorted, even negated, unless the vows are understood as powers, potencies for realizing communal living.

No doubt one of the life-long sacrifices which the religious experiences is her surrender of conjugal love, the marital union which consummates this love, and the fruit of that union, the family. The surrender of this love *is* radical. The religious community can not substitute for it. The religious community is *sui generis.* But through this surrender, or more accurately through the living out of her vow of chastity, the religious accepts greater responsibility for salvific solidarity among Christians. The choice of a particular community is, I would like to suggest, not a

choice of a new family, but a choice of more responsible
fellowship (*Koinonia*) for the service of the family of God.
The title *sister* expresses this reality with succinct pre-
ciseness, provided we do not restrict its meaning or define
its truth within the limits of the familial concept. I would
carry this idea a step farther.

Do we really communicate the radical nature of our
choice of consecrated chastity when we identify, at least
by analogy, the terms *community* and *family?* Such an
analogy it seems to me denigrates our radical surrender
as well as the total involvement implicit in the word *community* as it refers to religious institutes. It is the very
communal dimension of the religious consecration that is
its awe-full responsibility and glory.

Am I not in danger of sacrificing the best in traditional
thinking when I question the identification by analogy of
family and community? I think not. For the very qualities
that we attribute to family *qua* family are not unique to
the family; they are not constitutive of family as family.
These qualities or virtues: respect, acceptance, understanding, interest, *et al*, are precisely Christian virtues and
become the Christian as a person.

An example might express my thought more concretely and show how fundamental is the distinction
between religious community and family. Recently, a
religious priest made the observation that two possible
relations an individual religious could establish with
a superior were either that of a manipulator or that
of a "freezer." In the first instance, the individual could
so use the person in authority that he would succeed in
getting all he wanted; in the second relationship, the religious would be so non-responsive to the superior, that
the superior would not be able to function as a superior.
The priest's solution to or preventive against such rela-

tions was the practice of filial *piety*. I question: Can we as Christian persons, as members in Christ, manipulate others? Can we as Christians be cold towards others? It is not *filial* piety that is lacking in these relationships; it is Christian reverence.

But is this not a pretentious distinction? Are not all Christians, first of all, members of the family of God? Thus, is not the analogy between family and community most fitting? Yes, I am willing to agree that we are all members of the family of God. But in that sense there is no longer an analogy. The identification between family and community is in this case a real identification: only God is Father; we are all brothers. It is precisely because we often fail to appreciate the full reality of this fact that the distinction between filial piety and Christian reverence as practiced within religious communities is misunderstood. Because the family symbol we ordinarily use in explaining community life is immediately identifiable with the human family as the basic unit of society, our relations with one another—religious with religious, religious with superiors—are deprived of their full significance and value. The whole of community life is scaled down, interpreted in terms of familial relations, familial structure. Yet it is precisely because we religious have opted for a nonfamilial mode of being, if you will, that we can, within the universal family of God and among this uinversal family, live as community persons. Thus to prevent an analogous identification when a real identification is intended (God is our Father; we are all brothers) would it not profit our living of the vows if we understood more exactly the depths of meanings in the term community? For community expresses primarily, I believe, the ontological unity and charity that obtains among the family of God. It signifies the active and the passive elements that create favorable conditions for the growth of this unity and charity: openness, receptivity—sharing, giving, receiving. *Community* connotes oneness without loss of identity, a sharing in the interiority of another without the sacrifice of personal integrity. Truly transcending these same values as they are embodied in each atomic unit we call the human family, the term *community* enriches our understanding of the relationships that bind a religious to her fellow religious and to all Christians. She is sister to all. Sister for her is a title of equality, that is, of oneness; it is an expression of mutuality; it is in fact the affirmation of myself only in relation to others. Religious vows, then, must be the means for the attainment of this oneness, this mutuality. The vows must be used for effecting community—*Koinonia*.

When we as religious choose a definite institute or community, we are choosing not a religious family, but a way of living the vows according to the specific *ratio*. Our choice indicates, moreover, that the communal or ecclesial element is essential to this living out of our vows. Thus in a very real sense the poverty and chastity of a religious are more radical than that of non-religious who choose to live a life of virginity and poverty. The religious places herself, her power, her apostolate at the disposition of the Church; she does this precisely in and through the vow of obedience. Poverty and chastity, receive a new form, a new *ratio* in and through this third vow. Truly evangelical virtues, they become essentially ecclesial in character. Obedience as it were ensures that poverty and virginity will not be only means for personal sanctity—although they are truly that. But obedience makes them more than that. Obedience as vowed within a given institute guarantees that the vows cease to be purely personal and private responsibilities; they take on a social, a public quality.

Obedience thus becomes the keystone in the structure of religious life. And it is precisely because it is the keystone, that obedience and its correlative, authority must be removed from the familial context and/or framework if this familial concept is limited to or defined by the basic unit in human society, the family. Obedience and authority will fulfill their purpose—making "the power invested in love, in gold, and in independence" available to the Church—if they are understood and lived within the context of community (*Koinonia*) and as the means of effecting this *Koinonia*.

Collegiality in the Community

In speaking of obedience and authority in this relationship, we realize that these two powers (and they are just that, powers or potencies for an ecclesial life) are best understood and lived if we appreciate the principle of collegiality. The unique value of collegiality as applied to the body of bishops is its affirmation of the primacy of Peter *and* its equally strong declaration of the basic unity and communion of the bishops among themselves and with the sovereign pontiff. Collegiality underscores the elements of variety, plurality, adaptability that are indispensable for true unity. Thus the power invested in authority and in obedience for the building up of the body, for effecting a community is unequivocally acknowledged. As Joseph Ratzinger so trenchantly observes, collegiality is the means for reproducing in a finite way the "eternal dynamic interchange and interpenetration of Spirit and Spirit, of love and love." In fact, collegiality leaves no doubt that the Church, the People of God, is a community of service, of responsible service. Those who govern and those who obey govern and obey to create a community so that the family of God may be served, and

in this service learn to love one another and so live in communion with one another. Father Ratzinger summarizes
the primary effect of collegiality: "The 'I' is in all things
fitted into more comprehensive 'We' from which and for
which it lives."

I am not suggesting a literal application of the principle
of episcopal collegiality for religious communities. Such a
suggestion would indeed be temerity. Religious superiors
are not other Peters; religious themselves are not bishops.
The episcopal body is a college *sui generis* and *sui juris*.
But the principles and the dynamics which underlie this
social structure are certainly valid for religious living today, especially for effecting a true community by means
of the vow of obedience.

It is the interchange, the interaction, the communication
and thus the communion which collegiality demands that
break the conventional image of "authority as the un-
moved mover and the subordinate as the one who is wholly moved." The dynamics inherent in a life of obedience,
if not negated in this image, are reduced to impotence. To
ensure this vital exchange between those who govern and
those who obey, I believe we religious must abandon the
matriarchal orientation when speaking of a life of obedience. Would it not be better and in fact closer to reality
of we defined the structure within each local religious
community as that of a peer group among whom one is
first? This it seems to me is a workable concept for understanding the relationships, the dynamics of the relationships, and the responsibilities of the relationships which
obtain among members of a given religious community.

By defining each local unit as a peer group, the equality
among the members is recognized. This equality is not
to be identified with sameness. Religious sisters are not
all the same. Each is unique. Rather this is an equality

which takes into account the adult Christian and religious status of each member. Each member is responsible, responsive, mature; each member is oriented to and informed by Christian principles, goals and objectives; each member has chosen radical means for realizing her part in salvation history. She cannot be un-involved, unconcerned. Thus her relationship to each member of the community and to the community as such and to the whole Church is one of responsible concern. The dynamics at work ineffecting this relationship are the powers operative in a life of faith, hope and charity. For the mature religious not only believes in and trusts God; but she also believes in and trusts his presence operating in and through others. This belief and this trust are the ground of her love. She can thus respond to each situation, each value in life as a *Kairos*, as a moment of grace. Given that this is the basic and fundamental equality which creates a religious community, it is only an appreciation of this equality that will guarantee a mature obedience, a mature authority.

Moreover, appreciating the reality that the Church is, and the expression of that reality as it is signified by the religious life, authority and obedience cannot simply be defined or identified with these same powers as they are understood in secular society. Congar states this most exactly when he speaks of power within the Church: "There is never simply a relationship of subordination or superiority as in secular society, but always a loving obedience to Christ." He concludes: "Whether as leaders or as simple members of the brotherhood (we) are wholly engaged in the service of Christ and the brethren." The primary responsibility of all religious—those who govern, those who obey—is obedience to Christ for the building up of the Body that is Christ. Thus authority and obedience exist for service.

Correlative Authority

Does this not imply a real negation of the need for authority? Certainly not. No mature person will deny such a need. There must be some *locus*, some center for coordinating the actions of a group come together for a common good or a common purpose, and so sharing in common responsibilities. Whether authority is defined by its Latin equivalents—*auctoritas*: signifying influence, authorship, or *ob audire*: to listen to—authority is the *locus* for decision making. Because the person possessing authority stands among the peer group as first in decision making—thus authoring the life forces of the community, so to speak—authority must be in communion with, responsive to, as well as influenced by, those who share responsibilities for the common good. Authority does not stand alone; authority is not an office apart. Authority *is* because the group *is*. Without the common end, the common goals, the shared responsibilities, authority would be an anomaly. And contrariwise, without authority the common end and shared responsibilities would be a fiction. Authority and obedience are correlatives, not disjunctives.

Does not this mutuality destroy the spirit of faith that inspires a life of obedience? Hardly. Such mutuality is only possible where faith is active. Faith is not non-knowledge. Faith means in one sense limited knowledge, but more precisely faith transcends the limitedness of knowledge. Faith immerses man in the reality of salvation history—community salvation. Thus those who govern and those who obey must, if they are true to the faith that informs them, respect their mutual responsibilities. Faith precludes "all autonomous planning on the part of man." Authority's decisions must be informed acts; the cooperation and submission or surrender of the religious must be informed acts. These acts must express the faith from which they spring: the decisive option for the will of Christ in all things.

From this mutuality, which is a concrete expression of a dynamic faith, will result a respect on authority's part which supports and encourages those who are governed in their responsibilities for achieving the common good. Legitimate channels for communication will be established so that both the superior and the governed will have an opportunity for on-going dialogues, dialogues which are occasion for greater understanding and greater love. But religious obedience is not merely a matter of dialogue. It is most importantly a matter of respecting the movements of the Spirit, of respecting, in the words of Father Piet Fransen, "the charisms through which the moving inspirations of the Holy Ghost are given to all members of the Church." This respect will ensure what I like to term a supportive, active obedience; a supportive, active authority. Both those who govern and those who obey indicate by their manner and attitude in governing and obeying that neither is guiding the other towards herself. Neither is seeking to subordinate the other to herself. Freed from egoism, both respond unhesitatingly to the grace of the present moment.

Are there not dangers in this principle of mutuality? Yes. Authority under the guise of service, of humility, may abandon its unique responsibility, decision-making for an ever fuller religious and apostolic life. Under the pretext of fidelity to the Spirit, those obeying may confuse personal interests with community interests, personal good with the common good. Yet to deny the principle of mutuality implicit in a life of obedience is to court another danger: the razing of the very structure which can support a life of selfless love in the service of others. But as Father Fransen so realistically affirms, a danger never destroys a truth. The dangers involved in this principle of mutuality as it relates to obedience and authority alert us to the need for prudence, but prudence understood as an eschatological power—an habitual awareness of and response to the grace of the present moment. Prudence, as Father Häring affirms, "is the attitude of the spiritual man who recognizes the signs of the time and who answers *yes* . . . to the task assigned to this instant." Prudence thus demands on the part of those who command and those who obey a complete dispossession of self, a constant inner purification of self—God-centeredness. Prudence is then not only an antidote against real dangers, but also a power effecting a true spirit of obedience, a spirit of lived mutuality.

If the principle of collegiality affects, and profoundly affects, our understanding of obedience and authority, it also affects relationships among communities. Just as each bishop must be in communion with other bishops, so religious communities within a given institute, and among other institutes must be in communion with one another. Major superiors' conferences and sister formation groups are practical means for ensuring this total sense of communion. While respecting the differences which distinguish each institute in the Church, religious can learn from one another, share resources with one another, support one another. Sister-experts selected from among many communities could be organized in commissions for an on-going study of a theology of vows and a theology of apostolate. With diocesan commissions, sisters could share in a corporate study of the needs of local churches and the needs of the universal Church. Our apostolic vocation, our mandate to be of service, would then be more realistically fulfilled. The whole body would be strengthened.

RENEWAL OF THE RULE

Fundamental to all the propositions, all the suggestions in this essay, is a critical rethinking by each member of the community of the rule, the constitutions of the community. In this regard Daniélou writes tellingly: "Criticism is not legitimate unless it is constructive. One has the right to judge only what one loves." Questions then, when raised, must be raised from a spirit of love. Loving the values which the rule was intended to enflesh, we can speak with integrity of renewal. Renewal implies both a return to the original values and openness to the grace of the present moment in reference to those values. A return to the gospel and a return to the vision of the founder or foundress are imperatives for any serious re-evaluation of the rule. But equally necessary is an incorporation into these original values of the irruptions of the divine in the values of our *today,* our *Kairos.* Such a critical analysis, such a profound *aggiornamento* in the recasting of the rule is only possible, I submit, if each sister, each community question: Is the rule based on a theology of vocation for apostolic communities?

In formulating the question in this way, I realize the very limitedness of the vocabulary. All religious communities are apostolic. It may be that contemplative communities are more apostolically effective than those communities most directly involved in active works. And again, is not prayer a most active work? Erich Fromm beautifully and realistically writes of contemplation, even in a purely natural order, that it "is the highest activity there is, an activity of the soul, which is possible only under conditions of inner freedom and independence."

Yet, my question stands. We must appreciate the precise and real distinction between contemplative communities and active ones. There is a distinction within the basic unity of these forms of religious life. Do our rules express what is distinctly ours or do our rules express values unique to contemplative or monastic communities?

In reassessing the rule, we must also ask if in an effort to embody the spirit which is proper to each order, we have not in fact delimited the spirit which gave birth to our communities. True, the rule must express that which is unique to each order. But it must do so within biblical and ecclesial perspectives. Each community *is* because the gospel *is*, because the Church *is*. The evangelical and ecclesial dimensions intrinsic to the life of each community must be incorporated into the rule. The specific or distinct expression of these elements constitutes the unique character of each community. In any reworking, restructuring or rewording of the rule, serious study must be given to these biblical and ecclesial qualities as they are to be lived in each community.

Moreover, in re-evaluating the rule, scope must be allowed for experimentation. Quick and untried changes may prove fatal. Only after a period of trial are we in a position to evaluate the positive and negative values of new ideas, new structures, new practices. Experimentation allows for that flexibility which true stability demands, which life demands. In fine, experimentation will prevent what John Tracy Ellis terms, the curse of "presentism."

Truly, the curse of presentism, a curse of sterility—forces us to realize that while the religious is called to be a woman of today she must be a woman of *today* understood not as an isolated atomic reality. Rather she must be a woman of the today which shares in the legacies of the past, of this today which anticipates the possibilities of tomorrow: the today which is a *Kairos*, a moment of salvific responsibility for each participant in salvation history.

Thus, without being simplistic, can we not conclude as we began that the most formidable and challenging responsibility facing the American sister today is *to be* the person she is called to be, that she has chosen to be in this salvific unfolding? Before any other challenges— and they are legion—can be met and answered satisfactorily, the person as religious must find her own integrity. From this ground of her being she can move out to handle the towering problems of perpetual renovation, the need for which cannot be minimized. Open she must be to new programs for Christian formation, new techniques for the apostolate, new research and experimentation for implementing the *aggiornamento*. Committed she must be to liturgical reform, to a kerygmatic religious formation of our people, to ecumenical objectives, to social justice and inner-city renewal. Religious have no choice but to continue to up-date professional standards, horarium and habit. But without an on-going look at the *self* from the perspective of salvation history, the involvement in renewal will provoke the indictment once uttered by Paul— You are "as sounding brass or a tinkling cymbal" (1 Cor 13:1). A Christian world, and thus a person-oriented world, is shouting that the religious must know what is happening to her and to others in Christ in this our *Kairos*, our today.

BIBLIOGRAPHY

The reader of this essay is well aware that the writings of Pierre Teilhard de Chardin, Jean Daniélou and E. Schillebeeckx were sources for this chapter. The works of Yves M. J. Congar, F. X. Durrwell, Karl Rahner and J. M. R. Tillard, as well as the papers presented by Fathers Piet Francen and Robert Johann at the Georgetown Symposium on "Freedom and Man," were likewise drawn upon. Thus, rather than make special mention of them here I prefer to cite periodicals that speak about our *Kairos,* our today in truly contemporary terms.

Chicago Studies—An Archdiocesan Review
  Box 665
  Mundelein, Illinois 60060

Cross Currents—Quarterly
  103 Van Houten Fields
  West Nyack, N. Y.

Donum Dei—A Publication of the Canadian Religious Conference
    Canadian Religious Conference
    324 Laurier Avenue East
    Ottawa 2, Canada

Envoy—A *M*onthly Newsletter
  Duquesne University Press
  Pittsburgh, Pennsylvania 15219

Grail Review—Quarterly
  The Grail International Secretariat
  22, rue du Dr. Germain See
  Paris XVIe, France

Herder Correspondence—A Monthly Review for the Christian World
  Herder and Herder
  232 Madison Avenue
  New York, N. Y.

New City—Man in Metropolis: A Christian Response
  21 West Superior Street
  Chicago, Illinois 60610

Perspectives—A Magazine relating Religion to our Times
  21 West Superior Street
  Chicago, Illinois 60610

The Living Light—A Catechetical Review
    The National Center of C.C.D. - N.C.W.C.
    1312 Massachusetts Avenue
    Washington, D.C. 20005

The Theology Digest—Quarterly
    St. Mary's College
    St. Mary's, Kansas

Bibliography

Barrosse, Thomas, C.S.C. *Christianity, Mystery of Love*. Fides, Notre Dame, Indiana, 1964.

Berdyaev, N. *The Destiny of Man*. Harper Torchbooks, New York, 1960. Especially Chapter III, "The Ethics of Creativeness."

Buber, Martin. *I and Thou*. Translated by Ronald Gregor Smith. Charles Scribner's Sons, New York, 1958.

Burns, Patrick., (Ed.) *Mission and Witness*. The Newman Press, Westminster, 1964.

Cage, J. *Silence*. Wesleyan University Press, 1961.

Camus, A. *Resistance, Rebellion, and Death*. Knopf, 1961.

Chardin, Pierre Teilhard de. *The Divine Milieu*. Harper and Row, New York, 1964.

_____ *The Future of Man*. Harper and Row, New York, 1964.

Congar, Yves. *Power and Poverty in the Church*. Translated by Jennifer Nicholson. Helicon Press, Baltimore, 1964.

Constitution On The Church, Vatican II.

Constitution On The Sacred Liturgy, Vatican II.

Crichton, J.D. *The Church's Worship*. Sheed and Ward, New York, 1964.

Davis, Charles. *Sacraments of Initiation*. Sheed and Ward, New York, 1963.

_____ *Liturgy and Doctrine*. Sheed and Ward, New York, 1960.

DeSmedt, Bishop Emile-Joseph. *The Priesthood of the Faithful*. Paulist Press, New York, 1962.

Dewey, J. *Art as Experience*. G. P. Putnam's Sons, New York, (Capricorn) 1958.

Durrwell, F.X., C.SS.R. "Christian Virginity," Chapter 11 in *In the Redeeming Christ*. Sheed and Ward, New York, 1963.

———————— *The Resurrection*. Translated by Rosemary Sheed. Sheed and Ward, New York, 1960.

Erikson, Erik. *Insight and Responsibility*. W.W. Norton & Co., 1964.

Fuller, R.B. *Education Automation*. Southern Illinois University Press, 1962.

Gelin, Albert. *The Psalms are our Prayers*. The Liturgical Press, Collegeville, Minn., 1964.

Gerkin, John. *Toward a Theology of the Layman*. Herder and Herder, New York, 1963.

Gilleman, Gerard. *Primacy of Charity in Moral Theology*. Newman Press, Westminster, Md., 1961.

Grelot, Pierre. *Man and Wife in Scripture*. Herder and Herder, New York, 1964.

Halstead, Ronald. Trans. *Apostolic Life*. Newman Press, Westminster, Md., 1958.

Houtart, Francois. *The Challenge to Change*. Sheed and Ward, New York, 1964.

Kerns, Joseph E., S.J. *The Theology of Marriage*. Sheed and Ward, New York, 1964.

Kerr, W. *The Decline of Pleasure*. Simon and Schuster, New York, 1962.

LaPierre, Albert (et al), (Ed.) *The Church: Readings in Theology*. P. J. Kenedy Sons, New York, 1963.

———————— *The Word: Readings in Theology*. P. J. Kenedy Sons, New York, 1964.

Legrand, Lucien. *The Biblical Doctrine of Virginity*. Sheed and Ward, New York, 1963.

Lynch, E. *The Image Industries*. Sheed and Ward, New York, 1959.

Marcel, Gabriel. *Creative Fidelity*. Translated and with an Introduction by Robert Rosthal. The Noonday Press, New York, 1964.

———————— *Homo Viator*. Translated by Emma Craufurd. Harper Torchbooks, New York, 1962.

Martimort, Aime. *The Signs of the New Covenant*. The Liturgical Press, Collegeville, Minn., 1963.

Maslow, A. *Toward a Psychology of Being*. D. Van Nostrand, New York, 1962.

Mehl, Roger. *De l'autorité des valeurs*. Presses Universitaires de France, Paris, 1957.

Morgan, Douglass. *Love: Plato, The Bible, Freud*. Prentice-Hall, Englewood Cliffs, N.J., 1964.

Nedoncelle, Maurice. *God's Encounter with Man*. Sheed and Ward, New York, 1964.

Rahner, Karl, S.J. *The Christian Commitment*. Translated by Cecily Hastings. Sheed and Ward, New York, 1964.

_____ *The Dynamic Element in the Church*. Herder and Herder, New York, 1964.

_____ *Theology for Renewal*. Sheed and Ward, New York, 1964.

Ricoeur, Paul. *Finitude et culpabilité*. Tome I: *L'homme faillible*. Tome II: *La symbolique de mal*. Aubier, Paris, 1960.

Riga, Peter. *Catholic Thought in Crisis*. Bruce, Milwaukee, 1962.

Salm, Luke. *Studies in Salvation History*. Prentice-Hall, Inc., Englewood Cliffs, N.J., 1964.

Schillebeeckx, E., O.P. *Christ the Sacrament of the Encounter with God*. Sheed and Ward, New York, 1963.

_____ *Mary, Mother of the Redemption*. Sheed and Ward, New York, 1964.

_____ *The Church and Mankind*. Dogma, Vol. I Glen Rock: Paulist Press, 1964.

_____ *The Layman in the Church and other Essays*. Translated by Colman O'Neill, O.P. Alba House, New York, 1963.

Schoonenberg, Peter, S.J. "Marriage in the Perspective of the History of Salvation." Chapter 4 in *God's Word in the Making*. Duquesne University Press, Pittsburgh, Pa., 1964.

Schutz, Roger. *Living Today for God*. Translated by Stephen McNierney and Louis Evrad. Helicon Press, Baltimore, 1962.

Short, R. *The Gospel According to Peanuts*. John Knox, Richmond, Va., 1965.

Spicq, Ceslaus, O.P. *Agape in the New Testament*. B. Herder Book Co., St. Louis, 1963.

Stuhlmueller, Carroll, C.P. "Osee and the Mystery of Love," Chapter 3 in *The Prophets and the Word of God*. Fides, Notre Dame, Ind., 1964.

Suenens, Leo Cardinal. *The Church in Dialogue*. Fides, Notre Dame, Ind., 1965.

Thils, Gustave. *Christian Holiness*. Lannoo Publishers, Tielt, Belgium, 1961.

Van Kaam, Adrian, C.S.Sp. *Religion and Personality*. Prentice-Hall, Inc., Englewood Cliffs, N.J., 1964.

Vann, Gerald. *The Paradise Tree*. Sheed and Ward, New York, 1959.

——————————— *The Water and the Fire*. Sheed and Ward, New York, 1954.

243   m   6183

Muckenhirn, Sr. Charles B.
ed.

The Changing Sister